Second World Congress on Land Policy, 1983

Books from the Lincoln Institute of Land Policy/OG&H

The Zoning Game—Revisited
Richard F. Babcock and Charles L. Siemon

Land Acquisition in Developing Countries: Policies and Procedures of the Public Sector
Michael G. Kitay

Introduction to Computer Assisted Valuation
Edited by Arlo Woolery and Sharon Shea

Advanced Industrial Development: Restructuring, Relocation, and Renewal
Donald Hicks

Land Market and Land Policy in a Metropolitan Area: A Case Study of Tokyo
Yuzuru Hanayama

Second World Congress on Land Policy, 1983

Edited by
Matthew Cullen
Sharon Woolery

 A Lincoln Institute of Land Policy Book

Published by
Oelgeschlager, Gunn & Hain
in association with the
Lincoln Institute of Land Policy

International Standard Book Number: 0-89946-195-6

Library of Congress Catalog Card Number: 85-10455

Printed in the U.S.A.

Oelgeschlager, Gunn & Hain, Publishers, Inc.
131 Clarendon Street
Boston, MA 02116

Library of Congress Cataloging in Publication Data

World Congress on Land Policy (2nd : 1983 : Harvard Law School)
  Second World Congress on Land Policy, 1983.

1. Land use—Government policy—Congresses. I. Cullen, Matthew. II. Woolery, Sharon. III. Title. HD105.W664 1983   333.73'13   85-10455
ISBN 0-89946-195-6

Contents

PART I

The Human Condition: Growth, Equity, Basic Human Needs, and the Land

Introduction to First Session

Isaac M. Ofori

As we welcome you to the Second World Congress on Land Policy, and as we begin our deliberations on today's theme, "The Human Condition: Growth, Equity, Basic Human Needs, and the Land," let us imagine that we have among us visitors from the planet Mars. They are keenly interested in knowing how we humans on our planet Earth have been coping with these basic human needs; what policies we have evolved with special reference to our land resources, their use, misuse, and nonuse, their ownership; and what changes we propose to adopt to achieve equity and growth.

It is agreed that the basic needs of every human being consist of food, clothing, shelter, leisure, and some means of mobility. The need for food is satisfied by agricultural practices which have evolved in all societies from the earliest times, from the gathering of food and the hunting of animals to the present sedentary forms of agriculture. Material for clothing has similarly developed over many centuries, from fibers of the bark of trees to the most modern synthetics. Shelter probably originated with the first caveman who sought refuge from the elements, and has proceeded to the most modern forms of architecture. Mobility has perhaps developed most dramatically of all. It is the satisfaction of the need for mobility and the developments in quest of it which have enabled us all to assemble here this morning.

Man has been endeavoring over the centuries to meet his basic needs by utilizing a factor which for many years has not had much serious academic study: *land*. One may wonder why this important factor, which has always been used to satisfy the human condition, has been so long neglected. I think the answer lies partly in the fact that until quite recently we have taken our land resources for granted. Land has always seemed so plentiful, compared to the number of beings who have inhabited it. In such situations of plenitude, our basic considerations of land resources, if we ever gave the matter any thought, always centered on the question, Are we running out? And the answer to that question has always been an emphatic, No!

The picture, we have to agree, is changing. In absolute terms, both quantitatively and qualitatively, we now appreciate that we are running out of land resources to satisfy man's basic needs. We know now that desertification, which is the process of environmental degradation of our natural resources with associated reduction or loss of land productivity, has been threatening many countries of the world. The UN Conference on Desertification (UNCOD) has made the assessment that productive land was being lost at the rate of 60,000 square kilometers per year, and that 30 million square kilometers in some 100 countries were prone to desertification, threatening the livelihood of some 628 million people. In the area of satisfying man's need for shelter, we are all aware of the tremendous pace of urbanization in the world, a phenomenon which has been accelerating in recent years. A United Nations report on urbanization warned a few years ago that by 1980, the world would be on the verge of becoming predominantly urban. Whereas only 110 million people were urban in the developing regions in 1920, 930 million are expected to be urban in 1980—a ninefold growth in but sixty years. Similarly, in the other basic needs like amenities and transportation, we are faced with pressing and frightening prospects.

The increasing number of human beings which inhabit the world and the demands for more and better satisfaction of the basic needs of man have helped us, in a more serious way than ever before, to focus our attention more sharply on the factor of land. We can no longer predicate our discussions of land resources on the notion that we are in no danger of running out. We must now put our land resources on the pedestal where they belong and agree that our land resources are central to almost all our endeavors to satisfy our basic needs, and that every capital combination is a combination of land and other resources.

Our task in the next few days is to try to focus our attention on the land factor and evolve sound policies to guide its use, misuse, nonuse, and ownership.

Chapter 1

Land Policy: A Global Outlook

*Aurelio Peccei**

Mr. Chairman, Mr. Moderator, my dear friends. It is a great pleasure for me to be here this morning and to have the privilege of addressing you. I am grateful to both Mr. Matthew Cullen and my old friend Pierre Laconte for this opportunity.

I am somewhat hesitant to speak before such a distinguished audience of knowledgeable experts and eminent scholars—I, a poor generalist—and therefore I ask for your patience if I am not able to fully put forward my case as I stress what I think is important in a global outlook in our relationship with land. I will talk, in fact, of the imperative of responsible global land use in our small journey through this planet, and I will touch upon three main points. One is the changing human condition—that is, the decline in the state of the planet and humankind. The second one concerns new perceptions of the future. And the third point concerns two imperatives which, in my view, are required to turn around the present degenerating situation on the planet.

As to the first point, the present human condition and its dynamics of change, I will share with you some of the ideas that we in the Club of Rome have about this subject. Even looking at the very recent past, say the last 15 years, we can detect that there has

*This manuscript is derived from a transcript of oral remarks. Please see "In Memoriam" to Aurelio Peccei, pp. 299-300.

7

been a decline in the overall human condition. The Club of Rome, which I take as a reference at the moment, was formed in 1968, and that was still *la belle époque par excellence.* It was a period of euphoria during which we were enthusiastic about splendid scientific discoveries, about the consequences of marvelous technological advances, and about steady economic growth. Our optimism at that time was so great that we were even expecting to find around the corner a new El Dorado—that old problems of humankind were something of the past and that new ones could have an easy solution. We in the Club of Rome wanted to issue a warning against this complacency of industrial civilization, and we promoted a study which came out under the title *The Limits to Growth.* The objective was to show that not all human problems can be solved by technological means, that the human system could not continue its exponential growth without facing great trouble, and that there was too much ferment, too many tensions and gaps in human society not to take notice of them. For all its shortcomings, I think that study hit the nail on the head.

Ten years after the formation of the Club of Rome, in 1978, we wanted to check whether our opinions were correct or not, so we gathered again and examined the situation of the world. Ten years are nothing, just a fleeting moment on the clock of history, and yet in those ten years we found, or thought we found, that all major indicators showed that there had been a decline in the human condition. Not one single major problem of the world had been attacked efficiently, let alone solved—perhaps not even understood. And more problems, new ones, had emerged, intertwining with the old ones to form what we call the global problematic. We can argue whether these opinions are right or not. However I submit to you that, from all viewpoints—from the viewpoint of population, of economy, of security, of the environment—the human condition has not gotten any better since the end of the 1960s.

Again, more recently, we checked our findings and were concerned to find that, in our opinion, humankind had entered a phase of decline. But we also thought, and think, that if present trends continue, the global crisis will become ever bigger until we may be facing disasters of some kind or another in many countries. We cannot say when, how, or at what moment they may occur, but only that they are likely to occur. Today we find that many political, scientific, and even religious leaders share this opinion. If there is one factor which has improved in this period, that is human awareness—the sense that something important must be changed in society and in the way we conduct human affairs. Changed, of course, in a democratic, nonviolent way, but it must be changed.

Now we may ask ourselves, what is the matter with humankind at this advanced stage of its evolution that it is in such a plight? Of course there are many factors which contribute, but if I had to indicate one—a major one, the main one—I would say that this is the discrepancy of the material revolutions—the industrial, scientific, and technological revolutions which have given us such tremendous knowledge and power, and given us welfare which our forefathers could not even have dreamed of, but which have not given us the vision and the wisdom to control them and to apply them only to good ends. This mismatch between our tremendous knowledge and power and our capacity to use them for good purposes is probably at the root of the present-day crisis.

Two conclusions can be derived concerning the theme that we will be dealing with here. The first is that in applying our new assets, sometimes intelligently and sometimes not, misusing and abusing them, we have changed fundamentally the small corner of the universe in which we live, but we are not yet fit to support a population of 5 or 6 billion people, perhaps more. We have changed the world, but if we look at the world's surface, the world's resources, the world's state today, we may be convinced that we have not responsibly used our knowledge and our power. The second has to do not only with what we have done so far but with the future. For while we have changed our environment, we have failed to evolve, to change our values, our behavior, our ways of thinking, our institutions, our policies, our strategies, in order to be on a par with the new realities that we have created. We still have a frame of reference, a way of judgement, which comes from a past which is no more. Culturally we have remained behind the real world that we have created. Hence, our land policies, today and in the foreseeable future, will probably continue to degrade the planet on which we will have to live in ever greater numbers.

Let's take a look at the future. Our future is fundamentally different from the future which could have been foreseen by our forebears. Two main new characteristics of the future have to do with our topic. One is that for the first time the future will be almost totally a human product. In past centuries Homo sapiens was on the defensive, was a weakling. Today he is the most powerful agent for change on the planet. He dominates many natural phenomena. He is everywhere. He can change the shape and trends of things. Today the future is being formed by what 4.5 billion people—tomorrow 5 billion, the day after tomorrow 6 billion people—are doing, will be doing, day after day. Some have more influence, others less; but all together they will prepare the future for themselves and for their children and grandchildren. If the future so produced by us humans is to be the fruit of our disorderliness, our mediocrity, our pettiness, as is today the case, that future will be obscure and tempestuous. If instead the future springs out of our commitment to make it better than the present, then it will be a livable and a rewarding one. There are diverse possibilities for our future. Within limits, we can choose the future we want, because we will be building it.

The second characteristic is that, also for the first time, the future will be one. On a planet which is becoming smaller and smaller with respect to the number of its inhabitants and their power, their demands, their expectations, their mobility; on a planet which becomes ever more interdependent and integrated, where it is not a flight of fancy or rhetoric to say that there is such a thing as the oneness of humankind, irrespective of all its diversity—in that world there can be only one future. The present-day disparities between rich and poor, powerful and weak, developed and underdeveloped cannot exist anymore in that ever smaller, ever more tightly woven system which will be the world of tomorrow. And that should lead us to realize that we have a great stake in what others do and in their future, because their future will influence ours and vice versa. The spheres of solidarity in that world must expand from the city, the valley, the nation to the wider region, finally throughout the globe itself. If we can choose our future, we have to understand that others can also choose their future, and that all together we will end by choosing a common future.

From these two observations I think that we can draw a lesson pertinent to our theme. That is that land planning, use, and management, all land policies today, can no longer be conceived only in a fragmented way, apart from what others do. They must be envisioned in a planetary way, in a global way, seeing the planet as it is, not particularly well integrated but as a total system nonetheless.

Let me tell you how I see the concept of land. Land, in my view, should be considered in a very broad sense. The land space has to be comprehended with the entire natural endowment pertaining to it— climate, the soil, water, plant and animal life, and also mineral and fossil deposits, but chiefly the biological part of our planet which pertains to that land space. Also, it must be considered with the human artifacts, those already existing and those that will be built in the future. The land space of the world should be envisioned together with the elements which make it fit for human existence over time. If this is the concept of land, if we accept that the land has to be seen in this broad light, then I maintain that land is the most finite of all finite resources on a finite planet. And that land is also the most endangered of these resources. Therefore that land must be strongly defended against any waste, any mismanagement, so as to preserve as much as possible, and possibly improve, the carrying capacity of the planet.

Now let us consider the imperatives which may be derived from this view of the world, of our condition. Of course this is a partial view, for there are many other factors to be considered, and there are thousands of things of all kinds to be done everywhere, from the local to the small regional, to the national, to the large regional, to the continental, to the global level. But among these things some are primary, are necessary if we are to do the others, and these I call the imperatives of our age. I will mention just two of these imperatives which seem to be connected strictly with the theme of this conference. I said before that we humans have not adjusted to the advances or changes we have made in our planet. We have been, and are, lagging behind reality, running after our technologies, after our deeds. Now if this is so, it is an imperative to develop the human potential. We in the Club of Rome, following the majority of scientists, believe that there is a dormant potential within each human being, even the most marginal ones, a potential of understanding, of imagination, of creativity, of compassion, of tolerance, of conviviality, and moral energies which have been neglected, but which are the innate endowment of each human being. We think that this potential should be developed, is developable, and can become so if we devote our talent and treasure and time more to the human being than to the economy, technology, institutions—or at least to developing these in conjunction with developing the human being. If the protagonist of it all—the human being—continues to remain behind the reality of the world, this world cannot be put back on its stride again. This human development, which is possible—and which perhaps represents the most important resource at the disposal of humankind, a renewable resource, even an expandable resource—is necessary, because whatever enlightened land policies we may devise, we will discover that their implementation does not depend on the small elites who will determine the policies and strategies for land use in the future. We must have the participation of great masses of people. If they do not understand, if they are passive, if they do not see that the development of land in the proper way is in their interest, is something to which they may contribute, indeed must contribute, then all the policies and strategies which will be devised in the highest spheres will not be applied efficiently.

The second and last of the two imperatives that I will mention to you is that if the situation that I have depicted is true then we must as soon as possible outline the principles and study the feasibility of drawing guidelines for defining land policies on a global basis. There is a finite quantity of available land in the world at the disposal of this growing humankind, growing in number and in appetite. If we do not do so, it is hardly possible that the earth will be able to carry this population and afford them a quality of life, biological, physical, and cultural, which should be the right of modern men and women, and of our children.

We must think ahead, to the policies on a global span which would enable us to transmit to the next generation a planet able to give to them what we received from our forefathers. We know that today we are in the middle of a major ecological crisis. We know, as I said, that the number of people living on the earth and their needs, wants, and demands will be rapidly increasing. We know that the carrying capacity of any area of the planet also depends on the social and political structure and that, worldwide, these structures have little sensitivity to the needs of the environment—and even less ability to protect it. We know that both the poor and the rich of the world, though in different ways, are not making good use of their land. We know that there is no national or international institution or agency which plans to make comprehensive, systematic studies of the land use that should be adopted in the world. We know that such studies of our relationship with our planet and our responsibilities toward it should be made in an independent way. We know that this is something which should be done not by some existing world power, not in response to some ideology, to some sector interest, but in an open way, at the initiative of you—of us—scientists.

We know that such a study will be extremely difficult. It is also indispensable. There are so many data, such a vast bibliography, so many studies which can be used by a group of citizens of different cultures and convictions and conditions who wish to embark upon such a study. All these data are at their disposal. And, too, we know that such a study should not be so ambitious as to try to attack all the facets of the problem. This study can be phased in various steps and initiated with some philosophical, some moral, some scientific, and some ecological aspects which are amenable to our understanding, leaving the most difficult ones, the political and juridical aspects of a vast plan for the world's land, to be discussed.

In conclusion, I would like to leave with you the thought that perhaps it is worthwhile for you to examine during this conference, or perhaps after this conference, whether it is feasible to carry out a study of a global land policy aimed at preserving, at the highest level possible, over time, the failing capacity of our one and only earth; to see whether this study deserves encouragement. I think it is within the realm of possibility. You who know better may have another idea. But do not be discouraged. Do not be dispirited if there are difficulties. From now on the difficulties that we have to face in the world, in all things—talking about peace, about equality and justice, about development, about human fulfillment—will be greater than those that we have known in the past. But I think that you will decide that it is possible to make that study. I urge you to devote part of your time, your knowledge, to devising what could be the initial framework for launching this study. Who should take the initiative? As in many other cases, those who can, must. There is such strife in the world; we must feel our responsibility, our capacity to face it. And I think that we of the free world have the means, the freedom, the experience, the talent, the economic means, the scientific knowledge and information necessary to tackle this and many other problems. If we do not accept the challenge, we will pay for it.

Chapter 2

The Man/Land Relationship

*Arlo Woolery**

Thank you, ladies and gentlemen. Sitting in the front row, I had become so entranced with Dr. Peccei's remarks that I had completely forgotten what I was going to say. I have reassembled my thoughts, which I now hope will flow with a degree of continuity, but nevertheless may to you seem a bit random.

I was struck by Dr. Peccei's thoughts about the future, and I couldn't help but think of the motto of one of our great insurance companies, "The future belongs to those who prepare for it." Certainly Dr. Peccei has issued a clarion call and a real challenge to us in this Congress to prepare for a brighter future which only we can build. In reflecting on the preparation of my remarks, I must tell you that it was a most frustrating experience I have undergone. First I read the literature, and then I began to read the literature about the literature on the topics that we are discussing. And I found that there were so many different opinions that they ran the gamut all the way from the prophets of doom to the pure Pollyannish. There was stuff on the extreme left, there was material on the extreme right, and when I had assembled this material and tried to digest it, I determined that my proper place was in the extreme middle. So if there is an extreme middle, that is my platform today. I

*This manuscript is derived from a transcript of oral remarks.

must mention that I am doubly flattered to be here; first of all I am flattered to occupy the platform with people of such eminence as Dr. Peccei and the other speakers, and second I'm flattered to have an audience of the tremendous abilities, talent, and intellect that you represent.

There are certain perils of prophecy, and I would take my first thought about those perils from the world of baseball. Mr. Casey Stengel, manager for many years of the great New York Yankees, had a way with words. He said, "Prophecy is always dangerous. Especially when it involves the future." So I would caution you to be concerned about some of the prophecies that have been made. I certainly agree with Dr. Peccei that man has become a geographic factor in this world along with wind and water and climate. Man has now attained that tremendous power and that unique ability that allow him to modify his environment. Other members of the animal world either adapt to a changing environment or they perish. Man not only can change his environment but also can adapt to a changing environment, and I would ask you to hold that in the back of your mind as we go along. Also the concept of one world certainly will be a reiterated theme in my presentation after the reinforcement I received from Dr. Peccei's remarks. In this shrinking world, economies are more closely linked among countries than at any other time in history. With this economic linkage becoming tighter and tighter on a transnational basis, there is much less leeway for domestic options and policies for government leaders than there ever was in the past. So with that reduction in leeway we have to be more careful about the policies that we are talking about and about their transnational implications. I would also caution that there is a great deal of difference between knowing what you think the solution is and thinking you know what the solution is. It is so easy to think that we know the answer. But believe me, we must be clear about the difference, because we know so little and we forecast so badly. A German friend of mine said it better than anybody. He said, "We are too soon old and too late smart." And that may be why we forecast so badly.

As I talk I'm going to move around in time, and I hope you'll indulge me in that. I think time is a marvelous invention. It keeps everything from happening at once. First of all, let's drop back about 50 years, to a time when I was in high school. The United States had a population of about 130 million people. The Department of Agriculture forecast a 1980 population for the United States of about 180 million people. Currently we have nearly 240 million people; that forecast population increase was off by a factor of two to one. Fifty years ago I was on a debating team in an Iowa high school, and the debate topic was the problem of plenty. The agricultural problem facing us then, in 1933, was one of surplus, not of scarcity. I was debating in favor of what was called the ever-normal-granary plan, a plan that may have been conceived almost 4,000 years ago. The agricultural policy of that time called for killing 6 million young pigs, which we did. It called for plowing under millions of acres of immature cotton, which we did. And then we were promptly treated to dust and drought as if they were some kind of retribution for the profligate acts committed under our national agricultural policy. So I worry about policies of this type. At that time corn was ten cents a bushel, hogs were two cents a pound, and the farmers could not afford to haul the corn to town and buy coal to haul home to heat their houses. As a result, in our part of northern Iowa, the rich people burned corn and the poor people burned corn cobs after they had been shelled and the corn had been fed to the pigs and the pigs sold for two dollars a hundredweight. At the same time, I was reading newspaper stories about Detroit and Chicago and other industrial and commercial areas where there was hunger while we were killing 6 million young pigs and plowing under corn, wheat, and cotton.

Last week I had the opportunity to watch early morning television for 30 minutes. And what an interesting 30 minutes it was. Secretary of Agriculture Block was on the *Good Morning America* program. And the first question to him was, What is the problem with American agriculture? The Secretary's response was surplus and low prices. His solution: take 82 million acres out of production under a payment-in-kind program. The cost to the American taxpayer will be somewhere in the range of $20 to $30 billion. This kind of farm policy raises questions. This is the present, but it looks very much like the present of 50 years ago.

I was in Europe a couple of weeks ago and while reading the *International Herald* I was struck by this story: "French Take Farm Clash to Highways. Roads and Tollgates Blocked in the South." The dateline: Montpellier, France. The story:

> Farmers and wine growers caused traffic chaos across southwestern France Friday, blockading highways and major road junctions in support of demands for better prices for their products. Militant farmers occupied superhighway tollgates causing huge jams and blocked railroad lines between two cities, and at one tollgate, a radio report said, the farmers consoled the drivers for their delays by passing out free bottles of wine. In the past few days the French

farmers have also intercepted and destroyed shipments of fruit and vegetables from Spain and Italy, claiming unfair competition from cheap imports. In retaliation, about 20 Spanish farmers threw vegetables at the French Embassy in Madrid Friday, breaking several windows, and dumped truckloads of vegetables in the streets in front of the Embassy.

Now this is not the kind of fight for food that we had in mind when we convened this Congress.

As I mentioned, I would like to move around in time. Now, if you'll permit me I would like to take you back about 4,000 years in history to Old Testament times, to the story of Pharaoh and Joseph, the story of the seven fat years and the seven lean years. If you remember, Pharaoh said, "I had a dream last night," and the captain of Pharaoh's guard said, "There is a man, one of our slaves, who can interpret dreams." So Pharaoh summoned Joseph, who had been sold into captivity by his brothers, and asked him to interpret the dream. Pharaoh said, "I had this dream. I was by the side of a river. And there were seven fat cows that came up out of the river. Well favored, fat, and in fine condition. And then seven lean, hungry, ill favored kine came up from the river and ate the seven fat cows. And then I saw a stalk of corn and on this stalk of corn were seven fat ears. But then on another stalk of corn were seven ill favored ears, very poor, and those ill favored ears consumed the seven fat ears. What does this mean?" And Joseph said to Pharaoh, "The dream is one. The seven good kine are seven years, and the seven good ears are seven years, and the dream is one, as the future is one. And the seven thin and ill favored kine that came up after them are seven years and the seven empty ears blasted by the east wind shall be seven years of famine. And behold. There shall come seven years of great plenty throughout all the land of Egypt, and there shall arise after them seven years of famine, and all the plenty shall be forgotten in the land of Egypt, and the famine shall consume the land. And the plenty shall not be known in the land by reason of that famine following, for it shall be very grievous." And what was the solution to this dire prophecy of this slave who had been sold into captivity by his brothers? Joseph said, "Let Pharaoh do this. Let him appoint an officer over the land and take up a fifth part of the land of Egypt in the seven plenteous years. And let them gather all the food of that fifth part of those good years that come, and lay up corn under the hand of Pharaoh, and let them keep that food in the cities. And that food shall be for store in the land against the seven years of famine."

The problem is very similar to the one of 50 years ago, very similar to the one of the present: the problem of surplus and scarcity. But then in biblical times that surplus and scarcity was over time—seven good years and seven bad years over a 14-year span. It was not particularly over space at that time. But if you begin to examine our present predicament, you find that the surplus and scarcity are badly distributed over this planet on which we live—not distributed badly in time, but in space over wide geographic areas. I don't know the answers, but I do think we should be aware of history, lest we repeat its mistakes and fail to learn its lessons.

I have some cautions and caveats that I hope will be useful to you as you listen to other speakers throughout this Congress. One thing I would caution you to do is beware of statistics and linear extrapolations. I think payment in kind, regardless of the number, whether it be 8 million or 80 million acres out of production, is not really relevant. I also think that the withdrawal of the proposed 82 million acres from production will have virtually no effect on the total agriculture production of this country. If I know farmers, they are very wise, very sagacious, and very productive. They will take their least productive land out of cultivation and intensify their efforts on the remaining, more productive land, and as a result produce a greater crop yield than they have in past years, but on a diminished acreage of 15 to 20 percent of our total cultivated acreage. Then what happens to statistics? The average production per acre will increase substantially, and we can be misled by a statistical anomaly that may give aid and comfort to people who wish to prove points through the pure manipulation of mathematics.

I was on a program a few years ago with a distinguished group, and as part of the program there was a mathematical model offered that proved conclusively that as the size of the farm unit diminishes, production increases substantially per unit of area. However, when I looked at the mathematical equation it was plain that if you took the denominator to zero, the inevitable conclusion was that the productivity became infinite. I would submit to you, you must always look for zero in the denominator if people are projecting that Pollyannish world that would yield infinite fertility. As Dr. Peccei said, all of these things are finite, no matter how they are measured.

I was just at a meeting of the International Federation of Housing and Planning, and there was a competition among students of architecture to design the city of the future. I was struck by two things in that particular competition. I will tell you one now and I will tell you the other at the end of my speech. The first thing I was struck with in going through the exhibit of 55 different competitors who would design the city of the future was this: the large number of entries that seemed to suggest that the future lay in the direction of the past. The students had designed the city of the future to take us back to living conditions that prevailed 50 years ago. There was this desire to turn back the clock and go back to a simpler way of life. It was almost as if the past were what we call a "fraidy hole." I come from the Midwest, where we have tornadoes, and in order to avoid those severe storms we have cellars. You go underground, because the storm will not harm you if you are underground. Those underground holes throughout much of the Midwest are called "fraidy holes." If we are to take the past as our "fraidy hole," I would say we may as well close up this Congress and go to our own individual "fraidy holes," wherever they happen to be.

I also came back home to find a magazine in my pile of mail, containing an article by an architect. The architect, Frank Geary, wrote "Looking Backward instead of Forward." This is just a minor quote from his piece:

> Today we have the kind of free-for-all in architecture that is wonderful. Freedom of ideas is what this nation is supposed to be all about. Yet many architects seem to be looking for some kind of structure. In the process they are turning to a kind of imperial architecture that relates to an earlier time. They are looking backward instead of forward. They are dealing with a lot of nostalgia. And that bothers me. I find looking backward decadent. I find it negative. Nostalgia is an effort by some architects to humanize modernism. But for me nostalgia is not a real experience. It is a canned experience.

So I would submit, let us not fall in the trap of letting the past become our "fraidy hole," our place of refuge from the challenges that face us this week.

I was delighted to hear Dr. Peccei talk about the social and political economy. I think this is extremely important, because I feel that solutions to the problems we will discuss this week lie there more than in the field of pure technology. I think technology is easy. But getting technology implemented into our social, our political, and our economic system is the real challenge that faces this group and other groups around the world. So I would say as we analyze the presentations we will hear this week, we should analyze them for social, political, and economic viability, and then we'll be talking about the true conservation, restoration, and augmentation of our natural resources.

I'd like to take the remainder of my time to talk about the world as a package. Many years ago a politician who was then very old and very wise told me that in politics, as in life, you must take people as they are, not as you wish they were. And I think the world has the same messsge for us. It's a package—a package we must take as it is, not as we wish it were. It is a world filled with pleasure and pain, with surplus and scarcity, with problem creators and problem solvers (of which I hope we are in the latter category). But I think all of us are faced with the prospect of deciding whether we are going to be part of the problem or part of the solution. I think your very presence here indicates that you have opted for the second choice. We must look closely at the problems in the man/land equation. I think we're here to hold this Congress because we perceive problems in that relationship between man and land. The word *relationship* carries with it relativistic concepts. On a relative basis, does the problem which we are discussing here stem from too many people or too little land? If we say too little land, we may as well close down the Congress and go home. We are not going to emulate the Dutch and create more land. If we say too many people, I think we're being equally unrealistic. We are refusing to accept this world as a package, as it really is. We are beginning to think in terms of the world as we wish it were. In looking at that man/land relationship the question we should be asking is, How can we distribute the benefits that our land yields over the present population in a manner which will alleviate as much human suffering as possible without jeopardizing the land resource for the future? If we begin to break the problem down into its various aspects, to speak of the people who are out on the land removing that last vestige of vegetation to provide a cooking fire for tonight's dinner, and the people who are scratching barren hillsides to plant crops in areas where the next rainfall will carry the last remnants of fertile soil to some distant sea, then we are talking about hundreds of millions of people. And if those multitudes are creating land problems, and we few in this room are assembled to solve those problems, I would submit that the odds are overwhelming.

Some other questions occur to me. Are we expecting too much from our land? Have we really looked at the balance of the agents of production from two distinct points of view? First from a very narrow domestic point of view that may see plenty on a domestic basis, and then from a broad global point of view that sees land as the source of livelihood for a global population without geographic differentiation. I think there is a certain inevitability about the effect of basic economics. Certainly the strong US dollar which is paining many of you who are attending this Congress is a reflection of relativity—the relative strength of the United States economy and currency vis-à-vis the relative strengths, or perceived strengths, of other economies and other currencies. By definition, something that is strong must be compared to something that is weaker. The strong US dollar may simply be a reflection of weakness in other national currencies. But the one inescapable fact is this: the strong US dollar results in higher costs to countries importing food and fiber from the United States. And since the United States is currently producing a surplus of food roughly equivalent to a third or more of our domestic requirement, the relative currency strengths that I talked about have helped put that surplus food beyond the reach of people in need, and that is the result of the relative strength of the countries' currencies and economies. When I hear that a worker in our chairman Isaac Ofori's country must work a full week to acquire the wherewithal to buy one egg, I am very discouraged. A two-part question comes to mind: are eggs really that scarce in Ghana, or are cedis really that worthless?

This reminds me of a story that goes back a couple of hundred years. In a mid-European country a king was driving past a farmyard and saw chickens and thought how nice it would be to have some fresh eggs. So he had his driver stop, and he summoned the peasant and said, "I would like to buy some of your eggs. How much are they?" And the peasant, looking at the carriage, the trappings, and the king, said something like $50 per egg. The king replied, "Certainly eggs must be very scarce to command a price like that." And the peasant replied, "No, eggs are very plentiful. But kings are scarce." So I wonder, can a country like Ghana afford to treat its citizens like kings in its domestic food production and marketing? I think we've never really examined the economic cost versus the social cost of our agricultural policies. Man has the capacity to substantially modify his environment. He can do that in relatively short periods of time. He can modify it for good or for evil, for better or for worse. As I mentioned, all other forms of life must adapt to the changing environment that man has created, or they perish. It is only man who seems to have that ability to substantially enhance or destroy his own environment and then adapt to the environment that he has created.

I think we should also examine, as we will in one of the workshops this afternoon, land tenure systems. Does the land tenure system under which a man lives affect his personal relationship with land? The great land economist Arthur Young said, "The magic of property turns sand into gold. Give a man a barren piece of soil and private ownership, and he will convert it into a garden. But give him nine year's lease of a garden and he will convert it into a desert." I ask you, is it possible that we need to examine land tenure systems on a global basis to find out how we can provide each man who has dominion over the soil with greater incentive to convert sand into gold? Our land discussion should take place within a framework that can be moved from country to country. That framework for discussing land should include three dimensions. The first is the physical dimension, the simple geographical fact that each piece of land is unique, fixed in location, with characteristics that determine its productivity. Second, that land exists and is used within an institutional framework. Over the course of history in each country laws and customs have created institutional relationships between man and land. And third, there is that fundamental, inescapable economic relationship between man and land. That economic relationship is affected by global events, a great deal more than we are aware. When oil prices rise in the Middle East, land values change all the way from Tokyo to Timbuktu.

We must also insert time into our framework for analysis and look at it in its three elements: the past, the present, and the future. The past is useful only in helping us understand the present, and in providing information for predicting the future. If we fail to learn from the past, we may have no future. There are these lessons of history, and if they are properly learned, we should be able to chart future courses that yield universal benefits from the man/land relationship. We also have the problem of the present. For the millions upon millions of people who are facing the specter of famine today, if we talk only about problems that may become acute two decades from now, for them we offer no hope whatsoever. For these people the present is all that matters. Unless they are fed today, they have no future. Even so, the future cannot be ignored, because if we mortgage the future too heavily to solve present problems, there will be no future when we get there.

We must also learn to distinguish between real reasons and good reasons. And that is a very important distinction. Too often when we are asked why we do things the way we do them we say, because that's the way we've always done them. Also, when we're asked why we are doing something the way we are doing it, we feel constrained to give good reasons, not real reasons. Around the world, legislators—the men who make our policy decisions, who write our laws—hear much of statistics and logic from you in the audience. They hear much about research and your research findings and conclusions. But they formulate policy on the basis of philosophy and ethics and their own particular political bent. And then when they are asked why they voted the way they did, they will cite statistics and logic and the good reasons, not the real reasons. Perhaps we who should be providing better input are guilty of a certain amount of academic failure. Do we in this room state the wrong goal in encouraging land policy formulations that can bring us to a brighter future for mankind?

I mentioned earlier that I had been struck by two things in the program in Lisbon of the IFHP. The first was the desire of the young competitors and designers of the city of the future to retreat to the past, to that dim, dark "fraidy hole" that would yield very little progress. The second thing I found so striking was the candor of the jury that had examined these competition entries. The jury pulled no punches in its analysis and critique of the more than 50 entries in the competition. The winner received a great deal of praise, but also this statement was included: "Creation of ecological conditions indispensable to a balanced human life are envisioned in a rather simplistic way." About the second-prize winner, the following quotation was included in the jury statement: "The submission's weakest aspect is its inadequate attention to implementation. The authors assume a level of self-sufficiency and neighborliness that is long gone. They also ignore price." There were statements of this kind attached to each of the 55 entries. I would submit to this group that if we are any less candid in the analysis of the presentations we hear during this week, we'll be doing a disservice to the participants and the philosophy of the Congress.

In moving toward a conclusion, I must admit that I have a certain set of preconceived notions about the problem we are talking about. And I stand before you with a complete set of biases that is part of the human package we label Arlo Woolery. If you perceive these characteristics as fundamental flaws in me or in what I've said, then I would say, good for you. It is good that we are here. And if you can subject yourself, your views, and your biases to the same critical scrutiny, then I think you can avoid some of the pitfalls into which I may have stumbled. I think we should take some givens and quit arguing about them. I think all of us are in favor of soil conservation, and there is no reason to mount a major argument about things on which we all agree. I think we are all against hunger—real hunger and privation—so there is no reason to debate that issue. I think that we have developed agricultural technology that allows many countries to produce food supplies far in excess of their domestic needs. Alphabetically, I might just tick off Argentina, which could feed 100 million people; America, which we know can feed almost 300 million people; Australia, which I am sure could feed many more than its present 14 million inhabitants. Also, not every country needs to be self-sufficient in every product. If you go back in history, you'll find that trading in food and spices and things that are not perishable has gone on between countries for millenia. If we can learn to produce an economic system that lets us make exchanges of surplus among countries, we certainly are all richer for that discovery.

I think this Congress will be unproductive if we fall into the trap of debating whose prophecies are best, or embark upon a course of evaluating differential agricultural technologies. We should be looking at political, social, and economic solutions as part, perhaps a major part, of our deliberations.

Now some of you may be saying, well that was more a sermon than a speech. And if that has offended anyone, I offer my apologies. But I also should remind you that sometimes sermons are given when you have to say something, and sometimes sermons are given when you have something to say. I hope that my remarks have fallen into the latter category. May I also encourage you to rub your ideas together, to generate some intellectual friction. Great ideas are neither culture bound nor time and site specific. They are building blocks of a better tomorrow. And as we come together let us not be bogged down in argument over the completely unknowable, but rather let us look for that latent intellectual spark which can be fanned into a flame in which we can forge the kind of world that approaches the ideal which brings us all together—an improved relationship between man and land, with the earth's abundance insured for the future and divided more equally among the people who inhabit it today.

Chapter 3

Towards Land Policy for Human Survival

Nathaniel Lichfield

In this Congress we are not concerned with land merely in the popular meaning of terra firma. Rather the word comprises, as generally understood in land resource economics, those God- or Nature-given resources of the planet which sustain man by providing him with food, fiber, energy, shelter, and recreation. We are thus concerned with minerals, topsoil, rivers, oceans, crops, livestock, fish, and the air and sun, which make life possible.

That land in this sense has crucial importance in human survival, the focus of this Congress, is thus not surprising. Nor is it new. Since the 1960s the hypothesis of doom has been urged: unless man conserves natural resources, he is the most threatened of animal species.[1] Indeed, our Congress takes place in a year which will see publications of the World Conservation Strategy for the Earth's Survival, which is spelling out the message.[2]

In the opposite camp are many who do not accept this hypothesis. It gives, they argue, insufficient place to the possibilities of substitution among the earth's scarce resources,[3] to the adaptability of man himself to cope with the conflict between resource development and resource conservation,[4] and it ignores the political impossibility of slowing down resource development at a time when the South is demanding greater equality in standard of living with the North.[5]

But even this opposite camp accepts the proposition that *land resource* is critical for the human condition. And whether it be finite in quantity or not, it must be husbanded. Its abundance in, for example, the vast territories of the United States or Brazil should not leave us with sickening experiences there of waste, pollution, erosion, and neglect. Thus, the real controversy is not about the existence of the problem but about its nature, size, and urgency, and how to cope with it.

But while this is the focus of the Congress, our objective is not just further discussion and proceedings on the topic. Rather, it is to concentrate on one particular theme within the focus, and one which no other international bodies can discharge. This is expressed in the statement in the Congress program on its desired results, namely: "An appraisal of whether realistic land policies can be fashioned successfully to manage the land resource and satisfy human needs for shelter and food," leading to specific conclusions, with recommendations and suggestions for future action.

If these desired results can be achieved, this Congress will make an important and distinctive contribution to the wiser use of land in the human condition. If the doom hypothesis is correct, it will be a vital contribution to human survival. And if not, it will still be a valuable contribution in diminishing degradation in the quality and standard of life for our people.

These desired results will be better achieved the more the contributing authors and the participants address themselves to the land policy theme. While the focus of the Congress covers familiar, well-documented ground, its theme—the land policies required to meet the management objectives—does not. This is not because land policy is a new topic. It is not. Each and every country has evolved land policies of its own over the centuries to meet its needs and objectives. What is new is the comparatively recent attempt, stimulated by the United Nations, to create an international awareness of the importance and significance of land policy.[6] And this has been followed by recent essays in institutional, professional, and academic circles to deepen and enrich the subject.[7] In this the two sponsor organizations of this Congress have made their contribution.[8]

My own paper contains two themes, which we consider in turn. The first is resource management. Since land policy is here seen in the context of the management of natural resources to sustain human needs, I introduce this as a context, and the need for a resource management strategy for conserved use and development. The second theme is that of land policy and its instruments in the execution of such a strategy.

RESOURCE MANAGEMENT

Since our focus is the wiser management of natural resources to meet growing human needs, and since, doomsday or not, it is the conservation of the resources consistent with their use for human needs which must be our target, it is useful to describe the resources by categorizing them in terms of resource realities and conservation goals. Here the basic criterion in conservation is relative renewability or sustainability over time. From this flows the following classifications:

fund or stock resources (nonrenewable)
flow resources (renewable)
both fund and flow: biological resources, soil resources, and man-made improvements attached to the land.[9]

Whether God- or Nature-given or man-made, natural resources of all these categories have to some degree or another become appropriated as "property." It is this dual aspect of natural resources which has given rise to controversy. Simply stated, the question becomes, Is land a resource or property? A resource or a commodity for exchange?

While a telling and vivid contrast, and one which goes to the root of the land problem, the distinction is not too meaningful. The two are complementary. Where a private owner regards his land as a "resource" to sustain *him* (and not society) into the future, in the management of that resource for private gain he knows that short-term exploitation is not necessarily more profitable to him than longer-term conservation. And many a private owner, particularly of large landed estates, rural or urban, has taken a long and wide view of his objectives and practiced resource management on lines which leave little to be desired for the community. More than that, just as for utilization of a resource it is necessary to have an owner of the land interest (what farmer would grow crops if they were subject to legal pillage?), for conservation to be implemented it is necessary to have an owner with an eye to the longer term, for otherwise no one has an interest in pursuing conservation. Tenure is a critical element in development, management, and conservation.

Conserved Use and Development

There can be no question but that additional large-scale utilization of natural resources is inevitable over the foreseeable future. Consider the expected doubling of the world's population in 25 years; the pressures for full employment; the rising standards of consumption of food, fiber, energy, shelter, and leisure; the demands of the underprivileged in every country, and of the developing world, to catch up.

We are thus faced with the need for a strategy which recognizes the inevitability of growth married to conservation, which ensures the wise use of resources, in the long-term interests of mankind. This will mean a great adjustment in the relative weight of these twin goals in man's use of the earth. Whereas previously the driving emphasis has been on development and growth with somewhat belated and relatively weak attempts at control, in the wider and longer-term interests of society there now has to be a redressing of the balance. Conservation must have greater weight, based not only on considerations of efficiency but equity and social justice as well.

We are thus seeking a strategy of management for land, within the reasonably well established field and discipline recognized as resource management: the formulation of objectives, and the devising of operational policies, plans, and programs to achieve them, with the appropriate instruments and institutions for their implementation.[10]

But if the devising of a resource management strategy of itself should not create insurmountable difficulties in the light of contemporary knowledge, its implementation would be more daunting. For one thing, we live in a world where plan, policy, and program making are strong, but implementation is the Achilles heel. For another, we have the need to develop greater awareness of the role of conservation economics and policies in the use of the land resources through development and growth. For yet another, the requirements of conservation as part of the human condition necessitate a new consciousness on the part of each producer and consumer of the earth's resources, which has been formulated as a need for a new ethic.

All of these aspects of the new strategy require innovation in the application of what is known,[11] even though practiced by some resource owners and not by others, both public and private. But what is also needed is the extension of such knowledge to management on behalf of society—nationally in the first instance and then internationally, through current and emerging world agencies. The need is to advance this consciousness and to develop the philosophy, methods, and institutions.

LAND POLICY

Having set the scene for conserved use and development of the land resource, with development and conservation having equal weight, let us now explore the second theme of the paper: the role of land policy in this endeavor.[12]

We start with the concept of the "proprietary land unit," which defines the essential decision-making unit in terms of particular land and its tenure.[13] By definition, the management of the resource relates to that land according to the management objectives of the proprietor, which are conditioned by his tenure. These could include the rapid exploitation of the dust-bowl farmer or short-term speculative urban or mineral development; or it could cover the long-term view of management and administration of landed property with an eye to successive generations. Such long-term management carries with it the concept of a plan based on the objective of optimum return over the future which is the context for the management operations, it being recognized that the return can be seen not only in financial terms but also in terms of pride of ownership, status, political power, and, in these days, self-sufficiency in food, utilities, and energy. It is the art and science of such land management which has become established, certainly in Britain, as a professional and academic discipline of standing, under the synonyms of estate management, land management, land economy, and land administration.[14]

In such management the guiding principle is that land resources can sustain man over a longer period if properly conserved (in maximum sustained use), having regard to the kind of resource in question—renewable, nonrenewable, and so on. Within such management of the "private proprietary land unit" it has been necessary to introduce "private" land policy on the following lines. For landed property to discharge its functions there must be some recognition in law of property rights; of the owner's need, in a durable asset of fixed location, to be able to subdivide the ownership into tenancies, leases, easements, and so on; of the mutual obligations of adjoining and nearby owners (for example, rights of way, rights of light); of the obligations of those in possession to those to whom possession will revert in future (for example, to restore the property to conditions which have not suffered from exploitation).

The legal basis of private land policy is clearly a matter for government and the courts. But government has also needed to introduce "public" land policy to ensure that the public interest is protected. Examples dating from the last century are the setting of standards for the construction of dwellings to avoid health hazards; the avoidance of pollution of watercourses; the need to discharge sewerage into proper systems; the need to regulate the spacing of buildings to avoid overshadowing, lack of sunlight; the need to reduce pollution from factory waste; and so on.

In such urban and regional planning the impact tends to be on land as terra firma (including the minerals below the surface and the man-made improvements above it). The development of such resources is more easily controllable by governmental institutions than that of other natural resources, such as biological resources. Accordingly, such planning has tended to relate to land use policy, since it makes its main and most decided impact on the utilization of the earth's surface. And in the implementation of such land use policy there have been developed public land policy measures or instruments.[15] Examples are the acquisition of land by government to enable current unsuitable ownership patterns to be pooled; the control of the use of land without the need for government to take up part of the land; the advance purchase or banking of land to ensure that it is available for suitable development in needed quantities, appropriate locations, appropriate tenure, at the right time and at the appropriate prices. And while these land policy measures have been aimed at the *efficiency* of land utilization, others (such as taxation) have been aimed at the *equity of distribution* of the profit from the utilization and development of land, as between the proprietary owners and developers and the community at large.

But while urban and regional planning has of necessity primarily confined itself to making an impact on physical development and minerals, there have grown up in parallel government policies in relation to other aspects and elements of natural resources. Examples are controls for the minimizing of resource depletion (replanting of felled forests, reclamation of derelict land, protection of fish and livestock) and for control of environmental pollution (in effluent to rivers, noise, toxic emissions, fuel burning). Insofar as these resources come within our opening definition of *land*, they are also land policies, although they could equally well be termed land resource policies.

Also in parallel, and of even greater vintage, is the march of land reform. While land tenure has impeded what government has considered to be effective resource management, it has intervened to change tenure patterns. One direction is the breaking up of large landed estates to offer peasant proprietors the incentive to increase production (and the social justice of retaining their product). But another direction is the pooling of small ownerships, where this has impeded, for example, required increases in agricultural productivity in rural areas, or the benefits of comprehensive renewal in urban areas.

SUMMARY: THE NEED TO COORDINATE LAND RESOURCE POLICIES

In human settlements the function of the management of land resources thus arises in various quarters. It exists in both the private and public sectors in the ongoing management of proprietary land units; in the planned development of the land resources, be it by the private or the public sector; in the public urban and regional planning agency whose function is to control evolution of human settlements; in public policies to regulate environmental disruption; in socially and economically oriented land reform.

In all this diversity of natural resource management there have grown up land policies and instruments, both private and public, from varied sources. But despite this, they all relate to the one resource—the land—which requires their coordination in the interests of wise management. Instances of this coordination in practice are seen in urban and rural planning.

The Dividing Line Between Private and Public Land Policy

The dividing line between private and public land policy is certainly not a tidy one, as the following instances show:

(1) Houston, Texas, it is argued, has been developed under sale covenants in no worse way than could have been achieved under conventional urban planning. Why, then, the need for a public land policy beyond the essentials?[16]

(2) The increasing involvement of public bodies in the management of enterprises (ports, forests) and the planning and development of human settlements (rural or urban) has meant the

increasing ownership of land resources in public proprietary land units by public agencies whose aim is to discharge their own corporate objectives.

However untidy, it is important to be clear about facts on both sides of the dividing line if land resource management is to be effective. It is thus helpful to spell out some of the considerations affecting either side.[17]

(1) However vigorous the defenders of the private market, they nonetheless recognize that there are limitations in its achieving social goals, and that state intervention is necessary for certain functions (such as defense, roads, policing). In addition, they would accept that the private market does not have full regard to externalities, and that state intervention is needed on this account also.

(2) Since the above is arguable, there is needed for effective intervention some logic which considers both the costs of intervention and its benefits. This would be in contrast to intervention through ideology, which simply regards the imperfections of the market alone as justification for intervention by the state.

(3) Intervention not based on ideology would recognize the strengths of the market and also the importance of giving it the maximum opportunity to carry out its role effectively. Therefore, the government might set out to assist the market rather than intervene. A clear case here is the better dissemination of information, on which the market function relies; one of the roles of urban planning, perversely enough, is to help the market by supplying more comprehensive information about urban entities than any individual entrepreneur can hope to amass. Another is to recognize that part of the inefficiency of the market arises when the negotiations that could take place are inhibited through the sheer cost of transactions, whether the amount of legal work involved, government charges and duties, time delays, or the like.

(4) But even if government intervention is justified, it brings with it a price. The argument that the market is inefficient in achieving social objectives does not immediately *pari passu* make the intervening government efficient or even more efficient than the market. Governmental administration and bureaucracy can be wasteful and clumsy. Put more kindly, this is not necessarily an indictment of government but rather a statement that the art and science of governmental intervention is more complex and so, relatively speaking, just not as advanced as the practice of market transactions. There is government failure as well as market failure.

(5) Even if, nonetheless, government intervention in land policy is justified, a price is paid in terms of individual freedom. Here we are not concerned simply with the freedom of the market to deploy its own resources but also with the deep attachment that the individual proprietor or tenant has to his land. Freedom to own and exploit part of the land resources is a deeply rooted ethic. While state intervention implies that it is necessary for the freedom of the individual to be subverted to the freedom of the remainder of the community, toward whom exploitation of the land resource could be inimical, as it could be to their children, nonetheless freedom of proprietorship in land needs to be respected.

(6) One of the features of public intervention is the view that the increase in land values does not originate from the passive landowner but rather in the growth of population, production, and consumption, in the active development by government, and in its regulation in the market. Accordingly, all increases in land value, or a proportion, should be the property of the state. There should thus be a redistribution of land value increments from owners to the public, under one or another scheme for the public ownership of land value.[18] But whatever the logic here, there is one possible consequence to be avoided: such redistribution of the product can have its repercussions on the allocation of resources in production and so stultify the operations of the land market and the development process itself. This is but one instance of the need for care in selecting the appropriate land policy and instruments.[19]

Thus the private/public land policy relationship needs to be explored with care. And since each of the variables mentioned differs from country to country, there can be no uniform prescriptions or rules applying to all countries. Perhaps it was here that the weakness of the otherwise splendid UN Habitat Recommendations, adopted by 132 governments, was to be seen.[20] They were uniform and allowed little latitude for local, national, or state variations.

Beyond Resource and Property

Even if land can be managed successfully as both a resource and property in conserved use and development, there is still a further dimension: the management of the resource as property, with its economic connotations, is still an unsatisfying situation to those to whom land has a much greater significance in society. Karl Polanyi has written:

What we call land is an element of nature inextricably interwoven with man's institutions...Land is thus tied up with the organization of kinship, neighborhood, craft and creed—with tribe and temple, village, guild and church...the economic function is but one of the many vital functions of land. It invests man's life with stability; it is the site of his habitation; it is a condition of his physical safety; it is the landscape and the seasons.[21]

There is also the identification of land with nationhood and freedom from oppression, the notion of access to the land independent of a foreign government; and, given independence, access to it by right and not as a function of wealth.

All in all, land in the human condition is not only crucial to serving needs in the growth and development of human society. It also strikes deep in human history, ideology, and conflict. This deeper dimension adds to the urgency of the need to formulate successful land policy. It thus adds to the responsibilities falling on this Congress.

NOTES

1. See Rachel Carson, *Silent Spring* (Boston: Houghton, Mifflin, 1962); Donella H. Meadows et al., *The Limits to Growth* (New York: Universe Books, 1972); and Lester R. Brown, *Building a Sustainable Society* (New York: W. W. Norton and Company, 1981).
2. Various country reports are as of this writing in draft on the way to publication. The sponsoring body is IUCN-UNEP-WWF, *World Conservation Strategy*, Living Resource Conservation for Sustainable Development, 1980.
3. Harold E. Goeller and Alvin M. Weinberg, "The Age of Substitutability," in Maurice Goldsmith et al., eds., *A Strategy for Resources* (Amsterdam: North Holland Publishing Co., 1977).
4. Julian L. Simon, *The Ultimate Resource* (Princeton, N.J.: Princeton University Press, 1981).
5. Wilfred Beckerman, *In Defence of Economic Growth* (London: Jonathan Cape, 1974).
6. UN, Dept. of Economics and Social Affairs, *Urban Land Policies and Land Use Control Measures*, 7 vols. (ST/ECA/167), 1973; UN, *Report of Habitat: United Nations Conference on Human Settlements*, Vancouver, B.C., May 31-June 11, 1976.
7. For example, John Ratcliffe, *Land Policy* (London: Hutchinson, 1976); Haim Darin-Drabkin, *Land Policy and Urban Growth* (Oxford: Pergamon Press, 1977); *Urban Land Policy Issues and Opportunities: World Bank Staff Working Paper No. 283*, 2 vols. (Washington, D.C.: The World Bank, 1978); ICLPS, *Newsletters* 1-17 (1979-1983); Nathaniel Lichfield and Haim Darin-Drabkin, *Land Policy in Planning* (London: Allen & Unwin, 1980); O. H. Koenigsberger, S. Groak, and Nathaniel Lichfield, eds., *A Review of Land Policies* (Oxford: Pergamon Press, 1980).

8. Matthew Cullen and Sharon Woolery, eds., *World Congress on Land Policy, 1980* (Lexington, Mass.: Lexington Books, 1982).
9. For various treatments see S. V. Ciriacy Wantrup, *Resource Conservation: Economics and Policies* (Berkeley: University of California Press, 1952); Raleigh Barlowe, *Land Resource Economics* (Englewood Cliffs, N.J.: Prentice Hall, 1958); D. W. Pearce, *Environmental Economics* (New York: Longman, 1976).
10. See, for example, A. Warren and F. B. Goldsmith, *Conservation in Practice* (New York: John Wiley and Sons, 1974).
11. See, for example, Randall W. Scott, ed., *Management and Control of Growth: Issues, Techniques, Problems, Trends*, 3 vols. (Washington, D.C.: Urban Land Institute, 1975); Wantrup, *Resource Conservation*; Barlowe, *Land Resource Economics*.
12. The following is a development of Nathaniel Lichfield, "Towards a Comprehension of Land Policy," in Koenigsberger et al., eds., *A Review of Land Policies*.
13. D. R. Denman and Sylvio Prodano, *Land Use: an Introduction to Proprietary Land Use Analysis* (London: Allen & Unwin, 1972).
14. Michael Thorncroft, *Principles of Urban Estate Management* (London: Estates Gazette, 1968); John Ratcliffe, *An Introduction to Urban Land Administration* (London: Estates Gazette, 1978); Tim Stapleton, *Estate Management Practise* (London: Estates Gazette, 1981).
15. See Lichfield and Darin-Drabkin, *Land Policy in Planning*.
16. B. Siegan, *Land Use without Zoning* (Lexington, Mass.: D. C. Heath, 1972).
17. The following is a development of Nathaniel Lichfield, "Land Policy: Seeking the Right Balance in Government Intervention—An Overview," in *Urban Law and Policy* (1980).
18. Lichfield and Darin-Drabkin, *Land Policy in Planning*, chaps. 5 and 6; D. Hagman and D. Misczynski, *Windfalls for Wipeouts: Land Value Capture and Compensation* (Chicago: American Society of Planning Officials, 1978).
19. Lichfield and Darin-Drabkin, *Land Policy in Planning*, Chap. 9.
20. UN, *Report on Habitat*.
21. Karl Polanyi, *The Great Transformation: The Political and Economic Origins of Our Time* (Boston: Beacon Press, 1957), quoted in Harold J. Barnet, "Pressures of Growth upon Environment," in Henry Jarrett, ed., *Environmental Quality in a Growing Economy* (Baltimore: Resources for the Future, 1966).

PART II

Worldwide Trends and Their Impact on the Provision of Food and Shelter

Introduction to
Second Session

Harold Dunkerley

Yesterday morning, as is right and proper for such an international meeting, the speakers provided a broad perspective on the subject of this Congress. Aurelio Peccei gave us a stimulating vision of the responsibilities of a liberated human race, in charge of its own destiny, but faced with finite constraints, not least of land, under the woefully inadequate comprehension of the dangers and issues.

Arlo Woolery, in an elegant homily, reminded us of our own limitations, including an addiction to statistics and extrapolations and to analytic fashions unconsciously biased by temporary phenomena. These can lead us to ignore the obvious inconsistencies, absurdities even, of current policies, and the uneven sharing of the world's resources.

Nat Lichfield reminded us that, while many factors are relevant, this is after all a Congress on land policy. We should not allow the many fascinating details affecting the magnitude of future demands for land to divert attention from the need to get on with the task of formulating more effective approaches to land resource management and land policy.

Later this week we will be giving detailed consideration to conflicts at the urban fringe and policies of managing land to meet basic needs. This morning's topic, "Worldwide Trends and Their

Impact on the Provision of Food and Shelter"—the two main but not the only contenders for land—provides a bridge from the wider to the narrower focus. In introducing the topic, I'd like to emphasize the urgency of the issues and their relevance to defining appropriate land policies. Better assessment of the emerging pressures on land is vital to evaluation of the trade-offs between alternative policies.

It is in the developing world that the problems are most stark, the pressures greatest, the resources smallest, and the choice between alternatives most agonizing. This or that conservation policy— involving, say, establishing a new town in a less fertile or less polluted area, or using neighboring nonagricultural land for expansion of an existing urban area—may appear highly desirable. But such policies very often result in much higher costs, at least in the short or medium term, and in using the peripheral agricultural land surrounding existing urban areas. And this means that fewer resources will be available for providing shelter for the poor.

What criteria are we to use in weighing the choice? What can we say about public responsibility for future generations as compared with the present? To what extent are market prices for land an adequate guide to relative scarcities or productivities? This issue cannot be avoided. In many developing countries, urban land area will double on present trends in less than a decade. Better use of vacant urban land and higher densities may ameliorate but clearly will not solve the problem.

I am confident that this morning's speakers will provide us with a better understanding of the compatibility of urban and agricultural claims on land: to what extent they are or can be complementary, to what extent inevitably competitive. I only wish to add a word of caution on the great variations between regions, between countries, and even within countries in the intensity of the problems and the resources available. That is, in the inherent flexibility to cope with the problems. One example only: net urban savings per additional family in some poor, fast-growing cities in Africa are as low as $2,000. Two thousand dollars, that is to say, is the maximum available for their dwellings, work places, additional roads, schools, and so on. In some cities in Latin America, where the ratio of urban growth is now one of the lowest of any major region in the world, the corresponding net savings per additional family may be over $200,000. In some developed world cities they may be over a million dollars. We must be very careful of generalizations about what can be done.

Chapter 4

Evolving Pressures on Land Resources

*Lester Brown**

Today I am going to talk about population, about land, about food, about energy, and about the changing relationships among these four resources. I will begin by making three simple points about population growth.

First, we have focused on the rate of population growth and have noted with some satisfaction and relief that the rate of world population growth is declining. In 1970, as best we can tell, it was about 1.9 percent per year. Today it is about 1.7 percent per year. Clearly, the rate is headed in the right direction—but not fast enough. The annual increment to our population is still increasing. In 1970 we added about 70 million people, and in 1982 about 78 million people to the world population. We must accelerate the decline in the rate in order to reduce the annual increment. I think that we have reached the point where we now have to concern ourselves with the absolute increment, because in many cases we are simply exceeding the long-term carrying capacity of many of the economy's basic support systems.

Second, both traditionally and recently, we have relied on economic improvements to reduce the rate of population growth. That is the foundation of the demographic transition. But, as we

*This manuscript is derived from a transcript of oral remarks.

move into a period of slower economic growth, the economic improvements that would lead to lower fertility may not exist as they have over the past generation. It looks as though we are moving into a period of much slower global economic growth. Instead of the 4-5 percent that we became accustomed to during the third quarter of this century, the growth rate may be closer to 2 percent. The significance of this is that when the world economy was expanding at 4-5 percent, any country that came close to the average was achieving a gain in per capita income. But if the world economy should average a 2 percent growth rate—and for the last four years it has been lower than that—then in many countries there will be no improvements in per capita living standards, and no contribution to the decline in fertility.

Third, for our purposes, population growth is particularly important because it generates a demand for more crop land while simultaneously generating pressures to convert crop land to nonfarm uses. Where land policy is concerned, population growth is a double-edged sword.

This introduces an issue with which most of you are quite familiar: crop land conversion. We convert crop land to many uses. One is urbanization—the growth of cities. The world's urban population in 1975 was about 1.5 billion. (It is projected to reach 3.1 billion by the end of the century, although I do not think it will.) This increase will require the urbanization of about 2 percent of the world's crop land. Two percent is not very much, unless you really need it. And we do and will. As it happens, that 2 percent represents some of our better crop land. The Canadians, for example, in analyzing this phenomenon, estimate that one-half of all the farm land they are losing to cities comes from the top 5 percent of their land in terms of fertility. Not only cities but villages also grow. In an interesting study, Akef Quasi from Bangladesh, looking at many years of data, concluded that in a society that used bamboo and thatch for home construction, the conversion of crop land or the expansion of villages was directly proportional to the growth in population. If we look at a country like India, with 600,000 villages, almost all of them growing, we can begin to sense the way in which residential uses compete with agricultural uses for crop land. I first went to India in 1956 and spent several months living in three different villages there. When I went back, the expansion of those villages had been noticeable.

In China the problem is perhaps as severe as anywhere in the world. China has most of its billion people squeezed into a thousand-mile-wide belt in the eastern part of the country. With a 10 percent rate of industrial growth that has been maintained in China since

1960 or so, tens of thousands of factories have been built. The problem is that these new factories have had to be built close to where the people are, and the people are close to where the good rice land is. So there are thousands of factory sites in southern China now on land that not too many years ago was producing two crops of rice per year. The Chinese are concerned about this issue.

I now turn to the question of soil erosion. The rate of soil erosion in the world today underlines the importance of preserving all the crop land we possibly can. New data are becoming available to help us understand the dimensions of the erosion problem. What we are beginning to see is that mounting economic pressure in the form of demand for food and other agricultural commodities is being transmitted to the resource base, to our soils, and this is leading in many areas to their degradation through erosion.

We take great pride in the fact that world food output doubled between 1950 and 1973—in less than a generation. It had never happened before. But we can now see in looking back that many of the agricultural practices that were adopted in that ambitious effort are leading to the excessive loss of topsoil. We see it in our own Midwest, where the continuous row cropping of corn has replaced long-term rotations that included hay and grassland. We see it in the slash-and-burn cycle in Nigeria and Thailand and Venezuela; where farmers used to wait 20 to 25 years before replanting a site, the interval has been shortened to ten years, and even less in some areas. The soils do not have a chance to completely regenerate. One gets the feeling, when looking at the reports on soil erosion, that farmers are being pushed up the hillsides everywhere. The pressures are not limited to one particular country or another; they are worldwide. Food is a global commodity, and the increases in the demand for food affect all countries.

We are beginning to get some feel for the scale of topsoil loss. In 1968 Sheldon Judson, a geologist, published an article in *The American Scientist* in which he estimated that before agriculture, grazing, and other more recent human activities, about 9 billion tons of soil per year were moved from the continents to the oceans in the form of sediment. In 1968 he estimated that had increased at least two-, perhaps two and a half-fold. As best we can tell, in 1983 the loss is triple that original pre-agricultural 9 billion tons. This means that man has become a geological agent in his own right, overwhelming the activities of nature. The important difference is that soil erosion through natural causes did not exceed the rate of new soil formation. But today, on more and more of the world's crop land, it does.

We now have data on soil erosion in many different forms. The

World Bank, interestingly, is launching a major new project and sector report in this area. We have data on the amount of soil carried to the ocean by about a hundred of the world's major rivers. And what we see is an accelerating and very large flow of topsoil, much of it from the world's crop lands. We now have data on the movement of soil by air. Four studies on the movement of soil particles from North Africa across the Atlantic have estimated that between 100 million and 400 million tons of soil are crossing the African coast and moving over the Atlantic Ocean each year. The most recent study is at the higher end of that range. We now see from satellite photographs, after two or three days of particularly strong winds blowing from North Africa out into the Atlantic, dust plumes move progressively across the Atlantic. They are visible from the air. We now have data on a similar process occurring in the Pacific. The scientists at Mauna Loa Observatory in Hawaii have been gathering data for eight years on soil particles in the air from air samples that they take on the mountain. Those samples show a continuous flow of airborne soil from the Asian mainland some 2,000 miles away across the Pacific. The studies, covering eight years, document a very distinct annual cycle, with the amount of airborne soil going up in March, April, and May. The scientists in Mauna Loa can now tell when spring plowing starts in North China.

We have undertaken at the Worldwatch Institute a report (1984) on progress toward a sustainable society. We are attempting for the first time an estimate of the excessive loss of topsoil from the world's crop lands. (By excessive we mean a loss of topsoil that exceeds the rate of natural soil formation—the tolerance, or T-factor, as soil scientists describe it.) This worldwide estimate is based on national data but is by necessity filled out with many assumptions. (There is no table, for example, in the FAO Production Yearbook that lists by country the amount of topsoil lost in crop land.) But there is enough data to make an estimate, and we think it's better to make an estimate, however incomplete, than to make projections of world food production omitting soil erosion as an influence.

For the United States, based on good data from a 1977 soil inventory of some 200,000 samplings, we estimate a loss of 1.5 billion tons of topsoil from our crop lands each year in excess of the rate of natural soil formation. For India, based on data gathered by the local field stations of the Indian Center for Agricultural Research, the figure is 4.7 billion tons per year. For the Soviet Union, based on a combination of data and assumptions, 2.3 billion tons. For China, 3.3 billion tons. For the world as a whole, our preliminary estimate shows an annual loss—an excessive loss—of topsoil from crop land of 22.7 billion tons.

How much, in round figures, is 23 billion tons? If you assume, on the 3.2 billion acres of crop land in the world, that seven inches of topsoil remain, that comes to just over 1,000 tons per acre. So of the roughly 3.5 trillion tons of topsoil on our global crop land base, about 23 billion tons are lost per year, or .7 percent. This loss does not come from the entire crop-land base; it is concentrated on a fraction of it. It is interesting to contrast the situation with that of oil. Estimates of the ultimately recoverable reserves of oil in the world converge somewhere around 2 trillion barrels. Producing about 20 billion barrels a year, we are depleting our oil resources at about 1 percent per year. The difference is that we know what we are doing with oil; we have national policies and programs in almost every country to respond to oil depletion. Not so with soil.

The erosion of soil is the erosion of productivity. There has been all too little research in most of the world on the relationship between these losses. How does the loss of an inch of topsoil from a typical six- to eight-inch topsoil base affect productivity? There have been fourteen studies in the United States on the relationship, direct or indirect, between soil erosion and corn yields. The average result shows that, all other things being equal, the loss of an inch of topsoil reduces corn yields by 6 percent. For wheat the result is the same: twelve studies show that the loss of one inch of topsoil reduces average yields by about 6 percent.

In the southern conservation district of the state of Iowa, a team of agronomists, economists, and engineers has undertaken the most detailed analysis I've seen on the long-term economic consequences of soil erosion. They looked, for example, at how soil erosion will affect fertilizer demand. They point out that in going from a situation of slight erosion to one of moderate erosion, the fertilizer requirements per acre of corn will increase by 18 pounds per acre. In going from moderate to severe erosion, the fertilizer requirements will increase by an additional 38 pounds per acre to maintain a given level of productivity. They have even gone so far as to measure the increase in fuel required as soil erosion progresses and farmers are plowing up more and more subsoil. In going from a situation of slight erosion to one of severe erosion, fuel requirements will grow by 38 percent, as tillage becomes much more difficult where the soil is more compact and less friable. This is the kind of research we need if we are to understand the long-term consequences of soil erosion.

Secretary of Agriculture Block recognizes that soil erosion is a problem, but he says that he cannot argue in the councils of the administration for the sort of increase in budget resources needed to stabilize our soils. I feel that this is a matter of national security. We need to put the additional $1 billion, roughly double current expenditures on programs, on the table with two more B-1s or one more MX or whatever else we think about when we think about our long-term national security. Then and only then will we get the right answer.

Unfortunately, this problem is not unique to the US Government. It is a problem that plagues governments everywhere. The loss of 23 billion tons of topsoil per year represents a massive agronomic deficit. It represents a debt that our children will pay off in the form of higher food prices. There are other deficits, too: balance of payments deficits; corporate deficits that lead to bankruptcy; the fiscal deficit in Washington of about $200 billion this year. There is a difference between these deficits, however. If a corporation goes into bankruptcy, the distribution of wealth changes, but there is no real loss in productive capacity. If Argentina is declared insolvent, there is no automatic loss in global productive capacity. But the loss of 25 billion tons of topsoil per year represents a real loss in productivity. That is the difference between this deficit and most of the other deficits that we read about on the financial pages.

Let me raise another point. We have been substituting energy for land, sometimes with great abandon. Up until 1950 most of the increases in world food output came from increasing the area under cultivation. Since 1950 four-fifths of the increase have come from intensifying land use. Intensifying land use invariably means using more energy. In 1950 the world's farmers used 14 million tons of chemical fertilizers. In 1982 they used 117 million tons. This is probably the best single indicator we have about the growing intensity of modern agriculture. Fertilizer factories have become the new frontier. They have taken the place of the frontiers of agricultural settlement. But we are beginning to experience diminishing returns on the additional use of fertilizer in the more agriculturally advanced parts of the world. That is to say, in the American Midwest, back in the 1950s a pound of nitrogen fertilizer might have resulted in another 15 or 20 pounds of corn yield. Today it would produce an increase of only five or seven or eight. That is true in Europe, in Japan, and to a lesser degree in other areas. The returns on the use of fertilizer are diminishing, and the long-term real cost of energy embodied in that fertilizer is rising. The substitution of energy for land, although it has been very successful over the past generation, will not continue to be successful over the long term.

Another point: except in urban areas, the value of most land has been determined by its food-producing capacity. But as we move beyond the age of oil, land will acquire an energy collection value. As the curtain falls on the age of oil, we are moving more and more toward renewable energy resources. Renewable energy is solar energy in some form or another. Whether it is in biological form—firewood or energy crops—or in mechanical form—hydropower, wind energy, photovoltaics—it takes space to collect solar energy.

One of the most ambitious efforts to produce energy from crops is now under way in Brazil, as most of you know. Brazil now has over a million hectares of land in sugar cane planted for the purpose of producing alcohol to fuel automobiles. This year Brazil will be getting one-fourth of its automotive fuel in the form of alcohol from sugar cane, up from about 2-3 percent five years ago. The International Monetary Fund, as one of the conditions for continuing its latest loan to Brazil, required that the price of all petroleum products, including gasoline, be raised very substantially. That will further reinforce this trend toward producing liquid fuel from crops.

In this country, the biggest and perhaps most impressive development in renewable energy has been in firewood. A few years ago I was talking to an economist from Poland about a range of issues including energy. I showed him the trend on wood-stove sales in the United States from 1970 to 1981 or so, going up to well over a million a year. He said, "No, this is the past. That's past." I answered, "No, this is the future." I told him, much to his surprise, that we now get twice as much delivered energy from firewood as we do from nuclear power, without the $36 billion subsidy. Although the focus in the media is on the use of wood as a residential fuel, industry is using more wood for fuel than are all the households in this country put together. Some 15 million Americans, out of 83 million, use wood to some degree. Five million use it exclusively as their only source of space heat. I could go on at length about the future role of wood, and biomass generally, as an energy source. For example, the World Bank now has firewood plantation projects in about 30 Third World countries. Eight years ago I doubt if there were any.

Collecting solar energy in mechanical form also takes space. The global breakthrough in wind electrical generation is occurring in California. At the end of last year, there were some 4,600 commercial-scale wind electric generators in operation. Most were built in the last two years. There are now 26 wind farms in California—wind farms with wind generators planted like rows of corn. In California there are now land booms in the mountain passes that connect the coastal region with the interior valleys. People are beginning to realize that whoever owns the land in those mountain passes will own the wind energy that passes through them. The Altamont Pass north of San Francisco is now filled with wind electric generators, with the electricity purchased by Pacific Gas and Electric, the utility in northern California.

Hydropower, large-scale and small-scale, is going to increase. It is a renewable source of energy and one toward which the world, and particularly developing countries, is moving quite rapidly since the oil pricing increases. The problem with hydropower is that every time a dam is built to create a reservoir, some land is inundated. The largest potential population displacement I know of is being considered in China. If the Chinese proceed with the Three Gorges Project on the Yellow River, which will have enormous generating capacity, they estimate that it will displace 2 million people. Even in China, 2 million people is a lot of people to relocate. But the capacity of the system would be about 30,000 megawatts. That is the equivalent of 30 large nuclear power plants. There are many reservoirs around the world that are now covering a half million to a million hectares of land, some of it prime crop land: the Volta River Project in Ghana; Aswan; the Itaipu project between Brazil and Paraguay.

So land is acquiring an energy collection value. I will be surprised if within another decade we do not see ranchers in the Great Plains of the United States marketing both wind-generated electricity and beef from the same land at the same time. Those happen to be land uses that do not conflict in any important sense. Farmers can have rows of windmills on the land and still graze the land with cattle without any particular trouble. These farmers are already tied into the grid that serves Denver, for example.

There are a few thoughts that I'd like to leave with you. One is that there will be more of us in the future than there are today, and that is going to put additional pressure on land resources. Second, in the post-petroleum era we will be even more dependent on land than we are today. Third, I think governments everywhere will be seized with the urgency of putting the brakes on population growth. China, as most of you know, is moving very aggressively toward the one-child family as a national norm. The difference between China and Bangladesh, India, Egypt, Nigeria, and Mexico is that the Chinese have made the calculations. They have looked ahead to the end of the century and beyond, at population, land, energy, water, jobs. And what they have seen has scared them. One of the responses to that set of projections is the one-child family.

Finally, I think in our technological, urbanizing society, we have lost sight of our dependence on land. A world that will soon have 5 billion inhabitants desperately needs a land ethic—a new reverence for land and a better understanding of our dependence on it.

Further Comments in
Response to Questions from
the Audience

Question: What causes the soil erosion that you mentioned in your remarks?

Mr. Brown: The soil that is showing up in river sediment analyses, that is ending up in hydroelectric reservoirs, is coming largely from two sources. One is the plowing of land that is sloping and which is not protected and therefore is eroding. The other source is land that has been deforested simply because of the demand for wood for fuel. It is being increasingly recognized that soil erosion has two costs: (1) the cost of losing it from where you need it; and (2) the cost of ending up with the soil in a reservoir or some other place where you don't want it—where you lose irrigation and hydrogenerating capacity. Increasingly we are beginning to recognize in the international development community, including the World Bank, that you can't just have a group of engineers build a hydroelectric dam and then forget it. It has to be part of a larger project that considers soil erosion and deforestation, or in some cases fairly ambitious reforestation programs in the watershed that feeds the dam. Otherwise the dam might have a life expectancy of 60 years, but it will be filled with silt in 20 years, which is what is happening in other countries.

Question: In a book on the dispossessed of the earth, Erik Eckholm argues that inadequate land tenure systems have a negative impact on all of the situations that you mentioned this morning, plus forests and other areas. How can a sound land reform system or program—land to the tiller, or land taxation, or any of those programs—aid in the achievement of the goals of the sustainable society, as you mentioned in your own report?

Mr. Brown: As Erik indicated in that paper, almost all the important issues we concern ourselves with in redevelopment, whether it be productivity or income distribution, are influenced by land-tenure patterns. My guess is that over the long term, as the employment problem worsens, it is going to lead, directly or indirectly, to a lot of soul searching in national capitals on the land distribution question. What is not clear to me is whether the reforms will come directly, as a result of enlightened public policy and strong political leadership, or indirectly, as a result of civil war and political instability and overthrow of governments. There is not much question in my mind that land reform is going to come in a lot of places. The question is how. And I think analytically it is difficult to pick this up because it cuts across disciplines. But at least some people—Elliot Richardson, for example, speaking of the situation in El Salvador in Congressional testimony, says you can't separate the political conflict there from the issue of land ownership and land distribution. And he says that until that land question is addressed, there may not be any lasting solution to the first problem.

Question: How much of a threat does acid rain pose for our environment?

Mr. Brown: I did not mention acid rain this morning, but for some years now it has become increasingly apparent that the freshwater base is very vulnerable to acid rain. There are thousands of lakes in New England, Canada, Scandinavia where there are no fish today because of increased acidity. What we are now beginning to discover is that forests are also vulnerable, and particularly coniferous species. In Czechoslovakia there is a substantial area—I've forgotten how many thousand or maybe even hundred thousand hectares of forest land—that is dead, apparently from acid rain. Efforts to replant there have been to no avail. In West Germany, where some of the best research has been done, they think they now have established a mechanism that links acid rain with the death of coniferous species. It apparently has to do with aluminum released in the soil as acidity rises. There was a German scientist in Washington a couple of weeks ago from the German equivalent of the Environmental Protection Agency whom someone asked about the fir trees in Germany. He said, "We don't have a problem with fir trees anymore because they're virtually all gone." He said it has happened almost within months, and that once you reach a certain critical threshold, then that's it. I think some 60 percent of Germany's forests are now affected. The German government has been shocked by this because, as you know, Germans are the world's leading foresters and take great pride in their forests. This discovery in recent months has led the Bundestag, the German legislature, to pass a regulation requiring that the pollution emissions from utility smokestacks be cut sharply, across the board. There was almost no debate on it. It just went like that because they are very concerned with what's happening to forests. I have seen a study in Poland in which scientists estimate that if the current industrial trend continues, 2 to 4 million hectares could be lost by 1990. Forests will be biological wastelands in a matter of years. Now, the next stage is: what happens to crop lands? There are now indications that crop yields in some areas are being measurably reduced by the acid rain effect. We used to look at it just in terms of how acid rain affected foliage, but it's clear now that something much more fundamental is at work here, and there needs to be more research on it. I'm told that in Washington there has been some change in attitude and they are at least prepared to recognize that acid rain may be a problem.

Chapter 5

Latin American Development and Its Environmental Manifestations

*Osvaldo Sunkel**

THE INTERNATIONAL CONTEXT AND THE STYLE OF DEVELOPMENT

I would like to give a brief description of the conditions under which the contemporary development style in Latin America has evolved during the past 30 years. With a view toward arriving at a central operational concept, I should recall two definitions which concern the characteristics and the effects of this development style. First, I consider it part of "a new type of global system originating from the worldwide expansion of oligopolistic techno-industrial capitalism in its new stage of transnational organization."[1] Second, as regards its ultimate effects, "the prevailing style leaves aside important sections of the population located in marginal rural areas and on the periphery of the cities, so that in absolute and even perhaps in relative terms, the number of nonparticipants remaining in a state of abject poverty increases."[2] The latter definition does not exclude the fact that the marginalized population "participates" in the sense that the style has a strong impact on their strategies and

*The author is Coordinator of the ECLA/UNEP Development and Environment Unit in Santiago, Chile. This paper draws heavily on his book, *La dimensión ambiental en los estilos de desarrollo de América Latina*, UN, Economic Commission for Latin America (E/CEPAL/G.1143), July 1981.

ways of living, while at the same time their presence affects the style itself, although they do not share in its benefits.

The first definition explicitly recognizes the existence of stages in the development of capitalism in Latin America. In order to appreciate this fully, it must be realized that the transnational style has followed upon other forms of capitalist "internationalization" in Latin America and, therefore, that it coexists with manifestations of such previous forms inherited from the nineteenth century, and even with precapitalist and noncapitalist processes in each of the countries considered, rooted in colonial and pre-Hispanic times. It should also be stressed that each country's development is the product of a process of penetration and dissemination of the new style and its interactions with pre-existing socioeconomic, political, cultural, and environmental characteristics. Each country is therefore a heterogeneous mix of these different historical phases.

Let us recall briefly the different periods through which contemporary Latin American development has passed since the end of the Second World War. The first stage, from 1945 until the period of international readjustment achieved in the mid-1950s, was essentially a continuation of the early industrialization process which began in the largest and most urbanized countries of the continent when the crisis of the 1930s and then the Second World War abruptly interrupted traditional trade relations between Latin America and the industrialized countries.

The second stage can be considered to have begun in the late 1950s with the vast international expansion of the United States' economy, the reassumption of prominent positions by the European and Japanese economies, and the ultimate ascendancy of the transnational development style.

A third and final stage can be identified with another boost to the transnationalization of development in an increasing number of countries as a consequence of the massive diffusion of the transnational patterns of consumption, greatly enhanced by the financial boom and permissiveness of the 1970s.

The overall result of these processes and phases was an unprecedented expansion of the region's economy: since 1950 the GNP has grown at an annual rate of 5.5 percent. This was higher than the growth rate of the world economy as a whole. This rapid expansion remained at relatively high levels until 1965 (5 percent), when many economies were still primarily involved in the production of goods to meet the unsatisfied demand for mass consumption within domestic markets, and while the ascendant style was beginning to penetrate into the larger countries of the region. The highest growth rates were seen in the following period. This was precisely the time when the style became dominant in the larger countries with broader markets such as Brazil, Mexico, and Argentina. At the same time, large-scale foreign investment, accompanied by monopolistic or oligopolistic national enterprises, concentrated the process of capital accumulation in those sectors which were most characteristic of the ascendant style. The stage of accelerated transnationalization took place between 1965 and 1974, when the rate reached 6.7 percent. Later, the recession in the developed capitalist countries and the energy crisis caused this rate to drop to around 4 percent between 1974 and 1980. At the same time, many countries of the region opened up their economies to the rest of the world in order to take advantage of the expansion of international financial markets that allowed them to sustain rapid rates of growth and consumption.

This rapid growth in production and consumption was accompanied by the diversification of the economic structure through industrialization, the population boom, the considerable geographic redistribution of the population owing to rapid urbanization, and the drastic change in the social relations of production, as the capitalist mode of production in its transnational phase spread through the continent. This is the process of internationalization of consumption patterns, investment, and technology, owing to its massive disseminatory effect on all social levels, economic sectors, and geographical areas of the countries of the region. This is in complete contrast to international investment during the stage prior to the 1930 crisis, which was of an enclave nature. It is also in contrast to the import substitution phase which involved primarily basic industries and light manufacturing.

The impact of this three-part process of rapid economic expansion, high levels of industrialization, and large-scale urbanization will be examined in the following pages. At all events, it is clear that in the phase of these transformations the biophysical environment was subject to drastic adjustments, changes, and alterations as a result of so many and such significant modifications. It is, therefore, not surprising to note that a style of development which has such a highly demanding and concentrating effect on capital, income distribution, and geographical location should put to the test the absorption capacity of an environment which traditionally had to adjust to much less demanding factors regarding its utilization and occupation.

THE INDUSTRIALIZATION PROCESS

The inclusion of the environmental aspect in the analysis of the industrialization process involves: (1) an examination of the process by which raw materials obtained from nature are transformed into manufactured products; (2) a study of the location of industrial activities and the extent of regional concentration or dispersion; and (3) an observation of the process by which industrial activities generate wastes, residues, and by-products, and their effects on the environment.

In regard to the first point, special note should be taken of Latin America's vast industrial growth and the extensive changes which the production structure has undergone. These transformations have affected not only the various manufacturing sectors and branches but also the processes and products which have been subject to technological changes, since all of this has a decisive impact on the reciprocal relationship between the industrialization process and the environment. In this regard, as will be seen later, one of the most noteworthy aspects of industrial development in recent decades has been the massive use of technology from the industrialized world, which is devoted to the local reproduction of the industrial features and living patterns of those countries. This transfer of technology has brought with it, on the one hand, the need to import raw materials, energy and other inputs, and capital equipment; while, on the other hand, there has been only a tenuous relationship between the industrialization process and the utilization of the region's natural resources. One result has been insufficient progress in local technology and in the identification and exploration of these resources.

In recent decades industrialization has played a paramount role in Latin American economic growth, determining the main changes undergone by society. Industrial modernization and the overall growth of the manufacturing market have arisen from the need for expansion of the new dominant social and economic groups in Latin America. These groups' principal source of accumulation has come to be the industrial sector. This expansion, as will be seen later, takes on the form and characteristics of the world capitalist system's current dominant industrial style of development.

Thus, while Latin America's overall gross domestic product grew by a factor of 4.5 between 1950 and 1978, the industrial product increased almost sixfold. Since the population doubled, the industrial product tripled in value per inhabitant. Together with these increases in the value of the various overall indicators, significant changes in the production structure also occurred which necessarily had a strong impact on the physical as well as the economic and social environment, with quantitatively and qualitatively different characteristics from those seen in previous stages.[3]

Let us examine briefly some of these transformations, first in reference to structural changes and then to characteristics of the dynamics of growth—including some aspects related to technology, productivity, and employment—which will help to form an approximate description of the tendencies of the system or style, as well as some of the environmental consequences.

Since the Latin American industrialization process began, there have been three groups of countries clearly differentiated according to the size of their domestic markets: large, medium-sized, and small countries. The structures and dynamics of these three groups' industrial sectors have intrinsically different features.

Table 5-1 clearly shows these differences in the metal manufacturing and machinery industry. This sector is made up of consumer durables (such as automobiles) and capital equipment (electrical and nonelectrical machinery). These are generally considered to be "industrializing" activities because their production processes have important linkages with input-producing and user sectors which create additional demand for locally produced manufactures. From a structural point of view, this sector was in 1950 twice as extensive in the large countries as in the medium-sized ones, and twelve times as great as in the small nations. By that time, therefore, the foundations were already laid which would differentiate the future development of the three groups of countries.

The consumer nondurables industry, which is normally the most important in the beginning phase of any manufacturing activity, was of a similar relative size in the large and medium-sized countries, but was less significant than in the small countries. By this stage, the medium-sized countries also had a structurally larger chemical industry, principally of oil derivatives (Venezuela), than the larger countries. In regard to the basic metal industry (iron and steel), its magnitude was comparable in large and medium-sized countries, but much greater than in the small countries.

These last two industry groups were an important component of the so-called basic industries, which, as their name implies, are generally the industries needed to start off any industrialization process. These industries perform the first steps in the processing of

Table 5-1. Typical Structure of Industrial Production in Latin America According to Type of Country, 1950 and 1975

Type of Country	Year	Percentages of value added of manufacturing sector				
		Consumer Nondurables[a]	Wood, Paper, Nonmetallic Mineral Products[b]	Chemicals, Rubber Products, Oil and Coal Derivatives[c]	Basic Metal Industries[d]	Metal Manufacturing and Machinery Industries[e]
Large	1950	64	10	10	4	12
	1975	35	9	21	7	28[f]
Medium-sized	1950	66	10	15	3	6
	1975	48	9	20	6	17
Small	1950	85	8	6	0	1
	1975	65	11	14	1	9

Source: CEPAL, based on official information from 13 countries (censuses and indexes of industrial production) regarding analysis and prospects of Latin American industrial development.

[a] Divisions 31, 32, and 39 and groups 332, 342, and 361 (ISIC Rev. 2).

[b] Groups 331, 341, 362, and 369 (ISIC Rev. 2).

[c] Division 35.

[d] Division 37.

[e] Division 38.

[f] Argentina, 27; Brazil, 31; Mexico, 24.

mineral resources into the intermediate goods used in the metal manufactures and machinery industries. These groups of industries, as will be seen further on, are also highly polluting industries.

It should be mentioned that, of the three largest countries, in 1950 Argentina was by far the most important nation in terms of industrial production. Its industrial added value was 25 percent higher than Brazil's, and 40 percent greater than Mexico's. Its metal manufactures and machinery sector was also larger than that of the other two countries. In view of the relative importance of the region's three largest nations, it is worth taking a moment to analyze their respective manufacturing structures as they were in the 1950s.

In relation to development styles and the physical environment, there is a certain correspondence between the availability of natural resources and the industrial structure (see Table 5-2). A comparison of these three countries' structures shows that Argentina's foodstuffs industry was considerably more highly developed than the other two countries', surely because of the characteristics and importance of agricultural and livestock production in that country. For its part, Brazil's textile and clothing industry had a much greater relative significance than in Argentina or Mexico, probably owing to the volume of cotton production in Brazil. Finally, Mexico's chemical and oil derivatives industries were of the same scope as Argentina's in 1950 but were much larger in 1960. As is well known, Mexico has ascribed a fundamental importance to this resource ever

Table 5-2. Relative Weight of Major Manufacturing Branches in Argentina, Brazil, and Mexico

Country	Year	Foodstuffs[a]	Textiles[b]	Petrochemicals[c]	Metal Manufacturing and Machinery[d]
Argentina	1950	36	24	13	13
	1976	23	12	21	27
Brazil	1950	26	32	5	10
	1976	14	10	21	31
Mexico	1950	30	20	14[e]	10
	1975	19	13	22	24

Source: CEPAL/UNIDO Joint Industrial Development Division.

[a] *ISIC Rev. 2, 311 to 314.*
[b] *ISIC Rev. 2, 321 to 324.*
[c] *ISIC Rev. 2, 351 to 356.*
[d] *ISIC Rev. 2, 381 to 385.*
[e] *Twenty in 1960.*

since the late 1930s and was one of the first countries to nationalize the oil industry and to found a large state company for oil production and marketing.

The organizational and technological characteristics representative of industry during that stage can be summed up, *inter alia*, as follows: the prevailing average size was small (fewer than 50 employees), which meant that cottage industries predominated; the capital/labor ratio was low; technological and production processes were not very complex, but there was a great deal of national involvement in technological inventions and progress; physical productivity was obviously lower than it is now.

In regard to pollution of the physical environment, the nondurable consumer industries prevailing at midcentury had certain characteristics which were very different from those of other industrial activities. This analysis will have to be confined to water resources.

The potential risk of water contamination[4] depends on many factors, particularly the polluting agents identified with each industrial process. Basically, there are three types of pollutants: organic and sedimentary pollutants, toxic substances, and those substances which have an effect on the aesthetics of the environment and, therefore, on the usefulness of a given zone as a recreational or residential area. Nondurable consumer industries are basically organic and aesthetic polluters. Their wastes absorb the oxygen in water, and when the tolerance of a given river, lake, or estuary is exceeded, they disturb the normal development of flora and fauna and thereby limit the possibilities for this water's later use for consumption by the population (at a reasonable treatment cost), agriculture, and other activities such as recreation. The effects of this pollution also alter the natural ecological cycles of the environment; these effects are more difficult to evaluate, but this does not make them any less important.

In addition, the liquid industrial residues from these production facilities contain suspended solids (rinds, fibers, and so on) which block the normal penetration of the sun's rays into the river depths. This diminishes the likelihood that the processes of photosynthesis will occur which are required by plant life in riverbeds in order to preserve the species and maintain the normal development of ecological cycles.

The degree of water pollution also depends on the industrial concentration along a given watercourse, since this resource has a certain capacity for absorption through dilution. In 1950 levels of industrial concentration were lower than they are today. Moreover, owing to the very characteristics of the industrial processes (many involved in agribusiness), industries used to be located near production areas in smaller cities rather than in major consumption centers (large cities), as is currently the case. Because the economies of scale are not as important in these production processes as they are in basic industries and metal manufacturing and machinery industries, companies were on the average smaller than they are now. Thus the amount of waste in the water was lower per production unit, thereby making it more likely that the environment could absorb the pollutants through dilution.

I have attempted to provide a brief picture of the dominant development style in the manufacturing industry during the middle part of this century while pointing out some of its relationships to the environment. Subsequent high growth rates brought about the gradual introduction of the new development style into this economic sector. A brief examination of the principal traits of the period's dynamics will be given below, followed by an identification of the elements of the emerging industrial structure.

As I have already mentioned, the value of the industrial product increased almost sixfold during the years between 1950 and 1978. This enormous change had a considerable effect on the physical environment. The effect was even greater in view of the fact that, to a large extent, this change was concentrated in a few metropolitan urban centers and was accompanied by significant structural transformations. There were differences in each group or set of countries, but in overall terms, few escaped assimilation of the transnational development style.

The growth rate did not remain constant during this period. Some studies have identified three different phases in this stage: during the first, from 1950 until the early 1960s, the growth rate was 6.3 percent; in the second, which lasted until 1973, it reached 8.2 percent, while the large countries attained a rate of almost 10 percent; in the third period, from 1973 to 1978, the rate dropped to 4.5 percent, partially as a consequence of problems connected with the crisis in the world capitalist system.[5]

There was only moderate growth in the first stage owing to the external supply difficulties faced by many countries in the region. These problems stemmed from the drop in commodity prices brought about by the readjustment which took place after the Korean War. The most rapid growth and the greatest momentum in the various forms of industrialization in the capitalist system as a whole occurred during the second stage. During this stage there was a trend towards consolidation of the social, political, and economic bases for the establishment of affiliates of the transnational corporations in key sectors of the manufacturing industry. This process made rapid advances during the period; thus, by the end of the 1970s the predominance of this form of ownership was very marked in the most dynamic branches which have shaped the new development style in the manufacturing industry.[6]

These affiliates increase the levels of indebtedness in the countries of the region through their negative balances of imports and exports; by developing a type of technology which is capital intensive and which therefore absorbs manpower at exceedingly low rates; and by transferring outside technological know-how for their activities, only a small percentage of which stays in the region. As will be seen further on, they also represent a high potential risk of environmental pollution.

The industries with the highest growth rates are those which produce commodities, consumer durables, and capital equipment, as a result of the demand by high- and middle-income sectors. Let us look at the industrial growth profile, taking Brazil as an example. Figure 5-1 indicates that automobile production grew at the extraordinary rate of 18 percent annually during the last decade, while the 3 percent cumulative annual rate of expansion in the production of buses used by lower-income sectors did not even exceed the population growth rate and was below the growth rate of the urban population who are the principal users of buses. The production of television sets, refrigerators, and other domestic appliances also showed high growth rates, which fluctuated between 12 percent and 15 percent annually. The production of other commodities (chemicals, cement, oil, steel) which are basic to the development of the above activities also exhibited high growth rates.

Meanwhile, some of the traditional outputs of the agriculture and livestock sector attained increases which varied between 0 percent and 6 percent. These rates were below the aggregate and industrial product growth rate and, in most cases, were also less than the urban population growth rate. The strong growth seen in wheat production is interesting in this regard, as it also reflects new eating habits, with bread replacing traditional crops. There has also been a marked increase in soya production, which is an export product, in contrast to the stagnation of other agricultural and livestock products.

As a consequence of these trends, which are present to a greater or lesser degree in most countries of the region, the Latin American manufacturing industry's share in the aggregate gross domestic

Figure 5-1.   Brazil: Growth Rates of Principal Agricultural, Manufactured, and Mineral Products, 1960 to 1970

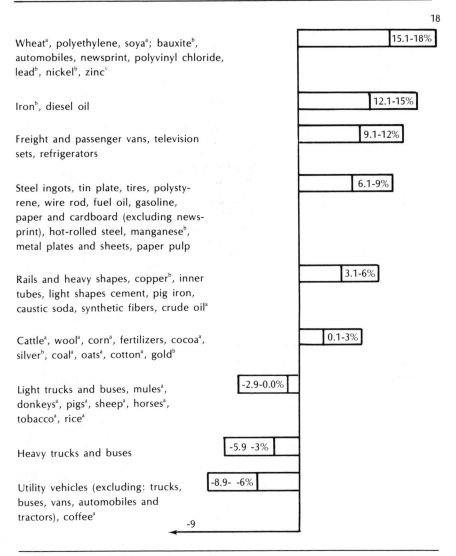

Wheat[a], polyethylene, soya[a]; bauxite[b], automobiles, newsprint, polyvinyl chloride, lead[b], nickel[b], zinc[c]

Iron[b], diesel oil

Freight and passenger vans, television sets, refrigerators

Steel ingots, tin plate, tires, polystyrene, wire rod, fuel oil, gasoline, paper and cardboard (excluding newsprint), hot-rolled steel, manganese[b], metal plates and sheets, paper pulp

Rails and heavy shapes, copper[b], inner tubes, light shapes cement, pig iron, caustic soda, synthetic fibers, crude oil[a]

Cattle[a], wool[a], corn[a], fertilizers, cocoa[a], silver[b], coal[a], oats[a], cotton[a], gold[b]

Light trucks and buses, mules[a], donkeys[a], pigs[a], sheep[a], horses[a], tobacco[a], rice[a]

Heavy trucks and buses

Utility vehicles (excluding: trucks, buses, vans, automobiles and tractors), coffee[a]

18

15.1-18%

12.1-15%

9.1-12%

6.1-9%

3.1-6%

0.1-3%

-2.9-0.0%

-5.9 -3%

-8.9- -6%

-9

Source: CEPAL, *Statistical Yearbook for Latin America, 1970, 1976 and 1977.*
[a] *The period considered is 1961-1965-1970.*
[b] *The period considered is 1961 to 1970.*
[c] *The period considered is 1967 to 1970.*

product increased from 20 percent to 26 percent between 1950 and 1978. The extent of structural changes in the manufacturing industry itself can be seen in Table 5-1. Within the context of the general upward trend with regard to the size of the metal manufactures and machinery industry, the large countries consolidated their position as the major producers of durable consumer goods and capital equipment in the region, and these activities came to represent 28 percent of total manufacturing output, in contrast to 12 percent in 1950. Among these countries, Brazil experienced the greatest growth. For their part, the smaller and medium-sized countries also expanded their manufacturing production, and did so at even higher rates in the most dynamic industrial branches, which is suggestive of the current development style.

After two decades of transnationalization it is interesting to analyze once again the industrial structures of the three largest countries in the region as they relate to the presence of natural resources (see Table 5-2). A consideration, for example, of Brazil's structure will show that the branches of the petrochemical industry continued to grow in importance, since this country is highly dependent on imports of oil, which is the major input and basic fuel for these activities.

It can also be seen that this industrial branch is of similar weight in the three countries—ranging from 21 percent to 22 percent—whereas the relative endowments of the relevant natural resources in these nations are very different. The same thing is true in the metal manufactures and machinery industries, which, since they correspond to the ascendant style, increased in relative importance from a level fluctuating from 10-13 percent to 24-31 percent, according to country. In this case also, as illustrated by Argentina, which almost totally lacks the mineral resources upon which the metal manufactures and machinery industry is based, the industrial profile is increasingly unrelated to the natural resources present.

When these two industrial branches—which are the most representative of the ascendant style—are taken together, they total roughly one-half of the industrial output of each of the three countries; in 1950 they represented less than one-fourth of industrial production. The foregoing should not be interpreted as a criticism of the industrialization process in and of itself. It does, however, suggest the need to give some thought to the style adopted by that process in Latin America in recent decades. This is particularly necessary since, as the industrial process becomes further removed from the natural resource base, it becomes more dependent on the importation of all types of inputs—raw materials, semifinished goods, energy (except for net exporters), and particularly capital equipment and technology—which makes the possibility for exporting to the world market more remote and the whole process highly vulnerable.

There were varied and important changes in technology during the period: the average size of enterprises has tended to increase; there has been an upward trend in productivity and employment; advances have taken place in automation of the management and control of production processes. At the same time, the greater integration and exchange of know-how among different industrial activities made possible by the large concept engineering firms have allowed marked progress to be made in mass production. These elements necessarily bring with them an exceedingly important qualitative change in the way technology is used. Today almost all know-how applied to these processes comes from engineering centers in the developed countries. In consequence, there has been a trend in the international division of labor which translates into a relative loss of the creative potential of Latin American scientists and technicians. An example will illustrate this situation. In Chile in 1937, 35 percent of the patents and licenses were owned by nationals, but in 1967 the proportion had dropped to 5.5 percent. In France, even though it is a developed country, the same indicator fell from 50 to 40 percent.[7]

In regard to technology transfer, defined as the process of selection, adaptation, and reproduction of technology, in the best of cases—when it is not a question of enterprises constructed under turnkey contracts—efforts are directed toward adapting some of the lesser aspects of production processes. In actual fact there are few selection alternatives, and the reproduction of technologies is practically nonexistent.

The fastest growing industries in the manufacturing sector also involve highly toxic substances. Among their wastes and residues, for example, are mercury, radioactive substances, lead, manganese, chromium, and cadmium. These are all elements which directly destroy the organic components in water environments. The treatments needed to eliminate or neutralize the effects of this type of pollution are more expensive than those used for organic pollution.

Another important feature of the dominant style deals with the high level of concentration of industrial activity. The intensive migration from rural to urban areas has made low-cost manpower available to industry. For example, the population in some municipalities of the city of São Paulo such as Diadema, Mauá and Osasco have had annual growth rates of 48.5, 21.9, and 22.9 percent, respectively, during the first years of this decade. Seven states and provinces (Buenos Aires, Santa Fe, Guanabara, Rio de Janeiro, São Paulo, Mexico City, and Monterrey) in three countries (Argentina, Brazil, and Mexico) provide 75 percent of Latin America's industrial product.[8] In Brazil, 55.7 percent of the chemicals industry, 80 percent of the transport materials industry, 90 percent of the rubber industry, 60 percent of the textile industry, 46 percent of the foodstuffs industry, and 66 percent of the paper industry are concentrated in São Paulo.[9]

From the standpoint of organic pollution, this high degree of industrial concentration amounts to an equivalent population of over 5 million inhabitants.[10] Obviously this high concentration greatly influences the pollution of rivers and bays near these urban centers and can create situations which make human use untenable in the medium term. These situations are difficult to put right owing to the high cost of the treatments which would make reuse possible.

THE RURAL MODERNIZATION PROCESS

In order to incorporate the environmental dimension adequately in the analysis of agricultural development, some basic ecological concepts should be remembered. First, a distinction must be made between the current production of an ecosystem and the accumulated biomass of the ecosystem over tens or hundreds of years. This clarification is crucial in order to differentiate that part of agricultural growth represented by the harvesting of biomass production accumulated over a long period of time from that which is attributable to annual production. Second, agricultural growth has in large part been achieved through progressive crop specialization, which is in turn attained through increasing artificialization. Latin American agricultural development is increasingly based on a highly specialized model which upsets ecosystem stability. When the potential for natural self-regulation is eliminated, the ecosystem becomes increasingly dependent upon outside inputs. This process is linked to the third concept of a subsidized environment: the increasing presence of artificialized ecosystems supported by energy subsidies, fertilizers, pesticides, mechanization, and so on. Last, ecosystems are affected by a wide variety of modifications, ranging from very intense and rapid catastrophes to slow processes which cannot be perceived in the span of one generation. It is important to recognize the processes of deterioration as they arise and to advance comprehensive long-range policies.

With the help of these concepts, let us now examine some of the major trends in volumes, intensities, structures, and modes of agricultural and livestock production. An analysis of Latin American agricultural development in recent decades reveals certain instances of continuity, but also shows up important differences with respect to previous periods.

The economic activity of the agricultural sector increased considerably during the period. Measured by its gross product, Latin American agriculture is 2.5 times larger than it was 25 years ago. This is in addition to a large increase in population: approximately 57 million people have been added to the 117 million who constituted the agricultural population in 1950, for a total of 174 million in 1975. This is equivalent to an annual increase of 1.6 percent, which is very high for the rural environment. Despite the fact that its share in the gross domestic product has progressively declined owing to greater growth in other sectors, it was still 12 percent in 1977. In that year agriculture generated 44.2 percent of foreign exchange earnings, showing the enormous importance which export crops continue to have in Latin American agriculture and in the overall development process.[11] This means that agricultural resources provide nearly half of the financing for the imported inputs which make the expansion of the development style possible.

Nevertheless, although agriculture has expanded, poverty levels have not changed significantly. Moreover, a polarization phenomenon has been observed between areas of modernization displaying a notable rise in capitalistic development and other areas corresponding to the peasant sectors. The increasing presence of transnational corporations in the use of land for new crops, as well as in the marketing and industrialization of products generated by that sector, has been another characteristic of this period. Partial agricultural modernization has raised labor productivity and, on many occasions, has influenced the reduction of employment in the sector. This factor has had a strong impact on the migratory flow toward urban centers or bordering areas.

The growth of Latin American agriculture has been achieved at the cost of the transformation, and in many cases deterioration, of ecosystems in which the modernization process has interfered. Up until the present decade, three-fourths of this growth was based on bringing new land into use. This allowed advantage to be taken of the natural fertility and, often, the accumulated production of previously untouched ecosystems. The relationship between growth owing to the extension of agricultural frontiers and growth stemming from an increase in productivity has now been reversed. This is the result of the gradual depletion of the best marginal land and is a factor in the intensification of ecosystem artificialization, a process which is heavily influenced by the transnational model of generation, adoption, and spread of technology.

With the penetration of capitalism into rural areas, this process has intensified and has taken the form of the predominance of production modes in which the profitability of investments increasingly eclipses ecological considerations. Peasant subsistence farming persists alongside these predominant modes.

Agricultural development has been subject to structural factors which have evolved appreciably in the last 25 to 30 years. In the postwar period, agriculture was characterized by a landholding system in which the latifundium-minifundium complex predominated. The different types of latifundia, traditional ranches, plantations, and enterprises in the first stages of modernization generated the rural power structures, the forms of peasant labor, and ways of organizing production. In traditionally agricultural areas, the latifundia generally underexploited the land while the minifundia overexploited it. In the marginal areas, the exhaustive exploitation of forest resources, the extensive livestock system, and the form of land clearing had serious repercussions in terms of resource deterioration.

Over the last 25 years the system of land ownership has undergone a significant evolution. The degree of land and income concentration has not diminished, except in Cuba, Bolivia, Peru, and Chile, but there have been considerable changes in rural capitalist development. The traditional latifundium has been modernized in many areas, and the modes of production arising out of these changes have come to condition development, imposing far more intensive forms of land use and so transforming a situation of underexploitation into one of overexploitation. When the traditional latifundium became modernized, it ceased to be the structural complement of the minifundium, owing to the increase in labor productivity and the shifts which occurred in areas where cultivation was being intensified. Consequently, the problem of the family unit of minifundium labor force tended to be exacerbated. In addition, the forms of landholding in the minifundium changed. Forms of land tenure such as tenant farming, *huasipungos*, and sharecropping diminished quite noticeably, but poverty levels in the peasant sector did not change significantly; around 1970, 63 percent of rural households were below the poverty line, and 34 percent were below the indigence line.[12]

With the penetration of the new style, the major socioeconomic factors were also altered. For the most part, new infrastructure works, especially in irrigation, were constructed for areas of medium- and large-scale farms. In Mexico, for example, between 1947-1955 and 1961-1965, 1,476,000 hectares of land were brought under irrigation, mainly benefiting the capitalist sector.[13] The main pricing and credit policies were also preferential. Marketing was organized around the predominant investments. Vertically integrated enterprises gradually arose out of the development of capitalist operations. These enterprises, associated with or transferred to transnational corporations, were the basis for transnational penetration in rural areas.

The differences among agricultural enterprises gradually became sharper. Those with comparative advantages directed their efforts toward export items; enterprises which produced for domestic consumption, however, frequently encountered serious obstacles to their development because of their low rate of return. The minifundium subsistence complex persisted alongside these other forms.

Together with this economic-structural situation, the modernization of rural areas penetrated by way of the model of the generation, adoption, and spread of technology. This model—which was greatly spurred on by capitalist development of the rural areas and state action—was largely a reproduction of the original model in industrial countries, particularly the United States, and frequently resulted in excessive artificialization. The varieties and strains of the Green Revolution, which showed spectacular results at first, subsequently declined in yield. This happened sometimes because the newly incorporated land was not as fertile as the land used earlier in this technological innovation, and sometimes simply because the seeds were not backed up by the necessary technology package. Use of tractors and agricultural machinery, symbols of progress and of technological advances in agriculture, increased at high rates. In the past 25 years the total number of tractors has grown by 7 percent annually.[14] The use of fertilizers has risen at the impressive rate of 13.8 percent annually.[15] An appreciation of the intensity of the process of capitalization and innovation in agricultural technology can be gained by comparing the above rates with the growth rate of the active rural population mentioned before: approximately 1.6 percent. The level of fertilizer use in Latin America is still far below the standards of developed countries; the use of pesticides, however, has been excessive in many cases, especially on crops such as cotton and sugar cane. In addition, mechanization which displaces manpower has not been in keeping with the labor supply. Equivalent unemployment in Latin American agriculture has been estimated at between 20 and 40 percent of the active population.[16]

The dynamics of capitalist penetration with the above technological model has resulted in the breakdown of the latifundium-minifundium system. The lack of work has prompted the peasantry to emigrate to urban areas and to marginal agricultural lands when they have not been forced to remain on their property, provoking an even greater overexploitation of the land.

Moreover, the new capital in agriculture has not been invested in response to the stimuli of earlier periods—social status, security, and so on—which resulted in underexploitation of the land, but rather is basically motivated by the rate of return on investment and the potential for generating surpluses. Consequently, capital mobility has become a new factor in the intensive use—and sometimes overuse—of the land.

During the last few decades, millions of hectares of virgin land have been brought into use. This extension of agricultural frontiers has primarily taken place in tropical and subtropical zones and is based on new technologies for clearing land. The peasant forms of land occupation, carried out manually with rustic methods, have been joined by the systems used in large enterprises, which involve the utilization of tractors and other heavy machinery.

It is difficult to gain an overall view of new land occupation, and even more so when this process is primarily a spontaneous one. However, one can form an idea of the pace of this expansion by observing, for example, the variation in the number of establishments in the Brazilian Amazon region, as seen in Table 5-3. The spontaneous occupation of new areas was spurred on by the planned construction in a number of countries of highways to provide access to the hinterlands. Notable examples are the population growth in the Amazon region and penetration into the most isolated secondary basins of the River Plate, such as the Upper Paraguay and the Pilcomayo.

Rural modernization and expansion have generated processes of erosion, salinization, deforestation, and so on, which have caused a serious deterioration of the physical environment. These processes,

Table 5-3. **Variation in the Number of Agricultural Establishments in the Amazon Region of Brazil**

Zone	Thousands of Units			Percentage Variation	
	1960	1970	1975	1960-1970	1970-1975
Northern region	138.1	260.9	337.4	88.8	29.4
Northern Mato Grosso	11.0	35.2	46.7	226.4	30.1
Northern Goias	27.9	37.2	41.1	33.3	10.5
Maranhao (west)	201.5	297.6	372.7	47.7	25.2
Total	378.5	631.0	798.0	66.9	26.3

Source: Charles Mueller, "La expansión de la frontera agrícola y el medio ambiente: La experiencia reciente del Brasil," in O. Sunkel and N. Gligo, eds., *Estilos de desarrollo y medio ambiente en la América Latina*, Fondo de Cultura Económica, Mexico, Serie Lecturas no. 36, 2 vols. (1981).

as well as their effects, are not new in Latin America. The occupation of space and new forms and systems of land use, incorporated over centuries, gave rise to processes of deterioration. However, the difference in the phenomenon seen in recent decades lies in its magnitude, the nature of the new technologies used, and the areas covered. The three most characteristic processes of the ascending development style are deforestation of land which is not well suited to cultivation or stock raising, unbalanced land use, and excessive ecosystemic artificialization.

The extent of deforestation is truly overwhelming, fluctuating between 5 and 10 million hectares per year. Salcedo and Leyton have estimated the average annual loss of dense forests between 1958 and 1973 at 6.5 million hectares[17] (see Table 5-4). Although this deforestation process is in large part due to colonization, transnational corporations have also contributed significantly, particularly in certain regions of Brazil and Central America.

As regards unbalanced land use, a notable underutilization of resources has existed side by side with a manifest overuse throughout Latin America. The underutilization characteristic of the traditional latifundium, as already indicated, has been replaced by overuse as the latifundium has given way to large-scale modern capitalist enterprises. Overuse in this form of land ownership and in the minifundium has basically been caused by three factors: overgrazing, single-crop farming, and farming crops which exceed the soil's natural capacity.

Overgrazing is most intense in areas which have been devoted to livestock activity for many years and in which there is also a water

Table 5-4. Estimate of Reduction in Latin America of Dense Forest, 1958-1973

Country	Total Decrease[a]	Average Annual Decrease[a]
Mexico	43,664	3,117
Central America	813	58
Caribbean Common Market	585	42
Other Caribbean countries	214	15
Andean Pact	21,315	1,523
Brazil	21,350	1,525
Southeastern South America	3,650	260
Total	91,591	6,560

Source: FAO, *Evaluación de los recursos forestales de la región latinoamericana,* 1975.
[a] Measured in thousands of hectares.

deficit. Overgrazing has been notable in the Andean region—particularly in the high plateaus—in almost all of Mexico, in southern Patagonia, in the Orinoco plains, in the Secas area of northeastern Brazil, and in the arid and semi-arid Chaco. The pampas of Argentina, like other humid regions, are not free from overgrazing.

Single-crop farming is an ancient cultural practice which has become more intense owing to the geographic specialization of the region within the context of international trade. The historical cycles of certain crops such as coffee, cotton, cocoa, and sugar cane are linked to the stages of single-crop production. Overcultivation has become widespread in Latin America and has also been closely related to the expansion of certain new crops. The division of property and the expulsion of population has also influenced the intensification of overcultivation.

The excessive artificialization of the ecosystem is the most characteristic process of recent modernization in rural areas. This is linked to the possibility of compensating for water deficits with irrigation, of enhancing the soil through the application of fertilizers, of controlling pests and diseases with pesticides, of creating genetic material capable of responding to supplementary production stimuli, and of using all sorts of agricultural machinery to improve soil preparation technologies, sowing, weed control, harvesting, and so on, as well as increasing labor productivity.

There is no doubt that with the necessary inputs and the technological and scientific know-how, agriculture must expand with artificialization. But an excessive point is reached when the system of technology generation and adoption is dominated by foreign models or by the interests of transnational and national corporations. The promotion and sale of the technology "package" is almost always behind the process of ecosystemic artificialization, and this being so, it is common to find excessive degrees of artificialization. The indiscriminate use of pesticides has resulted in the breakdown of food chains, the appearance of new pests and diseases, and the genetic resistance of species which are agricultural pests or which are vectors for diseases such as malaria. The excessive use of pesticides has also polluted basic resources, especially water. In some Central American countries, truly high use intensities have been detected. In 1973 in El Salvador, 512 kilograms per square kilometer were used in the cotton-growing area; this equaled 109 kilograms per inhabitant per year.[18]

These processes related to rural modernization, the extension of agricultural frontiers, and the overuse of land have helped accelerate the degradation of the Latin American environment. Erosion, the devastation of forests, and the overuse of land have been an influence in the overwhelming loss of land. When FAO published a map showing erosion in Latin America in 1954, 72 percent of Mexico's territory was shown to have suffered some degree of erosion; in Chile the figure was 62 percent.[19] Since that date, these percentages have risen, but the most serious aspect is that great expanses of surface area where erosion had been moderate now exhibit severe or very severe erosion.

An overall study of the region has not been carried out, but some national studies corroborate the exacerbation of this process. There is serious erosion of 200,000 hectares annually in Mexico, and the total affected area is around 200 million hectares.[20] A recent study indicates that the 34 million hectares of eroded soil in Argentina in 1957 have now increased to approximately 50 million.[21]

Sedimentation is very closely linked to erosion. The increase in erosion has had a direct impact on the amount of sediment in rivers. In addition, sedimentation combined with deforestation has had an effect on the fluctuation in the volume of their water flows. The elimination of forests and overgrazing diminish water retention capacity, the sponging action normally performed by forests is lost, and flooding becomes much more pronounced. In times of water shortages, the low watermark of rivers is much lower than normal, and areas irrigated directly from canals without reservoirs have less water than required. In this way it has been observed that in a large number of Latin American rivers the difference between maximum and minimum flows has been increasing, and therefore many agricultural areas have been lost due to droughts and abnormal flooding.

Salinization has accelerated noticeably in irrigated soils. According to FAO/UNESCO, in 1964 1,965,000 hectares were affected by salt in Central America and 120,163,000 hectares in South America.[22] In Peru, for example, 39 of the 52 coastal valleys contained 250,000 hectares affected by salinity, out of a total of 750,000 hectares.[23]

As regards soil depletion, widespread traditional practices, particularly in cattle raising, have caused a gradual loss of soil fertility. In the case of the humid pampas in Argentina, the experts agree that uninterrupted cultivation for around 50 years, without crop rotation and involving the burning-off of stubble and the practice of plowing furrows of the same depth, has provoked a loss of nutrients with a resultant drop in productivity. In tropical soils, processes of laterization have developed, resulting in the rapid loss of soil fertility.

Last, reference should be made to pollution, which in agriculture is produced by its own processes as well as by the effect of exogenous processes such as urban development, industrialization, and mineral extraction. The harmful effects of pesticide use, aside from the problems already mentioned, have resulted in direct poisoning, pollution of milk and other foods consumed by humans, and contamination of fish and other products from the sea.

The pronounced growth of cities and industry has meant that waste water is polluted with a great variety of residues. Sewer water carries diseases; water for domestic use has a high content of detergents, while industrial residues carry all sorts of suspended chemicals and materials which, for the most part, are not biodegradable. These effects can be observed in most Latin American cities. In Venezuela, for example, in the Federal District and the states of Miranda, Lara, Yaracuy, Aragua, Carabobo, Mérida, and Trujillo, 43,675 hectares of irrigated land were devoted to vegetables and industrial crops in 1973; of these, 77 percent, or 33,681 hectares, were irrigated with highly contaminated water.[24] There are many instances of air and soil pollution resulting from mining activity and of their effects on agriculture throughout the continent. For example, the effects of smoke from a copper foundry in Peru were studied in 1970; the smoke caused all vegetation to disappear in an area of 30,200 hectares.[25]

Total desertification can be considered the terminal process of environmental deterioration, a situation that is irreversible from a practical point of view. Deterioration has led to severe processes of desertification in many ecosystems. The loss of flora and fauna, erosion, depletion, alterations in river courses, and, primarily, desiccation have influenced this process. The total extinction of both animal and plant species deprives future generations of the genetic reserves which are potential resources that can contribute to scientific progress and to the fulfillment of many human needs. Currently 25 million inhabitants of Latin America live in severely desertified regions, a process which encompasses 17.5 million square kilometers.[26] The process, which was limited only to areas with a water shortage a few years ago, has begun to penetrate into areas where there is no such shortage. Predictions regarding the Amazon region continue to be alarming.[27]

Urban and industrial development and the development of tourism have been so intensive in recent decades that they have robbed agriculture of important resources. Almost all Latin American cities have grown out of agricultural or port settlements, in basins or valleys with the potential for cultivation. Urban growth, which has been characterized by the greatest degree of anarchy in regard to rational land use, has converted vast areas of agricultural land into residential sites, industrial centers, and transport networks. It is estimated that urban centers will occupy 1.5 million additional hectares of the best soil in the next 20 to 25 years in Latin America.[28] The growing need for recreation, vacation, and tourist areas has also had an impact on the use of land and water.

Aside from the deterioration of ecosystems, agriculture in Latin America loses more resources each day, whether as a result of defects in agricultural and livestock development itself or because these resources have been devoted to other activities. Bringing additional land into agricultural use is also increasingly expensive and problematical because of the serious ecological damage done to new resources incorporated into forestry, agricultural, and livestock activities.

THE URBANIZATION PROCESS

The rise of the transnational style has coincided with an acceleration of the growth and spatial redistribution of the population and changes in social and employment stratification and in patterns and levels of consumption. From 1950 to 1980 population grew at an annual rate of 2.8 percent, the highest of all the major world regions. In 1950 the total population of Latin

America was around 164 million; in 1980 it reached 358 million. Although the growth rate has begun to diminish slowly, it will continue to be high for many years to come. Thus, by the year 2000 a population of 595 million is expected, growing by nearly 2.4 percent per year.

From 1950 to 1980 the population of urban centers with more than 20,000 inhabitants increased fourfold, from 40 million to over 160 million inhabitants. The population of these centers is continuing to grow at an annual rate of 4.4 percent. In 1950 there were only six or seven cities in Latin America with more than 1 million inhabitants; in 1980 there were 25, and in the year 2000 there will probably be 46, housing 37 percent of the total population. There is already a city with more than 10 million inhabitants (Mexico City), and three more on the verge of reaching this size (Buenos Aires, Rio de Janeiro, and São Paulo).[29] Within a short period, several Latin American urban agglomerations will exceed the size of any megalopolis to date.

The proportion of the active urban population involved in nonmanual medium- and high-status occupations has greatly increased, although problems of defining and comparing data make it difficult to prepare general estimates.[30] These strata have received the majority of the per capita income increases which, moreover, are substantial in nearly all the countries.[31]

For the purposes of this work, it is not necessary to go into detail regarding demographic, employment, and income trends, or to discuss the differences between large, medium-sized, and small countries or between countries of early versus recent urbanization, since these data are easily obtainable in the publications of CEPAL, CELADE, and other institutions. Nor is it necessary to describe the typical environmental problems of large cities, which are well known in general terms; their local manifestations and causes, however, are too complex and diverse to be adequately considered here.[32] Clearly, such rapid and large-scale processes of growth and spatial concentration of population must have intensive repercussions on the ecosystems, the use of resources, and the quality of life under any development style. It must also be assumed that the various stages of peripheral capitalist development mentioned above have interacted with these processes, some of which have been in effect for some time, and affected their evolution; and that self-propelled trends with respect to the size, distribution, and structure of the population have also influenced the ascendant development style at the national level.

Returning to the focus of this work, it should be noted that by interacting with the remnants of other development styles or life styles and with demographic changes, the multifaceted penetration of the transnational style generates a group of phenomena which raises doubts about the future viability of the style and its acceptability from the point of view of environmental protection and human well-being. It also leads to partial reactions and solutions which may strengthen the style's viability or, through cumulative effects, transform its functioning. I shall highlight some of these phenomena in a very simplified way and attempt to determine what the contribution of the transnational style is, without attributing to it all the negative aspects of rapid and concentrated urbanization under conditions of extreme social inequality.

Development and its environmental consequences have been concentrated in small subsections of the various national territories, particularly in certain metropolitan areas of great demographic and economic weight. These areas

> generate the majority of the manufactures and the technical, infrastructure, commercial, and financial services which complement that activity. Moreover, they are the natural headquarters of the most powerful domestic and foreign entrepreneurial nuclei and, in the majority of cases, also serve as bases for individuals representing the domestic political power and much of the bureaucratic-administrative apparatus through which that power is expressed.[33]

From such national centers, the process of capital accumulation at the national level is directed by the most important foreign and domestic economic agents, and these centers reap the majority of the benefits from the dynamism of general economic and social growth. The greater capacity of such enterprises in the (domestic) "center" to generate surpluses is compounded by the transfer of income through trade in merchandise and remittance of benefits from the (domestic) "periphery." The fact that this spatial model, extremely concentrated from the geographic point of view, is intimately associated with the dominant development style is proven by the repeated failures of regional economic deconcentration policies instituted by many Latin American governments under differing political circumstances and at various times during the past 20 years.[34]

Capitalist agricultural modernization, combined with the high general rates of demographic growth, the attraction of new urban sources of labor, and patterns of consumption and services available principally in the metropolitan agglomerations, have stimulated migratory flows; as a result the population of these agglomerations has increased at annual rates of 5 to 10 percent. "Development" has been able to draw on a labor force priced below the cost of expanding it and constantly renewed by migration.[35] Much of the population has been excluded from employment in the modern enterprises and has undergone "regressive absorption" into personal services and artisanal activities with low rates of return but with great importance for the living patterns of the well-to-do urban strata. The development style has offered neither means nor incentives for the provision of housing, urban infrastructure, or social services in line with the needs of the lower-income strata.

The concentration of manufacturing, commercial, financial, communications, recreation, public administration, and other activities in metropolitan agglomerations, supplemented by the "spurious absorption" of well-paid jobs for those who have social power and educational advantages,[36] has generated a refined consumer market which is open to the constant diversification of consumption. The beneficiaries of the modern style of consumption make up a much larger share of the urban population than did the earlier elites and, under the influence of the mass communication media, marketing, and consumer credits, acquire attitudes strongly committed to the style which makes possible their privileged participation in the consumer market. Installment purchasing systems allow families from various income strata to become more deeply involved in the market for durable consumer goods than their financial capacity will allow, thus generating insecurity and a permanent gap between income and expectations.[37] Transnational corporations generally take a leading role in the promotion of consumption through television and other media, using techniques already tested in their countries of origin.[38]

The consumption of new manufactured products is also extended to the lower-income strata, probably leading to a large diversion of the resources required to meet their needs for foodstuffs and other basic items. In this market, manufacturing and marketing promote the consumption of goods such as transistor radios, plastic articles, cosmetics and pharmaceutical products, bottled carbonated beverages, and so on.

Patterns of settlement in the big agglomerations have been transformed owing to the combined impact of accelerated demographic growth, industrialization, and the assimilation by the medium- and high-income strata of life styles strongly influenced by the predominance of the automobile as a means of transport and a symbol of membership in the consumer society. This leads to a preference for suburban residences as a means of escaping from the deteriorating urban environment. All of the above has brought with it a series of important consequences.

(1) The area occupied by the large agglomerations has grown even more rapidly than the population, taking land away from agriculture and making infrastructure investments more expensive.

(2) The competition for space and the dynamism of rapid and constant urban expansion have led to speculation and monopolization of land, so that the price of urban real estate has increased much more rapidly than price levels in general. Financial capital plays an increasingly important role in the attraction of speculative investment in land, but owing to the predominating power relationship, state attempts to intervene in the real estate market have been consistently ineffective or counterproductive.[39]

(3) The cost of housing construction has also grown more rapidly than other costs because the market is controlled by large construction enterprises, and technical construction norms taken from the industrialized countries have been introduced. Public programs of housing incentives and subsidies have not been able to cut costs down to the level of the lower-income strata and have generally been diverted to the middle- or middle-to-low-income strata. As a result, in all the countries there has been a steady rise in the deficit of urban housing that meets modern standards.[40]

(4) The cost of land and construction makes it impossible for much of the urban population to obtain adequate housing. The consequences are: (a) the emergence of an illegal market selling extremely small building lots without urban infrastructure at prices which completely consume the savings of middle-to-lower-income families; (b) the establishment of irregular settlements, generally without property title or urban services, and often on land unfit for human habitation, which currently constitute the most rapidly growing areas in many large agglomerations; and (c) the relegation of the lower-income strata to areas especially afflicted by industrial pollution or areas at a great distance from their places of work and, moreover, badly served by public transport.

(5) The expansion of low-density residential areas inhabited by the most influential and moneyed portion of the urban population leads to strong pressure for public investment in high-speed highways, preferential public transport systems (metros, luxury buses), water (partially for swimming pools and garden watering), electricity, and so on. The size of the agglomerations and the simultaneous requirements of industry and agricultural irrigation are already creating acute water supply problems, and growing energy costs underscore the uneconomical aspects of these

settlement patterns. Public responses to these pressures rarely satisfy the residents of suburban areas completely, but at all events imply sharp discrimination against the poorest areas of the city as well as against provincial cities and rural areas, as far as investment distribution is concerned.[41]

(6) The spatial segregation of the urban population by level of income and degree of integration into the consumer society has become more extensive in the recent periods of penetration by the transnational style. Large construction enterprises and financial groups build "integrated" suburbs, with their own commercial centers, recreation and sports facilities, and security forces. Houses and apartments in these suburbs are sold through advertisements claiming that they combine the advantages of ultra-modern life, rural living, and protection against the dangers and inconveniences of the urban environment.

(7) Residential segregation, whether spontaneous or systematic, and discrimination against poor areas in respect of public services weaken any sense of community in the large agglomerations and promote the dissemination throughout the prosperous strata of stereotypes which justify discrimination and the denial of political rights. The lower-income population is perceived as a threat to "modern" consumption patterns and a source of delinquency, parasitism, and aggression against the urban environment. Flagrant contrasts between rich and poor have always existed in Latin American cities, but the fact that the relatively well-to-do strata constitute large minorities within urban populations of unprecedented size creates the conditions for new forms of class struggle.

(8) The spatial mobility associated with the automobile and consumerism in general is not limited to the cities. There has been an enormous increase in the use of space, water, and energy for recreation in coastal areas and others with tourist or sporting attractions, and this has had considerable environmental repercussions. International travel by highway or airline has also become a widespread phenomenon, although of minorities, and is being stimulated by differences in prices owing to inflationary processes and the national industrial policies associated with the development style. In these types of spatial mobility, there is a segregation by income comparable to urban segregation, with relatively low income groups attempting to follow the fashion of recreational travel, consequently leading to crowding and congestion on public transport and in parks and bathing areas, and considerable waste of petroleum.

(9) The combination of industrial growth and new patterns of consumption means that the production of wastes and contaminants will increase much more rapidly than the growth of the urban population. The resulting problems are well known, and it is not necessary to describe them here. It should be noted, however, as a symbol of the differences between the consumerist style in both the countries of origin and in Latin America, that in the latter the wastes of the well-to-do strata (paper, metal, tin cans, bottles) serve as the means of subsistence for large groups within the lower-income strata: a form of recycling made possible by poverty.

(10) The emergence of large areas, populated by low-income families, which are not equipped with an urban infrastructure and where no control is exercised over the adaptation of land for human occupation has naturally led to serious health problems, the scarcity of drinkable water and free space for parks and recreation, the accumulation of waste, industrial pollution, and vulnerability to disasters such as landslides and floods. In some cases the well-to-do suburbs have directly contributed to the deficiencies of the poor areas: the felling of forests and paving of higher areas have prevented the rains from being absorbed normally, leading to periodic floods in the lower areas. Where there is inadequate nourishment, these deficiencies seriously affect health. The sole major threat associated with this urban development style which is likely to affect both well-to-do families and poor ones equally is that of automobile accidents: overcrowded and badly maintained public transport probably causes as many injuries as private automobiles.

The poor areas present nearly insoluble problems with regard to meeting adequate health and quality of life standards unless sizable investments are made and the use of urban space is radically reorganized, together with profound changes in the distribution of income and patterns of consumption. There is not sufficient evidence, however, to justify the conclusion that the environmental and health levels of the poor areas are deteriorating everywhere and in all aspects. The most sensitive indicators, particularly infant mortality, are improving in some cases, although others are deteriorating. The authorities generally respond to emergency situations energetically enough to avoid disasters and possibly to eliminate some of the threats to physical health.[42] Moreover, the population itself shows an ability to solve some of its problems and create a relatively inhabitable environment, despite difficulties. In this field generalizations are especially open to debate.[43]

The most recent stages of penetration of the transnational style have entailed adverse consequences for the health of the lower-income strata, in addition to the expansion and diversification of industrial pollution. Medical treatment, following the trends of specialization and increasing costs observed in the central capitalist countries, has concentrated on the problems of the strata with the greatest economic resources. Generally, public health services have not been able to give increased attention to the problems of the poorest, and in some countries have reacted to the steady rise in costs and demand by reducing free treatment and allowing health services to be transferred to the private sector. Moreover, pharmaceutical companies are among the most aggressive and ubiquitous of the transnational corporations, causing overdiversification and excessive rises in the cost of medicines. The large-scale promotion of medicines leads poor families to set aside large shares of their spending for such products, while it has been noted that public control over the sale of harmful or useless drugs is patently ineffective. In some cases, transnational pharmaceutical corporations have continued to promote among the peripheral countries products banned as dangerous in the central countries.[44]

The large-scale exploitation of new mineral resources, the establishment of industries to process these resources, industrialized fishing, the building of huge hydroelectric dams, and the expansion of the agricultural frontier have led to the appearance of many mushrooming urban centers. These centers are a strong attraction for unskilled and underemployed labor, but they provide no facilities, owing to the nearly total lack of infrastructure and services. At all events, however, they have a great impact on local ecosystems because of the demographic growth and the industrial or mining processes which led to their creation. Generally, after several years of intense demand for labor in construction, the demand declines and is limited to technicians and skilled laborers for permanent, capital-intensive activities. Through inertia, however, the inflow of migrants persists, and rates of unemployment rise. Consequently, these centers are characterized by especially acute problems of segregation and a constant lack of infrastructure. The majority lack purchasing power, and the authorities are not interested in the "superfluous" population, since they must provide public services for the employed population. These mushrooming population centers seem to be exceptions to the concentration logic of the development style, since many of them arise during the preliminary stage—that of national capitalism—stimulated by large-scale projects financed by the state in its desire to create regional "bases of growth." More recently they have been set up as suppliers of intermediate goods for transnational industries.[45]

The experience of these centers raises doubts about many recommendations designed to alleviate pressures on the large agglomerations by setting up other poles of growth. The failure of many other attempts at industrial decentralization indicates that the establishment of such centers requires special conditions, but even when they are a success in economic terms, their consequences for the environment and the well-being of the population attracted to them may be worse than the growth of large agglomerations. Some of the centers of explosive growth (especially Ciudad Guayana in Venezuela) were established in line with the government's aim to initiate advanced social and spatial planning; however, this planning has had little effect on the results. In short, the administrative, material, and financial capacity of the state seems limited as far as organizing the growth of new centers under the capitalist style of development.

CONCLUDING REMARKS

The main purpose of the relatively detailed analysis of the effects of socioeconomic development on the environment, both overall and in the cases of the industrialization, rural modernization, and urbanization processes, has been to show the intimate relationship between the profound changes that have taken place in the last decades in population size and distribution, consumption and production patterns, technology, social structure and geographic location of sociopolitical and economic activity, and the use and abuse of natural resources and the environment. I have also attempted to show, conversely, that over-, under-, and malexploitation of resources, and the consequent environmental degradation and deterioration, have very serious consequences for the development process itself in contributing to some of its most undesirable characteristics: loss of employment opportunities, excessive rural-urban migration, worsening income distribution and poverty, increasing social costs, loss of productivity and capital accumulation capabilities, increasing external vulnerability and dependence, and therefore endangering the sustainability of the development process as regards both its environmental base and its sociopolitical viability.

There are fundamental theoretical and policy implications at which I can only hint in this concluding paragraph. With regard to the former, the development process can be seen as one of transforming the natural environment into an artificial, built environment, within a certain sociocultural organization and the application of capital, labor, technology, and energy. This provides a conceptual link for the integration of the social and natural sciences as well as the respective historical realities. In terms of policy, development plans, policies, and projects—global, sectorial, regional, urban, river basin—are in fact a form of environmental management. Since this is rarely perceived explicitly, it usually results in practice in mismanagement with negative social and environmental consequences, particularly in the longer run. Our task, therefore, is to bring this situation to the attention of policymakers, planners, development agencies, and the public at large, and to devise development policies, plans, and projects in such a way that they explicitly include adequate and wise environmental management.

NOTES

1. O. Sunkel and E. Fuenzalida, "Transnationalization and Its National Consequences," in J. J. Villamil, ed., *Transnational Capitalism and National Development* (London: Harvester Press, 1979).
2. A. Pinto, "Notas sobre los estilos de desarrollo en América Latina," *Revista de la CEPAL* (Santiago, first semester, 1976).
3. Hernán Durán, "Estilos de desarrollo de la industria manufacturera y medio ambiente en América Latina," *Estudios e Informes de la CEPAL*, no. 11 (Santiago, 1982).
4. Potential risk of contamination is understood to refer to the theoretical possibility of the contamination of an industrial plant deprived of waste treatment. The actual contamination will consequently depend on the effectiveness of the plants' treatment systems and the absorption capacity of the receptor. It can, therefore, only be measured in situ.
5. CEPAL, *Analysis and Prospects of Latin American Industrial Development* (ST/CEPAL/CONF.69/L.2), August 1979; CEPAL, *Statistical Yearbook for Latin America, 1978* (E/CEPAL/1086), June 1979.
6. For details see Durán, "Estilos de desarrollo."
7. Constantino Vaitsos, "La función de las patentes en los países en vías de desarrollo," *Trimestre económico* 40(1), no. 157 (January-March 1976):195-232.
8. See papers by Lucio Kowarick, "El precio del progreso: crecimiento económico, expoliación urbana y la cuestión del medio ambiente;" Alberto Uribe and F. Szekely, "Localización y tecnología industrial en América Latina y sus impactos en el medio ambiente;" and Armando Di Filippo, "Distribución espacial de la actividad económica, migraciones y concentración poblacional en América Latina," all in O. Sunkel and N. Gligo, eds., *Estilos de desarrollo y medio ambiente en la América Latina*, Fondo de Cultura Económica, México, Serie Lecturas no. 36, 2 vols. (1981).
9. Data from José Pérez Carrión, *Estudio de usos sanitarios y causas de la contaminación del agua en América Latina*, WADELA Project (Lima, February 1976).

10. Equivalent population is a measurement which allows an approximate ratio to be established between the effects of organic pollution compared to the pollution produced by a group of inhabitants in an urban center.

11. For details, see CEPAL, CEPAL/FAO Joint Agriculture Division, *Veinticinco años en la agricultura de América Latina. Rasgos principales, 1950-1975, Cuadernos de la CEPAL*, no. 21 (Santiago, 1975); CEPAL, *Long-term Trends and Projections of Latin American Economic Development* (E/CEPAL/1027), 1977; CEPAL, *Statistical Yearbook for Latin America, 1978.*

12. Oscar Altimir, "La dimensión de la pobreza en América Latina," *Cuadernos de la CEPAL*, no. 27 (Santiago, 1979).

13. CEPAL, CEPAL/FAO Joint Agriculture Division, *Veinticinco años.*

14. CEPAL, CEPAL/FAO Joint Agriculture Division, *Veinticinco años.*

15. CEPAL/FAO, *Consumption Prospects and Fertilizer Production in Latin America*, 4th FAO Regional Conference for Latin America and CEPAL/FAO Latin American Conference on Food (LARCC/76/7[d]), Lima, April 1976.

16. PREALC/ILO, *The Employment Problem in Latin America: Facts, Outlooks, and Policies* (Santiago: PREALC, 1975).

17. Sergio Salcedo and José Ignacio Leyton, "El sector forestal latinoamericano y sus relaciones con el medio ambiente," in O. Sunkel and N. Gligo, eds., *Estilos de desarrollo.*

18. UNEP, *Estudio de las consecuencias ambientales y económicas del uso de plaguicidas en la producción de algodón en Centro América* (Guatemala, September 1975).

19. FAO, "Studies on Soil Erosion in Latin America," *Journal of Soil and Water Conservation* (Mexico, July, August, September, November 1974).

20. Preparatory Commission for Mexico's Participation in the United Nations Conference on the Environment, *Informe Nacional* (October 1974).

21. Juan C. Mustó, *La degradación de los suelos en la República Argentina*, Secretariat for Agriculture and Livestock, National Institute for Agricultural Technology (INTA), Internal Series no. 67 (Buenos Aires, 1979).

22. FAO/UNESCO, *World Soil Map* (Paris, 1964).

23. Luis Masson Meiss, "Problemas de la zona árida peruana con especial referencia a la incidencia de la salinidad sobre su desarrollo económico," in *Primer Seminario Nacional de Sistemas Ecológicos, Recursos Naturales y Medio Ambiente* (Lima, June 1974).

24. Nelson Geigel Lope-Bello, "La experiencia venezolana en protección ambiental," in CEPAL, Natural Resources and Environment Division, *Información de Medio Ambiente en América Latina* (Santiago, 1974).

25. Ministry of Health, Peru, "Informe sobre el deterioro del medio ambiente" (Lima, 1971).

26. Margaret Biswas, "UN Conference on Desertification in Retrospect," *Environment Conservation* 4, no. 4 (Lausanne, 1978).

27. Robert Goodland and Howard Irwin, *A selva amazonica: do inferno verde ao deserto vermelho* (Belo Horizonte, Brazil: University of São Paulo, 1975).

28. Michael Nelson and Terence R. Lee, *Environmental Dimension of Water Management in Latin America*, CEPAL, based on the study *Water Development and Environment in Latin America* (1979).

29. CEPAL, *Tendencias y perspectivas a largo plazo del desarrollo de América Latina* (E/CEPAL/1076), 1979; Cesar Peláez, "Tendencias y perspectivas demográficas en América Latina 1950-2000" (draft, November 1978).

30. Carlos Filgueira and Carlo Geneletti, *Estratificación ocupacional, moderniza-*

ción social y desarrollo económico en América Latina (E/CEPAL/DS/185), November 1978.

31. CEPAL, *América Latina en el umbral de los años 80* (E/CEPAL/G.1106), November 1979.
32. CEPAL, *El medio ambiente en América Latina*, March 1976.
33. Armando Di Filippo, *Estilos de desarrollo económico y migraciones de fuerza de trabajo en América Latina* (Santiago: CELADE, May 1978).
34. Alejandro Rofman, "La interiorización espacial del estilo de desarrollo prevaleciente en la América Latina," in O.Sunkel and N. Gligo, eds., *Estilos de desarrollo*.
35. Kowarick, "El precio del progresso."
36. Raúl Prebisch, "A Critique of Peripheral Capitalism," *CEPAL Review* (first half, 1976).
37. Carlos Filgueira, "Notas sobre consumo y estilos de desarrollo," CEPAL (draft, 1977).
38. Jorge Wilheim, "Metropolización y medio ambiente," in O. Sunkel and N. Gligo, eds., *Estilos de desarrollo*.
39. Guillermo Geisse G. and Francisco Sabatini, "Renta de la tierra, heterogeneidad urbana y medio ambiente," in O. Sunkel and N. Gligo, eds., *Estilos de desarrollo*.
40. Guillermo Rosenblüth, *Necesidades de vivienda y demanda efectiva en América Latina* (E/CEPAL/PROY.1/R.37), November 1979.
41. In Santiago, Chile, the highest-income community (Las Condes), comprising only 8 percent of the metropolitan population, received 42 percent of public investment in local urban roads from 1965 to 1975, and 20 percent of the city's total road investments. This probably played a role in the growth of real estate prices, which increased much more there than in the rest of the city. See Geisse and Sabatini, "Renta de la tierra."
42. Wilheim, "Metropolización y medio ambiente."
43. Carlos Borsotti, *Estilos de desarrollo, medio ambiente y estrategias familiares* (E/CEPAL/PROY.2/R.5), August 1979.
44. Giorgio Solimano and Georgeanne Chapin, "Efecto del desarrollo socioeconómico y el cambio ecológico sobre la salud y la nutrición en la América Latina," in O. Sunkel and N. Gligo, eds., *Estilos de desarrollo*.
45. Juan Pablo Antún, *Centros de crecimiento explosivo en América Latina* (E/CEPAL/PROY.2/R.7).

Chapter 6

The City of the Future: A Worldwide View of Future Urbanization Patterns

P. Psomopoulos

During recent years, the international community has given much attention to climate, energy, quality of soil, food production, and so on in order to help establish well-being and a balanced development among human beings on this shrinking planet. These important issues are all interrelated. The task is to guide nations and the world toward a better understanding of important issues and of the relevant, meaningful, and necessary interconnections between them and other world problems and aspirations.

We should enable nations to come to a correct assessment of the problems, policies, and programs (or, in some cases, the lack of them) that affect the issue under discussion: to identify current trends and possible alternative futures, and to agree on operational proposals for efficient modes of action that can lead to an improvement in the general condition of human life, and of the other forms of life and natural resources on the globe.

Yet projects so far have inevitably concentrated upon certain fragments of the whole system of life which are of special concern, and probably rightly so, due to the complexity of phenomena, the limited knowledge available, and various methodological constraints. In fact, various aspects are highly technical and need to be examined systematically from economic, technological, or other points of view, involving intensive basic research, laboratory work, and/or test implementations in real life.

However, if all these issues are meant to have a bearing on man's system of life, by definition they also affect the network of human settlements which is the complex physical expression of this system of life. Therefore, any mobilization around themes of world importance, such as those included in nongovernmental organizations' (NGOs) programs, presents a unique opportunity to those interested in human settlements to try to identify and interrelate those aspects of human settlements' structure, functioning, and evolution that are most relevant to these themes.

Subjects such as the ones included in the agenda of this World Congress greatly affect the quality of every phase of human life. They affect individuals of all ages in their work, recreation, education, administration, participation, and self-development, as well as in their needs for shelter and other buildings, roads and other networks. In other words, these issues involve the entire human settlements system, now and in the future.

It is within this frame of thought that this short presentation on the "City of the Future" (COF) Research Project of the Athens Center of Ekistics is undertaken.

THE ACE'S "CITY OF THE FUTURE" RESEARCH PROJECT

The concept of the "City of the Future" as an interdisciplinary international research effort on the future of humanity was born in the Athens Center of Ekistics (ACE) in the year 1960. In simple terms, the project is an exercise in trying to formulate and test with available evidence a number of hypotheses on the possible image of human settlements 20, 50, 100, 150, 200 years from the present.

In 1961 a first document by C. A. Doxiadis giving project methodology and an initial formulation of fundamental hypotheses was published by ACE. It was mainly addressed to the collaborators of ACE and a limited number of world experts for their reactions. The project has been in progress for 23 years and is still continuing; it should never really end.

The COF, together with three more interdisciplinary research projects, "The Comparative Study of Metropolitan Areas," "The Human Community Study," and "The Ancient Greek City Project," attempts to study the evolution of human settlements over a very long period of time, from the most distant but accessible past to the most distant but accessible future.

The notes that follow draw on all these projects, but especially on the findings of the "City of the Future" project as presented in the book *Ecumenopolis: the Inevitable City of the Future*, by C. A. Doxiadis and J. G. Papaioannou; in a series of articles giving partial project results published in ACE's journal *EKISTICS*; in ACE's research monograph series; in various articles and books listed in the bibliography below; and in a large number of unpublished research reports.

Definitions and First Hypotheses

The "City of the Future" (COF) Research Project has attempted, and continues to attempt, the more accurate understanding of the process of the past, present, and future evolution of man's system of life and human settlements which are its expression in space. To clarify and understand the complex thinking procedure and methodology that were followed in the COF Project, it is necessary to state clearly some fundamental definitions and/or hypotheses which implicitly or explicitly constitute the basis of this research effort.

The use of the term *city* is simplified and symbolic, for the project's real concern is human settlements of all kinds, ranging from nomadic (whether with animals in the desert or trailers on the highways) to very large cities, from their overbuilt and overcrowded central parts to their farthermost outskirts.

Man lives in human settlements, which are the territorial arrangements made by him for his own benefit. Furthermore, with exception of very marginal clusters, "hunter" groups, or village dwellers, all settlements are more or less part of a broad human settlements system. People tend to cluster around central facilities according to more or less clear-cut patterns of interdependent communities of various scales. One of the most characteristic scales in any city, the neighborhood scale, is defined by the overlapping kinetic fields of the movements of the inhabitants to satisfy their daily needs.

Throughout human history man has been guided by the same five principles in every attempt he has made to live normally and survive:

1. *The maximization of potential contacts.* Man tries to have the

best possible contact with people and other elements such as water, food, houses, facilities, knowledge. This amounts to an operational definition of personal human freedom.

2. *The minimization of effort in terms of energy, time, and cost.* In his attempt to maximize his potential contacts, man tries to bring everything close to him. To achieve this in the best possible way he always selects the course requiring the minimum effort.

3. *Optimization of man's protective space* at every moment and in every locality, whether in temporary or permanent situations, whether he is alone or part of a group.

4. *Optimization of man's relationship with the other elements of his system of life*, that is, with nature, society, shells (buildings and houses of all sorts), and networks (from roads to telecommunications).

5. *Optimization of the synthesis* of the previous four principles. This depends on time and space, actual conditions, and man's ability to create the synthesis. Human settlements have been more successful, made their inhabitants happier, and lasted longer when this principle of balance has been applied.

In the present era old settlements, such as villages and cities (as they were structured in the past), are beginning to disappear, and new ones, such as daily urban systems and megalopolises, are beginning to appear. This clearly shows that human settlements follow evolutionary trends which, however, are not yet properly understood. The many different ways in which man has started his settlements could perhaps be called initial coincidental efforts. These he used as experiments; he learned which one served him best; and then he continued with many mutations until he eventually found the right direction. What is certain is that when a more satisfactory solution appeared, it was the only one that survived. We can see the truth of this statement in all types of units and at all scales of settlements.

The form, structure, and texture of human settlements of all scales can be attributed to several forces deriving either from man or directly from nature. When we move from the room (the smallest human settlement unit) to the house, the neighborhood, the city, and the metropolis, we discover that many forces are active, but their relationships change from case to case. The unit of the metropolis, for example, is too large to be influenced directly by man (in terms of his physical dimensions and senses), but it is influenced by the natural forces of gravity and geographic formation, by modes of transportation, and by the organization and growth of the system. Following this train of thought for all categories of human settlements, we can conclude that within every type of ekistic unit the changing forces of synthesis follow a certain pattern which, in terms of percentages, shows a decline of the forces derived from man's physical dimensions and personal energy, and a growth of those derived directly from nature itself as a developing and operating system.

In the future human settlements will be created by man guided by these five principles, which should not and cannot be changed. It is therefore our task to learn about them and prepare ourselves for the application of the fifth principle, the most difficult and complex of all: the achievement of balance between the others.

Experience has shown that human settlements find the correct road after many coincidental efforts or, in special cases, conscious goal-oriented efforts. Experience has also shown that this takes time, leading to many mistakes and much suffering. To quote C. A. Doxiadis:

> Our challenge now is to put aside all our personal dreams and create a goal-oriented effort representing the desires of man, our great master. To do this we must discover what the inevitable future is which has been decided by nature and man; what can be controlled by us; what the most desirable city for man is and finally how we can write the specifications for it, lay its foundations and build it. This is our great task: to help man find his own road.

Methodology and Basic Results of the COF Project

Long-range projection in general, and in particular in the field of human settlements, is unquestionably desirable. Human settlements all over the world are experiencing a period of increasing crisis; but they cannot be changed overnight. Their structure alone is likely to remain largely unchanged for periods of 50 or 100 years or more, predetermining future environment to an unacceptable degree. For many other reasons, the life of human settlements should be measured in terms of generations or centuries. Even in planning for the near future (say 10 or 20 years), plans should be set in the broader perspective of several generations if we are to comprehend the true nature and the scale of the problems involved and to conceive solutions. The intensive effort of the last 23 years within the frame of the COF project, and the results obtained so far, prove that such long-range projections are possible, meaningful, and relevant to present-day planning in the field of human settlements, provided we seek generalized patterns.

The validity and reliability of the general picture of future urbanization emerging from the COF project were tested using many independent methods, each of which gave approximately the same result: the recognition of certain trends and limitations shaping the future urbanization pattern. Three of the approaches used are described briefly here.

The "ultimate equilibrium" approach. The ultimate maximum population of the earth is estimated at some 20 billion, with a high level of urbanization, and an internal pattern of hierarchically arranged centers. Studies within the COF project indicate that the total population of the earth, which has been increasing at a constantly accelerating rate until now, is likely to continue growing well into the twenty-first century until a level of relative stabilization is reached.

Ecological considerations of balance between man and his environment (similar to other animal or plant communities within a limited enclosure) show that, given a sufficient period of time, man is likely to adapt his genetic mechanisms so as to conquer whatever space is available on earth. He is also likely to increase his densities if these are clearly below saturation level.

Although at present urban life has many ever-increasing disadvantages, urbanization can be regarded as an inevitable and even desirable universal trend. Rural dwellers, as well as inhabitants of small- and medium-sized cities, are irresistibly attracted to the largest cities by higher standards of living, the choices offered, the availability of highest-order functions, the variety of contacts, and many other considerations which far outweigh the disadvantages of urban life. There is every indication that this trend will strengthen as time goes on.

Even though available natural resources such as food, water, energy, and minerals are likely to become scarce in the near future, studies have shown—with relatively conservative projections of income growth and technological progress, and with efficient integration of such progress into the economic and administrative structure—that each of these resources is likely to be developed to such levels that within one or one and a half centuries very high population figures, of the order of magnitude of 50 billion, can be supported. However, such high population levels appear improbable. When maximum acceptable densities were applied to a number of future habitability levels, not including areas necessary for uses other than settlement (production, recreation, conservation, and so on), it was found that 100 or 150 years from now the earth could sustain a probable maximum population of some 20 billion, or within a probable range, 15 to 25 billion.

Habitable space has been computed for the present and projected for a sufficiently remote future—100 or 150 years—taking into account not only various grades of habitability related to climate, topography, soil condition, and other factors, but also an improvement of habitability conditions over the same areas and a reclaiming of further areas for habitation based on technological progress and income growth.

Maximum acceptable densities—with concepts like environmental control, maximum tolerable stress resulting from excessive complexity of life, and the like built-in—were computed on the basis of past and present trends. The study clearly shows an overall decrease in future average densities over large urbanized areas as incomes increase. In other words, the shape and size of the earth impose a limitation to the maximum population that it can accept. Population, therefore, can be regarded as a closed variable tending to move asymptotically through an S-shaped curve toward an ultimate equilibrium, which will be approached at a sufficiently remote future time.

Projections of the earth's total population levels, combined with a high degree of urbanization, in a remote future, result in a picture of certain basic characteristics of long-range urbanization projections. Finally, a purely geometric-mathematical study shows that a hierarchical concentration of facilities in centers of various orders proves much more economical than, say, a concentration in centers of uniform size or a uniform spread, or other theoretical alternative patterns. Such a hierarchical system of centers of various orders, therefore, is most likely to develop within the future urbanization pattern.

The "spatial pattern" approach indicates that the ultimate future human settlement system will take the form of a definite physical pattern: that is, Ecumenopolis, the city of the inhabited planet.

Until around 1940 the evolution of settlements resulted in large, more or less concentrated metropolises surrounded by suburbs, and representing the largest human settlement units at that time. After the Second World War the phenomenon of urbanization on a regional scale appeared. In areas where centers relatively close to each other exceeded a critical size of some 1 million inhabitants, a belt connecting these centers was progressively urbanized through the gravity effect; this belt was not continuously built up but contained a predominance of urban functions. This process resulted in the formation of a megalopolis—a multinuclear band formation with a population of several tens of millions and an area 10 to 1,000 times larger than the area of large metropolises.

On the basis of COF studies, 12 megalopolises have been

identified around the world, and five more are in the stages of formation. Projections of megalopolis structure and growth up to the beginning of the next century, using a mathematical model developed by the COF project, show (1) a great increase in their number, with over 160 megalopolises expected to exist around the year 2000, of which 53 will be interconnected into still larger megalopolitan networks or urbanized regions; and (2) a great increase in their average and maximum populations and areas, and in their complexity.

This rapid and large-scale increase will be one of the main factors intensifying the crisis of urban life until the year 2000, a period which is likely to be a most difficult one for humanity. A large number of serious problems is expected to accumulate, ranging from scarcity of basic vital resources to widespread deterioration of flora and fauna and of the quality of human life, particularly in poor regions of the world.

Such difficulties may impair the quality and efficient operation of major human settlement units, but are not expected to stop the formation and growth of megalopolises barring a total failure or catastrophe for humanity. Indeed, megalopolises attract population with a still greater force than isolated metropolises. COF estimates show that the advantages to be gained—multiple choices, such as proximity to two large centers; availability of highest-order functions; a standard of living considerably higher than in the areas outside, and so on—will more than compensate for the disadvantages, especially around the year 2000, when between 45 and 50 percent of the earth's population will be living in megalopolises.

In the twenty-first century technological progress will gradually increase the availability of resources and high-quality substitutes for them, and generally improve conditions of material comfort and wealth. Environmental control will become more efficient and restore the imbalance and deficiencies previously created. Higher incomes will make investments in large-scale technical projects possible, thus vastly improving man's control over his environment, the acquisition of resources, and the building of adequate settlements. In spite of many other difficulties, the overall balance will gradually become more and more steady, as indicated by the form of the S-shaped urbanization curve which flattens asymptotically toward a quasi-stable state during this period.

With the continuing increase of population, the improvement of communication and transportation systems, and greater scarcity of unused habitable space, settlements are expected to become more and more interconnected until:

(1) Toward the end of the first half of the twenty-first century, megalopolises will gradually be replaced by the next higher unit, the urbanized region.

(2) Around the middle of the twenty-first century, or later, the urbanized region will in its turn give way to a higher-order settlement, the urbanized continent, as the prevailing settlement pattern.

(3) Probably less than another generation later, all major settlement units will become fully interconnected in a new pattern representing a sort of ultimate equilibrium between human settlements and their wider environment. This highest unit in the hierarchy of settlements has been called Ecumenopolis, meaning a unified settlement system spanning the entire habitable area of the globe, not continuously, but in a totally interconnected network.

This concept of Ecumenopolis emerges as a smooth evolutionary result of the expanding systems of settlement patterns of the preceding periods. It is also consistent with the findings of the previous approach as to population levels, greatly increased urbanization, and an internal hierarchical pattern of centers.

Ecumenopolis, and all previous high-order formations, are characterized by a loose and discontinuous internal structure in spite of their relatively high regional densities. These are not built-up areas, but areas of intensely urbanized character. Within these high-order formations, large open areas are preserved for a variety of purposes, such as recreation, conservation, and production, again according to a hierarchical system.

The spaces between the formations are not empty; they only have lower densities, which allow for a large number of smaller settlements at all scales and other lower-order installations. According to various models, non-Ecumenopolis areas may contain from 7 to 20 percent of the earth's population, and will comprise land uses other than settlement, such as recreation, conservation of natural areas, production, and so on.

It is also projected that some 3 to 10 percent of the earth's population will probably live on water in floating settlements, perhaps closely related to the part of Ecumenopolis developing along appropriate coastal areas, which will acquire a special importance at that time.

Settlement both within and outside Ecumenopolis will occupy the proportion of habitable and semihabitable areas that is consistent with the other major land uses necessary for sustaining life, production, recreation, and so on for the entire global population.

Of the total 70 to 75 million square kilometers covered mainly by habitable and semihabitable land areas, settlements may occupy up to 10 or 15 million square kilometers, production 25 to 30 million, and recreation and conservation another 30 to 35 million, in addition to a further 75 to 85 million square kilometers of open conservation land, and the usable parts of the oceans' surface and underwater areas such as continental shelves.

A major organizing principle of the largely linear structure of Ecumenopolis is development along axes of urbanization, which should be considered general directions of growth and expansion along main transportation lines or connecting links between higher-order centers. According to the hierarchical concept, higher-order axes will link higher-order centers, which also will form at the crossings of these axes. The approximate probable location of these primary centers was determined using a mathematical model, and taking into account "practical" considerations about the importance of oceans and coasts, hinterland, population densities, habitability, and other factors; the locations were arrived at purely on the basis of achieving an ultimate global balance and bear no relation to the present political structure or its projected trends.

The "system of interrelated projections" approach used a limited group of key variables, lending themselves to more or less meaningful projections, to elaborate as many aspects of Ecumenopolis as possible, although with considerable variability. Since we are still unable to project many other important variables, this approach can and should provide only a partial view of possible and probable conditions in the world at this remote future time.

Interrelated projections were made for population, economic variables, water availability, energy, education, health and nutrition, and other variables.

For population, six models were developed: three for Ecumenopolis populations of 20, 35, and 50 billion for the years 2060, 2090, and 2120, respectively, and three with the same populations reached 30 years earlier. Population figures were worked out by 30-year intervals, and for each date total global population was broken down by settlement size, urban and rural areas, settlement formation and location types, densities, and broad geographic regions. These breakdowns are consistent with the characteristics of Ecumenopolis emerging from the other approaches. The areas and respective population densities of Ecumenopolis corresponding with these projections were then computed.

Economic projections based on a system of development curves were worked out, and retaining three of these (high, middle, and low), together with three population projections, nine economic models were developed. Although these models diverge considerably, especially in the remote future, they lead to interesting prospects. Very high per capita incomes and investment figures in the remote future mean, among the many possibilities, that engineering projects on an unprecedentedly large scale can be undertaken; areas such as oceans, deserts, underground areas, and outer space can be made more or less habitable; the battle against poverty can be supported; greater funds can be devoted to research and development; and higher-order functions such as art and science can be developed. These possibilities refer only to the latter part of the twenty-first century, not to the near future. The per capita income gap between rich and poor countries, for instance, was projected to increase until around 2000, shortly after which it will decrease, until it becomes greatly reduced by the time of Ecumenopolis.

The economic projections also indicate that the cumulative investment between 1960 and 2000 will probably be two to three times that of the period prior to 1960, from the beginning of history. The main problem is therefore not so much locating the source of funds as knowing of their eventual availability and choosing the correct investments to improve conditions within settlements.

From the water projections it was found that Ecumenopolis is unlikely to suffer from water scarcity, except for local arid pockets, even without exploiting new sources of supply such as melted polar ice or very deep water reserves. Traditional sources alone could adequately supply a population of 19 billion at the average present-day US level of consumption. Desalinated sea water could be pumped 1,000 kilometers inland up to an elevation of some 1,000 meters at reasonable cost.

Energy consumption projections were based on the finding of UN studies that a close correlation exists between per capita income and certain economic and social indicators, particularly if fairly large groups of countries with the same per capita income are selected. As a result it was found that while scarcity and the high cost of energy may create more difficult conditions in the near future, pressures will be considerably eased in the twenty-first century.

Correlations of education and health levels with per capita income indicate that not only will illiteracy be unknown long before Ecumenopolis, but also even the less developed areas of today will enjoy higher education levels at least comparable to those now existing in the United States and the United Kingdom. By midcentury nutritional levels in the least developed parts of the globe will be similar to those in advanced countries of today. Diseases known today will have been virtually eradicated, including those attributed to environmental pollution, over which strict controls will have been established before the end of this century.

Conclusions

In summary, the three methods outlined so far can draw only a probable but incomplete picture of the world in the remote future. Yet all three approaches, in addition to several other independent approaches for certain particular aspects, do concur and converge toward the same future image: that is, Ecumenopolis.

The large number of models that can be constructed for Ecumenopolis differ in spatial configuration—although with some more or less constant basic features such as main axes and centers—in population, income, and other aspects. Although ranging considerably between high and low, the models are useful in that what lies outside this range—lower than the low and higher than the high models—may be considered highly improbable.

There are several indications that many "desirable" models—in terms of providing satisfactory living conditions, or at least conditions better than those existing in cities today—can be worked out, using the three approaches already outlined; and with adequate planning humanity will be able to come close to one of these.

If Ecumenopolis is considered an inevitable general pattern of future urbanization, but with a large number of alternative interpretations, and if Ecumenopolis models are used as general targets for urban development, planners could try to connect present conditions and trends with projected future levels for certain basic variables. In fact, ACE has already used such an approach for projections of urban development on a regional scale in several areas (for example, the Great Lakes megalopolis of the United States and Canada, the south coast of France, Greece, the Japanese megalopolis, and many others). It was found that this technique was quite helpful and meaningful, and capable of being considerably improved in the future.

THE IMMEDIATE FUTURE

The COF study confirms that the period between now and the year 2000 is likely to be the most difficult one for humanity; a large number of problems are likely to accumulate, many of which already exist. Some of the most serious are: scarcity of food, water, and other natural resources for a growing population, reaching alarming proportions in many cases; slow rate of growth of the economy of most of the poor countries, leading to stagnation and dissatisfaction with the increasing gap that separates them from rich countries; environmental deterioration through air, water, and land pollution, and widespread danger to flora and fauna; intensification of dissatisfaction because of higher expectations and lower attainments; increasing tension and stress; violence; the possible collapse of prevailing social or political systems; and insufficient technological and organizational progress to cope with these problems efficiently.

Almost all—if not all—these problems and their multiple repercussions are already manifest within human settlements, are harming them, and are influencing the rate and degree of growth or deterioration of their structure, function, and distribution in space. Fundamentally, these problems are causing tremendous imbalance among the five elements of human settlement—man, society, shells, networks, and nature—in all sizes and types of settlements, and from all points of view—economic, social, political, administrative, and cultural.

Furthermore, many of these problems are also "caused" by human settlements: their distribution in relation to each other, their location on the surface of the earth, their function, and their growth or decline. To give a more specific example of this cause-effect relation in human settlements, let us examine two very concrete and timely issues that have attracted the attention of the world community during these last few years, and which are also closely connected with some of the major themes of this Congress: climate and soil, as connected with the UN Desertification Program, and the concern over loss of arable land.

As all activity in human settlements takes place in space, and any decision or action implies "location" and "connections," spatial considerations within and outside a settlement are of great importance.

Desertification, the process of spreading desert conditions across formerly more productive lands, is due to sudden (though probably temporary) climatic changes, increased pressures of population, inappropriate technologies, and the careless exhaustion of soil and water resources. The phenomenon occurs in a large number of rich and poor countries on all continents and affects some 15 percent of the world population distributed in a large number of human settlements.

An analysis of the degree to which the structure and distribution of human concentrations in space are related to the acuteness of the repercussions of desertification on people and productivity has shown that very small, isolated human settlements, with their necessarily limited resources and services and unidimensional economic base, have often suffered a total elimination of their raison d'être. Thousands of livestock and human beings have died. Whole populations have been forced into an exodus toward larger human settlements in search of better economic opportunities for survival and more favorable living conditions. The prevailing conditions of their earlier human settlement structure, function, and organization are responsible, in the main, for their objection to returning.

To encourage return, a new system of settlements must be developed at a different scale and with different characteristics, which can provide a full range of social services and more varied opportunities.

The success of programs and plans for agricultural reorganization will depend on the implementation of a major human settlement program to keep people where they are or to move them where they should be. This involves a system of a few larger settlements with improved transportation to the agricultural lands, or of many small settlements with improved transportation to an urban center. By changing the overall pattern of the distribution of people in space, and by considering broader human settlement systems (not necessarily larger, continuous built-up areas), one can lessen their vulnerability to desertification.

Human settlements are not only the most dramatic victims but are also themselves one of the main instruments of desertification. The physical expansion of human settlements due to the large-scale and high-speed population explosion and movement of people toward urban centers is a major factor in desertification.

Rural migration to urban centers may reduce the productivity of agricultural land in the areas of their origin, which in most cases consists of soils of poor quality. At the same time, urbanization desertifies very fertile land by overlaying it with all sorts of constructions. Every year, all over the planet, human settlements "eat up" about 140,000 square kilometers of arable land, 60,000 square kilometers of pasture, and 180,000 square kilometers of forest. Although expansion of built-up areas sometimes encourages an improvement of cultivation standards in their immediate vicinity, this is outweighed by the far larger destruction of agricultural land.

This overview shows that since it is necessary to reconcile the need for fertile land to feed the earth's growing population with the need for habitable land to accommodate this population, the serious conflict between agricultural and built-up urban land is likely to become more acute.

Need for Immediate Action

No matter how optimistic and how objective the COF study might have tried to be, and no matter how high a probability its statements or measurements have, there is no certainty that man will find and put into effect the right solutions to some of the very critical problems in time to save the situation. And *in time* means here and now, because whatever happens now decisively conditions the future.

The main question—and the essence of the whole COF effort—is: should we allow the transition to the future to go on by itself following the present trends, or should we try to understand what is happening, conceive clearly what we want our future to be, and then guide the forces in that direction, reducing friction as much as possible during this long period of evolution?

No doubt there is a need for action. There is also the possibility for efficient and immediate action which would greatly improve the overall conditions and the quality of life in human settlements. Somewhere on the earth examples exist of efficient methods successfully applied to solve problems, totally or partially, but these methods are not applied everywhere either because they are not widely known or because they are not given proper recognition. It is a fact that past and present failures to maintain a balanced relationship between human settlements and natural resources result from the inability to apply existing knowledge of processes rather than from any lack of understanding of the processes.

There are things we can change overnight, but we never do. There are tensions all over the globe, and there are margins in all situations for the possible release of these tensions that we never use. Instead of trying to find a new solution to the problems, or applying old solutions which have been unjustifiably abandoned, most of us tend to stick to fighting urbanization—an impossible task. Urbanization seems to provide a life style and a pattern of allocation of human effort and time which is desirable to most humans, even if it is not recognized as such by experts. However, taming urbanization by bringing existing rural and urban agglomerations together into urbanized systems is both desirable and feasible.

Satisfaction of many of the present global needs, particularly in respect to incompatible distribution of population and resources, might take many years, many decades, before a state of equilibrium and relaxation of tensions can be reached. But in order to do this, the process of conceiving the magnitude of the problem, collecting the necessary data, programming, planning, and implementation should start immediately.

Some problem areas, modes of action, and issues of high priority, as developed in the *City of the Future* study, are given here.

Action towards a global ecological balance. In the past, man has always been the dominant factor both in the initial creation of his environment and in maintaining a desirable balance between the various elements. However, he now finds himself in a complex world of limitless dimensions in which he has to cope with new problems increasing at an unprecedented and threatening rate. Studies of human settlements, both in the technologically advanced and in the developing countries, show that:

1. The balance between the five elements of human settlements has been dangerously upset and, in some respects, irrevocably damaged during recent years.

2. While this imbalance harms all elements, it is particularly harmful to man, who should be able to condition the environment to meet his own needs.

3. Despite the facilities provided by modern technology, man seems to have lost control over the tools, created by him, to form his environment on a human scale.

4. Even worse, man now seems to be oblivious as to what his real needs are, what be wants to do, and where he should go from here.

Balance, on the basis of human satisfaction, is man's ultimate goal in dealing with his system of life. The most important and most difficult to apply of the five principles serving human needs is that which guides man towards achieving the proper balance among the other principles.

There is imperative need for immediate action so that humanity can reach a new balance between man and nature, a balance that will no longer be expressed only at the village scale (this was the goal 10,000 years ago) or even at the city scale (this became the goal later) but at all scales, from man to the whole earth. This means that man, nature, and all the other elements will have to change direction and move towards the same goal.

This notion of achieving balance is not simple at all; it depends upon the demands of nature, man, society, as well as upon the requirements of shells and networks. Such a balance has to be guided by a decrease in the forces derived from man's physical dimensions and personal energy, and an increase in those derived directly from nature itself as a developing and operating system.

A proper effort to assess the total natural resources available in a given territory, be it for purposes of conservation, exploitation, or other uses, is a prerequisite and one of the fundamental tasks of any plan of action. We need land use planning with proper margins for adjustment within certain ranges that are definable. A first subdivision into four categories can and should be determined at a global, continental, regional, national, and subnational level:

1. Natural areas (wildlife, forests, and so on).

2. Cultivation areas, including animal breeding (using various degrees of mechanization).

3. Human settlement areas (which will interfere to various degrees with the first two areas).

4. Pollution areas: heavy industry, ports, airports (necessary because we cannot yet control pollution).

Each area will have many subzones, and within each there will be patches of uses belonging to other zones. Special COF studies have made calculations and defined probable and desirable ratios of subdivision of total and habitable land into zones (see Tables 6-1 and 6-2), each with a different degree of human intervention in the natural environment. Similar studies have been carried out on the desirability and feasibility of the subdivision of coastal areas and oceans into corresponding zones. The extent, location, and criteria for the definition of each subzone must depend greatly on prevailing conditions in each case.

Within the human settlement areas it is necessary to define the following: (1) areas of land suitable for various uses; (2) degrees of habitability; (3) definition of optimum combination of uses; and (4) definition of best feasible combinations of uses.

The best outcome of a concerted effort for the immediate future would lead to:

1. A set of maps defining the quality and productivity of soil and water for the whole territory of each nation.

2. The consequent grading of these areas in the categories of use for which they are most suitable.

3. Identification of conflict areas (arable land on which extension of settlement is inevitable because proper control machinery is not available; forest versus animal breeding areas; tourism versus preservation) and other problem areas such as those where desertification is likely or has already taken place.

4. Development of long-term alternative plans for the uses of

Table 6-1. The 12 Global Zones of Land

Zones	% of Nature and Wildlife in Each Zone	Type of Human Intervention	% of Cultivation	Role of the Machine	Shells (Buildings)	Networks
1	100	only scientists for research	0	none	none	none
2	100	crossing by foot or boat	0	none	none	none
3	95	crossing, staying temporarily	3	none	tents	none
4	95	crossing, staying temporarily	4	none	camps	none
5	90	crossing, staying temporarily	5	auto-mobiles	motels, houses	roads
6	20	staying permanently	70	auto-mobiles, tractors, light industry	houses, buildings of many kinds	roads
7	20	staying permanently	60	auto-mobiles, tractors, light industry	houses, buildings of many kinds, covered cultivation areas	roads, rail-roads
8	20	staying permanently	40	for enter-tainment	hotels, sports buildings	roads, railroads, airplanes
9	10	staying permanently	30	auto-mobiles	homes, second homes, buildings	railroads, airplanes
10	10	staying permanently	20	auto-mobiles	homes, second homes, buildings	railroads, airplanes
11	0	staying permanently	10	auto-mobiles	homes, buildings	railroads, airplanes
12	0	for work only	10	every possible role	industrial waste disposal	railroads, airplanes

Table 6-2. **The Role of Nature (Wildlife) and Total Nature (Wildlife and Cultivation)**

Zones	% Nature and Wildlife	% Global Land Area	% Wildlife on Global Basis	% Cultivation	% Cultivation on Global Basis	% Global Wildlife and Cultivation
1	100	40	40	0	0	40
2	100	17	17	0	0	17
3	95	10	9.5	3	.30	9.8
4	95	8	7.6	4	.32	7.92
5	90	7	6.3	5	.35	6.65
6	20	5.5	1.1	70	3.85	4.95
7	20	5	1	60	3	4
8	20	5	1	40	2	3
9	10	1.3	.13	30	.39	.52
10	10	.7	.07	20	.14	.21
11	0	.3	0	10	.03	.03
12	0	.2	0	10	.02	.02

national space (with an emphasis on social cost) and the selection of one alternative for immediate action.

5. Development of a short-term program of action for the selected alternative plan (time, human resources, money).

Action for settlements of all scales. Many millions of human settlements—small and large, dynamic and static, closely or loosely connected, or enclosed in major systems—are now spread over the surface of the globe. (See Table 6-3.) In the process of urbanization many of them may disappear, many may be embraced within major systems, many will grow at various levels. Action in each case needs special consideration of the various dimensions of problems within the limits of the settlement itself, but also within the broader system or systems with which it is connected.

Although there are no globally valid principles to guide identical action for cities and villages with similar characteristics, long worldwide experience and special studies within the frame of the *City of the Future* and ACE's other projects show that, in terms of probable priority, one could suggest specific action for prevailing problems by type of settlement, and corresponding ultimate and immediate goals and action (see Appendix 6-1).

Action for urbanization pressure areas. The major population

Table 6-3. Distribution of Types of Settlements by Number and Size

Type of Settlement	Population Range	Estimated Total Population	% of Total Population	Estimated Number of Settlements	% of Total Settlements
Very small	1-100	276 million	7.7	10,440,000	73.4
Village	100-5,000	1,569 million	43.6	3,747,610	26.3
Polis	5,000-200,000	807 million	22.4	40,692	0.3
Metropolis	200,000-10 million	455 million	12.6	560	—[b]
Megalopolis	10-500 million	490 million	13.6	19[a]	—[b]
Total		3,597 million	100	14,229,380	100

[a] These 19 megalopolises include an average estimated 518 settlements. This number has been subtracted where applicable from the other types of human settlements.
[b] Negligible fraction.

areas, it is believed, will experience the gravest and most pressing problems during the next 30 to 50 years, both for the settlements (and systems of settlements) in them and for their total environment, in view of (1) high densities of population (increasing with time), especially in selected core areas; (2) high total population (increasing with time); and (3) megalopolitan development, or development of large isolated megalopolises and, what is more important, of large interconnected systems of megalopolises (urbanized regions, or small eperopolises) that will tend to become the dominating feature within these areas. These characteristics are expected to grow spectacularly in size and complexity with time.

These major pressure areas are divided into four categories:

1. In this type megalopolitan systems are already developed and are evolving toward one unified, complex system expected to form in the future. Total population and core densities are high.

2. Total population is smaller than in type 1; megalopolitan development is simpler, in terms of overall linear formation, but already present.

3. Megalopolitan development in this type is still in its early stages, evolving toward several distinct megalopolitan systems which, however, have to be considered as one major unit within a unified study area because of the functional interrelations between these megalopolitan systems.

4. This type is the same as type 2, but megalopolitan development is still in its early stages.

Several types of problems can be distinguished within these pressure areas:

1. Problems of structure, function, and development of the megalopolitan systems within these areas, leading to proposals for the proper organization and governance of these systems.

2. Problems of changing land uses, the eating up of open land through expanding urbanization, and environmental deterioration because of the growing megalopolitan systems, leading to proposals of measures of environmental control and protection, distinguished according to zones of increasing human intervention in the natural environment.

3. Problems of overall regional structure and development studied in the light of the developing megalopolitan systems within these areas, leading to corresponding proposals for regional control and development.

For each area, partial studies and modes of action could be devised, dealing either with specific problems (or groups of problems), or with specific subareas; in any case, we should not lose sight of the overall perspective of the total area, and of the entire system of problems. This means that each partial study should always be considered as part of the total one for each major study area.

CONCLUSIONS

To start improving our system of life, we need to make radical changes in our values and priorities. The vital factors upon which all the necessary changes will depend are the new intellectual and cultural developments of mankind.

Ecumenopolis will come inevitably, but it will only come in its most desirable form if mankind guides events toward the forms man most deeply desires. Our efforts should focus upon reestablishing and maintaining harmony between the five elements that make up human settlements: man, nature, society, shells, and networks. Growth takes place naturally; harmony in the man-made environment can be achieved through man's conscious action.

The development of a rational and scientific approach, making a careful study of the complex system of life in which we live and of the factors which make man happy, is a fundamental prerequisite for any action.

Immediate action on a global scale requires a lot of courage, but it is feasible and desirable. Until we can manage to organize plans on this scale, action should be encouraged on as large a scale as possible. Action should always be based on the desire to serve man. Everything we build now lays the foundations for the city of the future.

Appendix 6-1
Part I: Action for Human Settlements

Human Settlements	Problems	Goals	Policies and Programs
A. General	Identify only problems connected with human settlements as systems of life.	The practical way to deal with goals in terms of time dimensions and contents is to set ultimate and immediate goals both points of a long development process:	To proceed to policies and programs, begin by defining the term *human settlements*, then define the problems, and conclude by defining ultimate and immediate goals.
	Define the extent of influence of problems on the human settlement territory and their relation to any broader territory.	1. Ultimate goals must be set for the foreseeable future in a realistic way, ranging from one generation to a considerably longer period.	Define policies and programs for only one human settlement or a specific group of human settlements.
	Classify the problems of human settlements in a systematic way.	2. Immediate goals can be implemented at once as a first step in the long development process, or as the foundation for a sound development process.	The larger the area of human settlement involved, the more general will be the policies and programs.
	Evaluate the problems clearly so as to identify priorities.		Define the human settlement within which the problems are created and the responsibilities this human settlement has for their solution. The implementation of programs to the administrative boundaries of the human settlement suffering from a particular problem cannot be limited.

(cont. on next page)

113

Appendix 6-1 (cont.)

Human Settlements	Problems	Goals	Policies and Programs
B. Elements 1. Nature	Types of problems of Nature and human settlements regarding the area they influence:	*Ultimate*: Bring Nature into balance with human settlements. *Immediate*: Control the use of Nature's limited resources.	
	1. Complete elimination of natural resources.	*Ultimate*: Prepare an environment that can survive forever. *Immediate*: Plan for ultimate goal requiring change in attitude.	
	2. Temporary elimination of natural resources.	*Ultimate*: Plan for a constant, desirable, and feasible environment. *Immediate*: Prepare an action plan.	
	3. Permanent pollution of natural resources.	*Ultimate*: Create special zones in isolated areas for waste material. *Immediate*: Study possibilities and prepare waste zones.	
	4. Temporary pollution of natural resources.	*Ultimate*: Develop technology to relieve human settlements from temporary pollution. *Immediate*: Start the process now.	
2. Anthropos (man)	Consider all problems of the existence of man to be human settlement problems until each specific case is investigated. Determine the proper human dimensions of the space needed by humans for physiological reasons.	*Ultimate and immediate*: Create human settlements which protect and develop man. To survive, fulfill all basic biological and physiological needs, starting with oxygen and temperature and ending with all other needs defined by experts in	

114

To understand problems of human settlements in terms of the human body and senses, international evolutionary trends must be understood. Then compare case study with the evolutionary phase that people in the case study could be expected to have reached or should be helped to reach.	*Ultimate:* Give every man adequate space, starting with room and extending to the area of his daily urban system.
Try to understand not only whether or not they are human settlement problems but whether or not they are problems of a normal evolutionary phase through which human settlements pass.	Give high quality to spaces made available to inhabitants, which quality must be related to the biological and physiological needs of inhabitants, their history, culture, and civilization.
The problems of human settlements in terms of mind and soul must be judged by the inhabitants of the human settlements themselves.	A science is needed, without which there is no hope for a clear definition of goals and, therefore, of their achievement.
3. Society	
Analyze each problem of interaction between people in the community.	*Ultimate and immediate:* Make everyone equal inside all areas of human settlements.
Locate problems by units defined by population size and territory.	Equal opportunities for all to visit any place they choose.
Classify problems in each unit by category (national, racial, economic, religious, age group, income group).	Separate pedestrians from machine vehicles.
	Automate machines so that everybody is served equally.

(cont. on next page)

Appendix 6-1 (cont.)

Human Settlements	Problems	Goals	Policies and Programs
	Define problems on basis of social units and categories, their being the centers in the network of relationships.	Guarantee safety and security. *Immediate*: Guarantee safety and security to the maximum possible extent. *Ultimate*: Arrange spatial organization of human settlements in a hierarchical way. *Immediate*: Define at least some levels of local authority for special tasks without overlapping boundaries.	
4. Shells	When existing number of shells is known, compare them with number of people and acquire first idea of real relationships. Estimate size and volume of needed shells on basis of a certain but only tentative standard. Estimate grouping of needed shells on basis of tentative standard. Many shells of the past have major problems caused by decline in their initial quality. The best shells must be saved. Refer both to existing and missing shells when defining problems.	*Ultimate and immediate*: These can be very different. The basic unit in any effort concerning houses should be room. The dimensions of human room will tend, in the long run, to meet assumed international standards. Shape of room tends to be orthogonal, with a flat, horizontal ceiling and floor. Quality of room depends on many factors not all mentioned here. Ultimate and immediate goals must be coordinated as well as possible.	

Ultimate: Some sectors exist where we can be very specific and others where we must remain prepared for all kinds of change. It may or may not be possible to coordinate immediate with ultimate goals.

Goals concerning quality can be defined only for immediate future and for certain proportion of total needs because full agreement is never certain on matters of quality.

Technologies are universally valid, but only for immediate future and not as ultimate goals, because new demands will arise.

Ultimate: Cannot be defined for organization of all kinds of buildings. But as society must be organized and people prepared for new demands in buildings, space to be conserved for all types of future shells must be estimated.

Ultimate and immediate: Enable old buildings of historical or cultural value to survive as living parts of whole system of shells and not as dead relics, in which case they are in great danger of being permanently lost.

(cont. on next page)

117

Appendix 6-1 (cont.)

Human Settlements	Problems	Goals	Policies and Programs
		Examine all existing buildings, including those which must die and those which should be helped to live forever, and then foresee the new shells necessary for tomorrow and more distant future. Only by making this overview can old and new demands be unified into a living system of shells.	
5. Networks	Understand that all types form part of total system.	*Ultimate:* Coordinate system.	
	Have an image of all existing networks. They can be measured against the number of people they serve for the first image of the real relationship.	*Immediate:* Serve urgent needs in spirit of ultimate goal.	
		Conceive whole system of networks, in order to lead it towards implementation, as a truly modern technological system related to anticipated population and income level.	
	Estimates of problems of networks must be based on standards which can only be considered as tentative.		
	Calculate problems of quality of existing and missing networks on basis of assumed standards, always considering the hypothetical nature of the calculations.	To succeed, the goal of coordinated system of networks must be rational and must define the future role of each part of the system; that is, whole human settlement must be very well planned for present and future needs.	

To achieve goals set for networks, all needs of past, present, and future must be considered to be connected in one balanced system.

Problems of total organization of networks as a system must be based on assumptions about systems lacking, always considering hypothetical nature of calculations.

Several networks of past, necessary for many human needs, are gradually being eliminated.

Problems of networks must be based on work on both existing and missing networks.

(cont. on next page)

Appendix 6.1 (cont.)
Part II: Classification of Human Settlements

Units	Population Range	Estimated Number of Units	% of Human Settlements	Estimated Population (in Millions)	% of Global Population	Problems	Goals
Temporary human settlements						Inhabitants live in a most primitive way. Changes of climate and human action threaten conditions. None of the elements of human settlements (man, society, shell, network) exist in a satisfactory way.	*Ultimate:* Settle the inhabitants as permanent residents in a given area as soon as this is reasonably feasible. *Immediate:* Select a plan of action: (1) urgent and immediate aid for survival; (2) long-term to assist people become permanent residents.
Very small human settlements	1-100	10,440,000	73.4	276	7.7		
Villages	100-5,000	3,747,610	26.3	1,569	43.6	Any definition of problem must begin by recognizing whether and when the general conditions which led to the village's existence may be changed. Analysis of problems should be related to elements in the following order: nature, shells, networks, society, man. Villages are abandoned and inhabitants move to higher-income areas. This problem remains despite many attempts to overcome it. Transition of village inhabitants	*Ultimate:* Give village inhabitants choices equal to those of the urban dwellers by making them part of daily urban system. This will bring a completely new urban system of human settlements which will house agricultural workers as members of an urban profession. *Immediate:* Acceptance of ultimate goal and a realistic analysis of its situation.

120

| Polises | 5,000-200,000 | 40,692 | .3 | 807 | 22.4 | The moving of villagers to a nearby metropolis transforms the village into a suburb (temporary, easy problem).

Most, perhaps all villages will change their character, even if their land is retained for cultivation or is expanded, and become parts of urban systems.

Many and varied, ranging from threatened extinction to explosive growth. They must be considered as parts of the whole system of human settlement.

In areas of agricultural decline most polises are doomed.

Creation of many new demands because of explosion of population, economy, mobility, and area. | temporary, and often helps new systems of agricultural life develop.

Ultimate: For most polises it is to become an organic part of the broader urban system. A few might decline if changing system of human settlements around them does not provide incentive for survival.

When ultimate goal is negative, set immediate goals as incentives for changing ultimate negative goals. |
| Metropolises | 200,000-10 M | 560 | | 455 | 12.6 | Creation of new demands and threatening of nature in and around polises which become parts of metropolises and megalopolises.

Never enough housing for all classes of people, or enough of any other type of building to satisfy all citizens' needs, in terms of quality in every | *Ultimate:* Acceptance of the facts about their existence and preparation for appropriate development and growth without any negative attitudes. |

(cont. on next page)

121

Appendix 6.1 (cont.)

Units	Population Range	Estimated Number of Units	% of Human Settlements	Estimated Population (in Millions)	% of Global Population	Problems	Goals
						reasonable aspect of this demand. The lack of shells is worsened by the difference between classes, which do not exist in polises. Two categories of network problems: (1) those increasing equality between areas; (2) those menacing the entire metropolis. Most metropolitan networks belong to the past and are incapable of serving new needs. Centers or metropolitan areas are abandoned because they suffer from pressure on road networks.	Plan for proper land uses, taking into consideration the need for two new types of areas: (1) for humans, (2) for industry, as well as the need to save and develop existing areas for wildlife and for agriculture. *Immediate:* Prepare accurate estimates of future growth and physical plans to guide it. Implementation of immediate goals should be the first step towards achieving the ultimate goal.
Megalopolises	10-500 million	19		490	13.6	We face them today without a sound understanding of their problems but with a general concept based on the scientific understanding of human settlements. Nature is in greater danger in a megalopolis than anywhere else. Complete lack of coordination of networks into a unified system in terms of operation and physical structure. Both	*Ultimate:* (1) Understand their territorial organization. (2) Coordinate their total system of networks with the total territorial organization. (3) First in importance and third in execution. Reestablishing balance between the four types of areas (Anthropareas, Industrareas, Cultivareas, Naturareas) leads to the proper conception of the

National systems	The failure officially to recognize the birth and growth of megalopolises means that many necessary measures, especially the organization of territory, are not taken. We are not yet prepared to deal with the national system of human settlements. Classifying and evaluating the problems and measuring the real number of people affected by them is the only way to form an accurate image of their importance at the national level.	To set national goals we must understand all problems and the degree to which humans are affected by them. Without national goals the system of human settlements will fail. *Ultimate*: Set national goals. *Immediate*: Begin working towards them.
International systems	Classifying and evaluating the problems and measuring the real numbers of people affected by them is the only way to form an image of their relative importance at the international level. International understanding is a prerequisite. And so is the acceptance of a systematic approach.	*Ultimate*: Fulfill all goals set by all nations and inspired by the principles of a global system of human settlements with equal rights. *Immediate*: All those dealing with human settlements should (1) accept a methodology for the understanding of human settlements, their problems, and their solutions; (2) train and develop experts on human settlements all over the globe; (3) provide capital needed to begin and continue action on human settlements; (4) create the mechanisms for supplying materials.

REFERENCES

Antonopoulou, M. 1971. "Habitability Study: A Basis for Physical Ecumenopolis (ECU)—Introductory." RR-ACE:178(COF), Internal Document (January 8). City of the Future Research Project. Athens Center of Ekistics.

————. 1971. "Habitability Study: A Basis for Physical Ecumenopolis (ECU)—Natural Criteria." RR-ACE:178(1)(COF). Internal Document (April 2). City of the Future Research Project. Athens Center of Ekistics.

————. 1971. "Definitions and Densities of Concentric Zones 0-9." RR-ACE:195(COF). Internal Document (December 17). City of the Future Research Project. Athens Center of Ekistics.

————. 1972. "Habitability—II: Demographic Criteria." RR-ACE:197 (COF). Internal Document (March 10). City of the Future Research Project. Athens Center of Ekistics.

Antonopoulou, M., and Ripman, Christopher. 1973. "The City of the Future—Ecumenopolis: Assumptions, Scope, Alternatives." *EKISTICS* 36, no. 207 (February):63-77.

Athens Center of Ekistics. 1970. *Megalopolis & Ecumenopolis*. Special Bibliography Series no. 1 (November). Mimeographed.

Berry, Brian J. L. 1971. *Megalopolitan Confluence Zones: New Growth Centers in the United States*. Research Report no. 10. Athens: Athens Center of Ekistics.

"The City of the Future." 1965. *EKISTICS* 20, no. 116 (July).

"The City of the Future." 1967. *EKISTICS* 24, no. 140 (July):5-62.

"The City of the Future." 1968. *EKISTICS* 26, no. 152 (July):4-99.

"The City of the Future." 1970. *EKISTICS* 29, no. 175 (June).

"The City of the Future." 1971. *EKISTICS* 32, no. 189 (August).

Doxiadis, C. A. 1966. *Between Dystopia and Utopia*. Hartford, Conn.: Trinity College Press.

————. 1966, 1967, 1970. *Emergence and Growth of an Urban Region: the Developing Urban Detroit Area*. Vols. 1-3. Detroit: The Detroit Edison Co.

————. 1967. "The Coming World-City: Ecumenopolis." In *Cities of Destiny*, edited by A. Toynbee. London: Thames and Hudson.

————. 1967. "Ecumenopolis, the Settlement of the Future." Research Report no. 1. Athens: Athens Center of Ekistics.

————. 1968. "Ecumenopolis, Tomorrow's City." In *Britannica Book of the Year 1968*. Chicago: Encyclopaedia Britannica.

————. 1968. *Ekistics: An Introduction to the Science of Human Settlements*. New York: Oxford University Press.

————. 1970. "Urban America and the Role of Industry." DUS-101. Report written for the National Association of Manufacturers. Washington, D.C.: Doxiadis Urban Systems, Inc.

————. 1974. *Anthropopolis*. Athens: Athens Center of Ekistics.

————. 1974. *Global Ecological Balance*. Athens: Athens Center of Ekistics.

————. 1975. *Building Entopia*. Athens: Athens Center of Ekistics.

_____. 1976. *Action for Human Settlements.* Athens: Athens Center of Ekistics.

_____. 1976. "Propositions pour l'avenir des etablissements humains." *Revue 2000,* no. 35:7-8.

_____. 1977. *Ecology and Ekistics.* London: Paul Elek, Ltd.

Doxiadis, C. A., and Papaioannou, J. G. 1974. *Ecumenopolis: the Inevitable City of the Future.* Athens: Athens Center of Ekistics.

_____. 1976. "Oecumenopolis" (extracts). *Revue 2000,* no. 35:13-17.

Eckardt, W. V. 1964. *The Challenge of Megalopolis.* London: Macmillan.

Eldredge, H. W., ed. 1967. *Taming Megalopolis.* 2 vols. New York: Doubleday.

EKISTICS. Mainly issues July 1965, February 1966, July 1966, May 1967, July 1967, July 1968, June 1969, June 1970, June 1972, January 1974.

Gottmann, J. 1961. *Megalopolis: The Urbanized Northeastern Seaboard of the United States.* Cambridge, Mass.: MIT Press.

_____. 1975. "The Concept of Megalopolis." In *Great Lakes Megalopolis Symposium.* City Hall, Toronto, March 24-27. Edited by Leman Group, Inc. Ottawa: Ministry of State for Urban Affairs.

_____. 1976. "Les poussées megalopolitaines dans le monde." *Revue 2000,* no. 35:3-6.

Great Lakes Megalopolis Symposium. 1975. Toronto City Hall, March 24-27. Edited by Leman Group, Inc. Ottawa: Ministry of State for Urban Affairs.

Hearne, Alan; Bell, Malcolm; and Van Rest, David. 1977. "The Physical and Economic Impact of Motorways on Agriculture." *International Journal of Environmental Studies* 11:29-33.

Kamrany, N. "Bibliography on Futurology Post-1960." Mimeographed.

"Land Development Policies." 1976. *EKISTICS* 41, no. 244 (March).

"Living with the Desert." 1977. *EKISTICS* 43, no. 258 (May).

"A Look to the Future and a Review of the Past." 1972. *EKISTICS* 34, no. 200 (July).

Meier, R. L. 1965. *Megalopolis Formation in the Midwest.* Ann Arbor: Department of Conservation, University of Michigan.

_____. 1967. *The Influence of Resource Constraints upon Planning for Worldwide Economic Development.* Research Report no. 3. Athens: Athens Center of Ekistics.

Murphy, E. F. 1977. *Bureaucracy and the Rules of Property: Regulating and Renewing Environment.* Amsterdam: North Holland Publishing Co.

Papageorgiou, G., and Papaioannou, J. G. 1970. "Growth Indicators for Athens, 1870-1970." RR-ACE:157(COF). Internal Document (January 15). Capital of Greece Research Project, Athens Center of Ekistics.

Papaioannou, J. G. 1967. "Megalopolises: A First Definition." Research Report no. 2. Athens: Athens Center of Ekistics.

_____. 1970. "Future Urbanization Patterns: A Long-Range, Worldwide View" (summary). In *Proceedings of the International Future Research Conference, Kyoto.* Vol. 2. Tokyo: Kodansha Ltd.

_____. 1971. "Future Urbanization Patterns in Europe." In *Mastery of Urban Growth.* Brussels: Mens en Ruimte.

———. 1975. "The Emergence of Megalopolis." *Contact* 7, no. 6 (December).
Pell, Claiborne. 1966. *Megalopolis Unbound.* New York: Praeger.
Pickard, J. P. 1962. "Urban Regions in the U.S." *Urban Land News and Trends* (April).
———. 1967. "Population Land Area Projection in the U.S. Megalopolis." *Urban Land News and Trends* (February).
———. 1969. *Metropolitanization in the U.S.* Research Monograph no. 8. Washington, D.C.: Urban Land Institute.
Psomopoulos, P. 1968. "New Dimensions in Public Works." In *The American Public Works Association Yearbook 1968.* Chicago: APWA.
———. 1973. "Disabled People in Disabling Settlements—The Quality of Life for the Handicapped." In *Models of Service for the Multi-Handicapped Adult.* New York: United Cerebral Palsy of New York City, Inc.
———. 1976. "Notes on Urban Expansion as a Major Factor of Soil Destruction" Paper presented at the IFIAS Workshop, Samarkand, USSR (June 12-21). R-ACE 156 (May 10). Athens: Athens Center of Ekistics.
———. 1977. "Desertification and Human Settlements." *EKISTICS* 43, no. 258 (May):245-248.
———. 1977. "Guiding the Growth of Metropolitan Athens." *EKISTICS* 44, no. 262 (September):120-133.
Sheather, G. D. 1969. *North and Central Lakes Region: A General Systems Theory Analysis.* Part 1. Research Report no. 7. Athens: Athens Center of Ekistics.
Swatridge, L. A. 1972. *The Bosnywash Megalopolis.* Toronto: McGraw-Hill.
Toynbee, A. 1970. *Cities on the Move.* New York: Oxford University Press.
Tyrwhitt, J., and Bell, G., eds. 1972. *Human Identity in the Urban Environment.* London: Penguin.
United Nations Conference on Desertification. 1977. "Desertification: An Overview." A/CONF.74/1/Rev.1. UN Conference on Desertification, Nairobi, 29 August-9 September.
Virirakis, J. 1972. "Communities as Units of Distribution and Use of Facilities—Minimization of Energy. Chapter 2: The Influence of Density on Community Size." RR-ACE:207(HUCO). Internal Document (September 21). Human Community Research Project, Athens Center of Ekistics.
———. 1972. "Communities as Units of Distribution and Use of Facilities—Minimization of Energy. Chapter 3: Mechanism of Adaptation of the Community Sizes to the Changes of Density Over Time." RR-ACE:208(HUCO). Internal Document (September 26). Human Community Research Project, Athens Center of Ekistics.
Wade, M., ed. 1969. *The International Megalopolis.* Toronto: University of Toronto Press.

Chapter 7

The Need for Public Awareness

Pierre Laconte*

After the three remarkably complete speeches of this morning about the quantitative changes in land use, little is left for me except maybe a few positive comments.

The first point I would like to make is that the resilience of the users of the land is probably much higher than we may believe. The human being alters his environment much more than the animal, but at the same time he has a greater ability to adapt to the changes of environment caused by his own collective actions. We may therefore affirm that this planet is already preparing itself to feed 10 billion people.

This presupposes, of course, that we do not consider the hypothsis of a nuclear cataclysm, which, according to an MIT scenario, would cover half of the planet with darkness and dust for six months and suppress most forms of life in this hemisphere for an indefinite period of time.

Unless we consider that kind of scenario, it seems likely that the population will increase exactly as Lester Brown has indicated. This will increase the reliance and the dependence of human beings on land and therefore, in the long run, increase the average market value of land because of the increased demand for it.

But one point which I think is important is that at the same time

*This manuscript is derived from a transcript of oral remarks.

that the demand for land increases, there will be an adaptation of the land supply. It is already happening. One major factor (only in its infancy now) is the increased accessibility of remote places through the new telecommunications technology. Satellites will bring the marginal cost of long-distance communication close to zero. From an isolated place it may be cheaper to use a satellite link to communicate with any city than to install a telephone line. Satellites will open up deserts or remote islands of the planet which up to now have been inaccessible to human settlements. This increased accessibility will create vast new land markets for places hitherto uninhabitable.

In Alaska today new communities are being opened up to information, cultural life, and civilization by communication through satellites. To take another example, India has been a pioneer in the use of satellites to bring culture and education to remote rural villages, enabling them to keep their young population on the land. Propinquity with the urban world is achieved without physical proximity, as Melvyn Webber predicted 20 years ago. Telecommunications will make more places livable. However, it will also increase the impact of dominant cultures.

Because of the adaptive process which I have just described, the supply of new land has to be monitored very carefully.

Besides the extension of the land supply, new uses for existing land are constantly emerging. As Lester Brown indicated, land will have, in addition to its use for food or shelter, a use for the collection of energy—for example wind energy, which would give a new value to windy places, hitherto less desirable.

Here also the satellites could have an influence by allowing new uses for existing land. The satellite is not only able to transmit data; it is also able to transmit energy. Large solar panels attached to satellites can concentrate energy, which can be collected on the ground by antennas, thereby vastly reducing the land area needed for solar panels placed on the ground or on top of buildings. Thus, an additional means will have been achieved to allow a higher and better use of the land.

Lester Brown also stressed the need for a new land use ethic. I fully share this view. Actually, I believe that this new ethic will grow naturally, as the energy ethic grew naturally from the energy crisis. People will never again think about energy as they did before 1973.

I feel that the same might become true for the land and natural resources. The environmentalists have put into the minds of the people a certain concern about natural resources which is here to stay. If Mr. Watt was unable to do what he would have liked, was it not because of that already deeply-rooted new concern for the conservation of resources? I personally feel that the land use ethic will grow out of the increased demand for land, its scarcity, and our increasing dependence on it.

Public awareness, however, has to be based on facts, and the facts about the depletion of resources must be brought to the public attention. With all the disciplines and experience we represent, we are able to monitor and publish changes in land use at the world level, using the inputs from international, governmental, and nongovernmental organizations all over the world. We possess a wealth of data, but the various sources sometimes give contradictory results. For example, the data about deforestation apparently diverge, mainly because of differences in definitions and parameters. There is a need to assess all available sources of information, including their apparent contradictions, in order to learn and understand the changes which are occurring, and to publicize the results of our investigation. This is the task which Aurelio Peccei has suggested we take on our shoulders. I feel he is right. It should be our international priority to work in this line. We should start now.

Comments by Speakers in Response to Questions from the Audience

Question: There has been a focus on settlements. I'd like to know what we can do about settlements in terms of regional demands.

Mr. Psomopoulos: Well, Professor Murphy, we can do a lot. And we are doing a lot internationally. It is certain that the most critical period is what we used to call the ecumenic settlement, and is now the period between the present and the years 2000-2010 according to all predictions. There is a practice and there are some principles.

Yesterday I spent almost the whole night reading all the papers we have available. There are 50. There is one very important point that I want to stress in addition to some of the ideas you have in your various books on the environment and management of land. It is one point that Dr. Honjo mentions. Because of the proximity, because we haven't yet witnessed the impact of communications, it is almost certain that communications will increase rather than decrease contacts, and will not allow regional location of detached settlements as it is anticipated. This was a hypothesis that was promoted when the telephone was invented, and in fact the outcome was just the opposite. Dr. Honjo says that if we are to avoid this kind of vicious circle and the continuous growth of both urban and rural settlements and the tendency to have rural settlements taken over by urban settlements and general expansion, we should think about developing settlements outside the reach of major concentrations that are attractive. This is a real idea, a very important idea, that is being implemented internationally.

We have a lot of resettlement projects in various countries. Many countries, encouraged by the World Bank and other international agencies, are thinking of exploiting new lands, very fertile. At the desertification conference people spoke about the various reasons for desertification, but they never spoke about settlements. Lester Brown mentioned it for the first time today. Wherever you do agricultural development, you also develop settlements and people.

I think if we don't create major settlements in wild areas never exploited before—not necessarily very precious for agriculture but for other uses—and if we don't classify land into categories ranging from pure virgin land to polluted land, and all the range in between, we shall never manage a meaningful approach to regional planning. We need new tools. And we need to accept that the maximum accessibility to the most advanced artifacts that humanity has produced is the only guarantee that villages and small settlements located in new areas will remain where they are. A lot of projects internationally are failing totally because of our ignoring this major hierarchy of settlements.

Mr. Dunkerley: Would other members of the troika like to respond?

Mr. Laconte: Professor Murphy probably wanted to get an institutional answer. I would say that there are two examples, both quite recent, which could be mentioned. One example is the Treaty of Rome, which has generated a certain number of regional policy instruments for the European community. Some have undoubtedly worked rather effectively. Much money, for example, has been spent on agricultural land policy. The results are debatable—it would be a long discussion—but no one can deny the impact of European federal policies.

The other example is the Barcelona Conference and Treaty on the pollution on the Mediterranean Sea, which has generated effective tools for pollution control which are bound to have some impact at the regional level.

Mr. Sunkel: I think there are many examples in Latin America for regional planning. In Mexico, in Venezuela, in Brazil there are enormous regional or spatial policies—building Brasília, for instance, building new towns in Venezuela, and so on. I would say that most of these planning efforts which have been going on for many years are tremendous failures. I couldn't give a full diagnosis, but I would try to say just two or three things. I mean failures in the sense that Brasília was designed to be a city, the capital of Brazil, for about 1 or 2 million people. Now the formal city of Brasília is already over that number of people, and it is basically unlivable. What is more important is that there is double that population around Brasília, which was never anticipated.

Growth poles, which were very important in Latin America at a certain stage, have never decentralized or restrained population from flowing to the main areas. So this is a dismal failure, and I would attribute it to many reasons. I think there is a tremendous problem in thinking about regional planning. We have had two kinds of approaches. One is the economist-sociologist-social science type of approach, which I think has absolutely no knowledge of the physical aspects, of the fact that a settlement is the center of a tremendous network of relationships with the environment. I think this is something that is lacking in almost all of the plans for regional development.

On the other hand, there are the physical planners—architects, urban designers, and so on. Those, I think, have dismally failed to anticipate the socioeconomic and political forces which, for instance, made architects plan Brasília but did not realize that they needed another city of double its size to make that city possible. So perhaps the bringing together of social scientists and physical planners is one way, at least, to start approaching this most important of subjects.

PART III

Exploding Cities and Agricultural Productivity: Conflicts at the Urban Fringe

Introduction to Third Session

William Lim

I am indeed honored to be invited to this Congress and to be a moderator for this session on exploding cities and agricultural productivity. For many years I have been intrigued by this controversial issue of allocating land for agriculture in urban areas, particularly in the free-market economies of Third World countries. I wish, therefore, to take this occasion to share some of my ideas with you on whether urban agriculture is a myth or a new ideology.

When urban land usage is determined solely by natural market forces, one major casualty is agricultural land. As the physical boundaries of urban centers increase in response to population and development pressure, agricultural land is often conveniently converted for built property development. This phenomenon applies equally to urban centers in both free-market and socialist economies. Currently accepted locational theories are often used to argue that the most efficient use of available land resources is established by the price mechanism in response to market demand and supply conditions. It is not disputed that in macroanalysis of land use planning locational factors are important. They must be given serious consideration.

Land use patterns and land prices in urban centers are greatly influenced by many factors, including transportation, availability of essential services, permissible usages and stipulated plot ratio and density, as well as provisions for access to communal recreational and other facilities. The intensity and types of land usages determine the kinds of infrastructure provisions. It is possible therefore to deliberately allocate certain land for specific purposes to fulfill the social and environmental needs and long-term interests of the community as a whole. It is even possible to achieve this without incurring unnecessary capital expenditure in the provision of infrastructure facilities.

In order to achieve cost-effective and meaningful land use planning, proper studies and deliberate policy decisions have to be made well in advance of development implementation. Land for public purposes, particularly land for housing and shelter for the majority in Third World urban centers, should be acquired by the authorities at reasonable cost. Providing land to achieve social justice and equity does not necessarily decrease the economic efficiency and utilization of land even in free-market economies.

During the last few decades, the concept of land ownership in free-market economies has been substantially modified. Rezoning controls, increment tax on development, and land acquisition laws demonstrate that landowners no longer enjoy the indisputable right to use the land. Private landowners are but catalysts who should effectively utilize and develop the land. In the process, the concept of land as an essential commodity to be used and developed for the benefit of the community is to be increasingly accepted. To ensure the quality of life in the urban environment, most responsible governments have allocated adequate land for public and civic buildings, educational and religious institutions, and parks and playgrounds, as well as communal and recreational facilities. Increasing attention has also been given to historical conservation and the provision of land for public housing and shelter for the poor. However, few countries today have deliberately allocated urban land for agricultural purposes. Perhaps policymakers are not yet convinced of the desirability of this course. Furthermore, the powerful urban elite in most free-market economies oppose the need to adopt a viable urban agricultural policy.

For urban agriculture to be viable there are four basic requirements: (1) maximization of the use of urban land with reference to the quality of life and the intensity of development, particularly in mass housing; (2) establishment of an ideological reorientation to yield a new concept of land and its utilization; (3) analysis and understanding of its effects on the urban infrastructure; and (4) provision of a comprehensive land policy definitive enough for immediate application and flexible enough to meet continuously changing conditions, particularly in rapidly expanding urban centers in the Third World.

The oil crisis has forced the world to consider the soft energy option and energy conservation. Do we need a major international food crisis before urban authorities, particularly those in Third World countries, decide to allocate sufficient suitable urban land for agriculture? It is in this context that we all should welcome the contribution of our speakers in this morning's session.

Chapter 8

Land Problems in Japan

Masahiko Honjo
Tokunosuke Hasegawa

The conflict between cities and rural communities over land arises essentially from urban expansion and the resulting elimination of agricultural land use due to the far greater profitability of urban land use. This has a direct effect on land use in areas around cities. But in countries with extensive frontiers where there is space for agriculture to develop, the conflict is mitigated. In Japan, however, land is already densely populated and intensively used, and furthermore great store is set on the ownership of land. Thus there is considerable resistance to changes in land use. With the Meiji Restoration of 1868, Japan entered a period of modernization and, at the same time, the era of urbanization. Large-scale urbanization advanced rapidly, particularly after the Second World War, and deepened this conflict between cities and rural communities.

It is in this context that the nature of the conflict over land that has developed in Japan between cities and rural communities will be discussed.

NATURAL CONDITIONS IN JAPAN

Japan is a long and narrow mountainous archipelago with an area of 370,000 square kilometers and stretching 2,000 kilometers into the Pacific in a north-south direction. It is located in the monsoon region, and heavy rains erode the mountains and deposit soil in the lowlands, creating wet delta plains on the coast suited to the cultivation of rice. From ancient times, agriculture centered around rice-paddy farming has flourished in these areas. Rice has a higher yield per unit area than other crops, such as wheat, and moreover a mild climate makes it possible in many regions to grow a second crop. Thus, a small area can support a fairly large population.

Table 8-1 and Table 8-2 show the situation in land use today. Two-thirds of all land is highland forest, and 15 percent is agricultural land; urban developed land accounts for less than 4 percent. Looked at from a topographical standpoint, 28 percent of the land is at or under 100 meters above sea level, 31 percent has a gradient of 8 percent or lower, and 15 percent is low, level land. There is thus only a small amount of land suitable for agricultural or urban use within the narrow borders of Japan.

Some of this is in potential flood areas, further restricting the development of large cities. Yet the long coastline and the many rivers have accommodated for ages the movement of goods and people and have made possible the intensive use of habitable land over the entire country. As Japan began to modernize, new infrastructural facilities such as railways and roads were constructed. Because these were built in regions which already had concentrations of people, investments proved highly cost effective and spurred further concentration. As world trade expanded after the Second World War, harbors and coastal industrial regions were developed which offered conditions favorable to the development of heavy and chemical industries. These conditions helped to sustain the high rate of growth of the Japanese economy and to effect the rapid changeover to a more intensive and urban land use.

THE DEVELOPMENT OF LAND USE IN RURAL AREAS

Before we proceed to a discussion of the conflict over land, we should take an overall look at how land use has evolved in rural areas.

Agricultural Production

As has been already mentioned, Japanese agriculture has centered from ancient times around the growing of rice. This has required a

Table 8-1. Land Use And Natural Conditions in Japan

Land Use	Area (10,000 ha.)			Percentage (%)		
	Japan	3 major metrop. regions	country-side	Japan	3 major metrop. regions	country-side
Agricultural land	564	66	498	14.9	16.8	14.7
Cropland	547	66	481	14.4	16.8	14.2
Pasture	17	0	17	0.5	0.	0.5
Forest	2,528	205	2,323	66.9	52.3	68.6
Plain	36	1	35	1.0	0.2	1.0
Body of water, river, channel	114	13	101	3.0	3.3	3.0
Road	103	19	84	2.7	4.8	2.5
Developed land	138	43	95	3.7	11.0	2.8
Residential	107	33	74	2.9	8.4	2.2
Factory	15	5	10	0.4	1.3	0.3
Office or commercial	16	5	11	0.4	1.3	0.3
Miscellaneous	294	45	249	7.8	11.6	7.4
Total	3,777	392	3,385	100.0	100.0	100.0

Source: *Wagakuni no kokudo riyō no genjō, (White Paper on National Land)*, 1980.

Table 8-2. Topographical Conditions in Japan by Percentage of Land Area

Altitude above sea level	100 meters or below (28%)	100 to 200 (14%)	200-600m. (35%)	600-1000m. (15%)	1000m. or above (8%)
Gradient	0-8° (31%)	8-15° (14%)	15-30° (38%)	30° or above (17%)	
Topo-graphical type	lowland (15%)	plateau (11%)	hill (11%)	mountain (63%)	

great deal of effort in flood prevention, irrigation, and drainage work, achieved through close cooperation. This has been the basis of Japan's tightly knit agricultural communities. Rice production has been central to Japan's economic organization, and throughout history this fact has governed the determination of landownership and cultivation rights, the establishment of systems of taxation, and the conduct of land surveys (land measurement and land registration).

The process of modernization during the Meiji era was also financially based on agricultural production, the land tax being an important means of absorbing earnings and providing funds. On the one hand, land registration and land tax systems were modernized, and on the other, irrigation drainage projects and projects to readjust arable land were actively undertaken in order to increase production. By 1898 the Farmland Readjustment Law had been enacted.

During the Second World War the delivery of rice to the government was made compulsory in order to promote self-sufficiency in foodstuffs, and this practice continued during the postwar era of food shortages. As incentive, however, the government had to provide various forms of assistance to farmers. As a legacy of those days, Japan continues to follow a policy that attaches great importance to rice production. This is an extremely important point, one that is related to postwar agrarian reform, and it has considerable bearing on present-day land use. This matter, however, is better left for discussion in the next session.

Besides rice, silk was another important agricultural product. It was a major export item during Japan's early period of modernization and a source of foreign exchange, and the industry was protected and nurtured. Mulberry fields were cultivated as a side business on steep highlands which were poorly watered and unsuited to the growing of rice. This crop was next to rice in importance as a source of income. From around 1930, however, the development of synthetic fibers lowered the economic value of silk in foreign markets, and today silk is significant only as a traditional industry. The mulberry fields too are disappearing.

Suburban agriculture developed in the course of modernization. This occurred because suburban agriculture enjoyed a twofold advantage: there were higher returns in producing fresh foodstuffs for the urban population than in growing rice, and productivity could be increased by using night soil from the city for fertilizer. As will be explained later, recent organizational changes in agricultural markets have made suburban agriculture less advantageous, and suburban farms are gradually disappearing. However, they are still in the forefront of the conflict between cities and rural areas.

Lowland Forests and Highland Forests

Many lowland forests were found on the plains. These were used for firewood, charcoal, and fertilizer, contributing to a self-sufficient system of agriculture. Many of these forests, called joint-use forests, were owned and used communally. They also provided a fringe of verdure on the outskirts of cities and were an important factor in maintaining an ecological equilibrium. However, the growing availability of gas, coal, and—particularly after the war—oil robbed lowland forests of their value as a source of fuel, and these lands were quickly turned to urban uses. The green landscapes retreated from the suburbs.

The mountainous areas that make up 70 percent of the country are largely covered by forests. Where possible, these forests have been used to provide lumber, firewood, and charcoal, but the increased importation of lumber, the changes in fuel use, and the departure of labor from mountain communities have undermined the management of these forests and are making it difficult to protect and cultivate forests and to maintain a natural environment in Japan.

THE ADVANCE OF URBANIZATION AND LAND POLICY

Next, let us consider the antithesis of the agricultural region: the urban region. Urbanization progressed as Japan underwent modernization beginning with the Meiji Restoration, and it gradually accelerated as Japan entered the twentieth century. In particular, there was an explosive growth of cities after the Second World War. Needless to say, this accompanied a change in industrial organization, away from primary industries to secondary and tertiary industries. What is exceptional about Japan compared to other advanced countries is the extreme rapidity with which this phenomenon occurred there.

The difficult task that confronted Japan in the process of urbanization was simultaneously undertaking the accumulation of capital to build up industries necessary for modernization, and in support of this, the basic development of the land. Transportation in the past had been by boat (along the coast or on rivers) or on foot;

wheeled transportation was virtually undeveloped. For example, the 600-kilometer-long Tokaido route between Tokyo and Osaka, which the Shinkansen now covers in three hours, used to have practically no bridges; travelers had to cross the many rivers on ferries or on people's shoulders. Conditions in cities and houses were equally primitive. Streets and water supply and sewerage systems were left over from the feudal period, and an administrative organization that could transform them into modern urban facilities did not yet exist.

In the process of urbanization, Japan had to upgrade the rapidly expanding cities with very limited capital and weak administrative powers; it was a case of muddling through. It was commonly accepted that priority was to be given to the construction of necessary—that is, basic—facilities. The building of other urban facilities and housing was of secondary importance. (The policy was to build first and then supplement or improve later on, when there was more financial leeway.) There were never systematic, far-sighted investments based on an anticipatory plan with the timely provision of urban facilities. City planning never managed to catch up with sprawl. Cities were densely packed with wood houses, and major disasters provided the only opportunities for altering these into well-ordered cityscapes. These circumstances account for the Japanese proclivity to view city planning as an activity engaged in only after a disaster such as an earthquake or a war.

Given this background, a bitter conflict between cities and rural areas would seem inevitable. In fact, however, the conflict was most often resolved quite commonsensibly with the two sides reaching some sort of agreement. Since the war, however, urbanization has become extremely rapid, and technological developments such as motorization and the advent of high-rise buildings have further promoted urbanization, making the conflict more serious.

Let us consider this process of urbanization and the consequent conflict in sequence.

First Stage: Early Modernization

A late arrival to the modern world, Japan first had to catch up with the advanced societies. The great powers were then following a policy of imperialist expansion, and the Industrial Revolution was nearing its culmination. Japan's goals in modernizing were to strengthen the country economically and militarily (*fukoku kyōhei*) as well as industrially (*shokusan kōgyō*). While developing its military strength, Japan made efforts to develop modern industries and advanced in short order from light to heavy industries. By the early twentieth century it had reached the stage of economic takeoff. Modernization led to urban growth and the increased concentration in cities of population and industries. The first urban development regulation established during this period was probably the 1898 Tokyo City Improvement Act. This provided a legal system for developing Tokyo into a modern city, with Paris serving as a model, befitting the capital of a civilized country. What was most notable about this regulation, however, was the direction that it indicated with regard to urban development policy. Kensei Yoshikawa, who as prefectural governor of Tokyo was responsible at the time for city improvement, presented a petition in connection with the draft of this regulation in which he asserted that "roads and rivers are basic. . .housing and sewerage are subsidiary." This statement suggests a tendency to favor infrastructure-oriented projects, particularly the construction of roads, and indicates how determined the bureaucrats of the time were to modernize Japanese cities, which were still feudal in their structure. This attitude has colored subsequent city planning in Japan up to the present day.

Second Stage: Industrialization

Tokyo was not the only Japanese city to undergo urbanization in the twentieth century; major cities throughout the country underwent this process and required urgent development. The enactment in 1919 of the old City Planning Law and its companion regulation, the Built-Up Area Building Law, were intended to deal with this situation.

The idea of widening the scope of urban development to include not just the built-up areas but the surrounding regions as well became accepted. In Tokyo, for example, the city planning district included areas that could be reached in approximately 60 minutes' travel time from central Tokyo, and the intention was to develop the entire area as a unit. What is notable is that the Farmland Readjustment Law, touched on in the previous section, was applied to the development of areas on the outskirts of expanding cities. Farmland readjustment was a project for improving agricultural land; farmers within a given district pooled their land, and each ceded a certain fraction of his land for the development of necessary infrastructural facilities. The result was orderly divided parcels of land. The farming associations played a central role in carrying out these projects, and the strong sense of solidarity that existed among farmers of a given district made the transactions possible. The experience gained from this was now to be put to use in transforming arable land into developed land.

This was in fact proposed in the City Planning Law of 1919, which introduced the idea of land readjustment. In land readjustment the public authority did not retain all the land; instead most of the land, apart from that set aside for public facilities, was returned to the original owners (who were at the time of the enactment mostly farmers). It was thus a project to systematically create developed land so that the benefits of development could be shared. The land required for public facilities and the construction funds were provided by the landowners of a district, each contributing a fixed percentage of his land in the form of a "land decrease." The land decrease was usually 30 to 50 percent, but this was acceptable to the farmers because the increase in the value of the land more than offset the loss. This became a widespread system, and land readjustment is regarded as the origin of city planning in Japan.

This method was not without its problems. Tenant farmers could not share in the benefits of development, and people who had moved out of the city to live on the outskirts had small properties which could not be "decreased;" consequently these groups tended to oppose land readjustment.

Nevertheless, during this period the urban area expanded, and agricultural land, encroached upon, fell back in this manner. The farmers, however, continued to own considerable areas of land, and even after land readjustment they could continue their agricultural operations, making up if need be for the land lost through land decrease by developing or buying new farmland nearby. The urban expansion, furthermore, created suburban agriculture on the outskirts, and the housing demand made it possible for farmers to engage in the business of providing rental housing. The urban work force also was able to absorb the surplus agricultural population. Although urbanization during this period was notable, particularly on the outskirts of metropolises like Tokyo and Osaka, it proceeded at a much slower pace than today's, and the retreat of rural areas was gradual. Thus the conflict between cities and rural areas was not yet critical.

Another urban problem of this period which should be mentioned is the 1923 earthquake in the Tokyo region. Tokyo and Yokohama were devastated by a powerful earthquake and the consequent fires. The Special City Planning Law was enacted for the purpose of promoting reconstruction, and based on this law the Capital Reconstruction Agency (later the Reconstruction Bureau) was established by the government to administer the work. Reconstruction worthy of being called city planning was carried out, creating much of the framework of Tokyo as it exists today.

The land readjustment method was used for the development of infrastructural facilities such as roads in urbanized areas, an application repeated in postwar reconstruction work, and it represented a major advance in Japanese city planning technique.

Third Stage: From Postwar Reconstruction to a High-Growth Economy

The Second World War ended in 1945, having caused enormous damage to many Japanese cities. The damaged area totaled 630 square kilometers, and 2.3 million homes, or 20 percent of all houses, had been destroyed. This provided an unparalleled opportunity for the implementation of city planning.

The War Damage Reconstruction Agency was established within the central government for overseeing the reconstruction of cities and housing. In 1946 the War Damage Reconstruction Special City Planning Law was enacted, and postwar reconstruction projects based on land readjustment methods were to be planned and promoted. The initial plans called for reconstruction projects covering 650 square kilometers, but as this was considered too ambitious in light of Japan's financial situation at the time, the scale of the projects was reduced to 280 square kilometers. Even so, postwar reconstruction projects played a major role in the advancement of city planning in Japan. In carrying out these projects the land readjustment method was used, and what began as a modified application of the Farmland Readjustment Law became a law of its own with the 1954 enactment of the Urban Land Readjustment Law.

One policy measure taken in the postwar era—that is, early in the third stage of urbanization—had enormous influence on land use, and that was agrarian reform. The Occupation demanded as early as 1946 that the government carry out the reform as part of its policy to democratize Japan. Much of the farmland that had been owned hitherto by a small number of landowners and cultivated by tenant farmers was distributed to the latter. As a result, large holdings disappeared in favor of many small holdings, numbering some 2 million in the first two years.

Agrarian reform was certainly effective in promoting democratization and in increasing farmer motivation, but it resulted in the division of farmland into small units amounting to no more than a hectare per household on the average. The farmers who had been made independent of the landowners organized themselves into agricultural cooperative associations which took over from the landlords of the past the role of farm administrators.

Following the period of postwar reconstruction there began in the latter half of the 1950s the era of rapid economic growth. This was a time of tremendous development centered on a shift to heavy and chemical industries, a period in which a revolutionary change in the industrial structure was effected. The population engaged in work in primary industries accounted for 48.3 percent of the total labor force in 1950 but rapidly decreased as people moved to secondary or tertiary industries; by 1980 they made up only 11.2 percent. At the same time, there was a movement of the population to the cities, amounting almost to a national migration. Urban regions rapidly expanded, particularly in the case of built-up areas within metropolitan regions. Land prices suddenly began to rise, and confusion reigned in land use.

To deal with this situation a National Land Agency, in charge of land policy at the national level, was established in 1974, and a National Land Utilization Planning Law was enacted that same year to provide a basic system for land use and transactions.

The most important step taken was the enactment in 1969 of the new City Planning Law. Fifty years had passed since the old law was first put into effect, and this new law incorporated measures to deal with the various problems that had arisen in the interim with the advance of urbanization, particularly in the postwar period. The most important of the measures were the Land Use Plan and the Development Permit System, which were intended to promote efficient urban development by separating city planning areas into "urbanizing areas" (areas that were already urbanized or were expected to be urbanized in ten years' time) and "controlled urbanization areas" (areas where urbanization was to be restricted) and concentrating urban development in the former. These measures were devised because it was necessary to deal with the sprawl that rapid urbanization had created and the accelerating increase in land prices. A land use plan and a land tax system logically ought to have been considered together, and it was argued that arable land in an urbanizing district should be taxed at a level equal to that on developed land.

Although this may have been correct theoretically, it was opposed by suburban cities, towns, villages, and rural areas, even where they desired incorporation into an urbanizing district. An equitable tax program therefore was never fully carried out. This was, at the time, the point of greatest contention between cities and rural areas and constituted a part of the political power game.

We will discuss in a separate section the two most critical issues in the conflict that thus evolved between cities and rural areas: the change in the rural community itself and the upsetting of the ecological balance.

CONFLICT ON THE OUTSKIRTS OF CITIES

The Transformation of Rural Communities and Households

Postwar urbanization radically changed the nature of the rural community which had provided the basic support for the operation of farms; at the same time, economic growth largely altered the organization of Japanese agriculture. These developments were most conspicuous on the outskirts of cities. By *conflict* we mean precisely a structural change of this nature. The essentials of this clash are as follows.

First, there was a change in the nature of the rural community. The transformation of the industrial structure meant not only that the city drew large numbers of people away from the rural community but also that urban-type employment opportunities increased within the rural community itself as local industries developed. As income rose in the rural community, the level of education and welfare also rose, radically changing people's lives. As a result, the number of farmers with side businesses increased sharply, and the number of those who were exclusively farmers dropped from 21.5 percent in 1965 to 13.4 percent in 1980.

In this manner the agricultural labor force which had been the basic underpinning of Japanese agriculture shrank markedly and became centered around those who were unsuited for work in other occupations, namely the women and the elderly. People from the cities, meanwhile, moved into the rural communities and were an anomalous, alien population. The majority of these new residents were employed in the city, and it was the city which held their interest. Their pattern of life and their values differed from those of the natives. The management of farms had depended hitherto on the cooperation of farm households, and this had bound the rural community together; these new developments, however, made such cooperation and coordination difficult.

Second, there was the bias that existed in agricultural policy and the consequence of that bias. As previously mentioned, the policy in Japan with regard to agriculture has been to place great importance on rice production and to protect and nurture it. This tendency was strengthened by a policy aimed at achieving self-sufficiency in staples, which can be traced back to wartime measures, and is apparent in the continued maintenance of a government system of rice supervision.

The government engages in the supervision of foodstuffs; that is, it buys rice from farmers and then sells the rice to consumers. The price at which rice is bought, however, is higher than the price at which rice is sold, and the cost difference is paid for by the government, which means that the price of rice is kept very high— more than twice the international rate.

Furthermore, large supplementary funds are given to farmers through what are called "projects for the improvement of agricultural organization," public projects for the improvement of agricultural land or agricultural operation.

Because such a policy guarantees a very stable price of rice and makes rice growing profitable, rice production is kept at a high level, resulting in surpluses. For this reason, restrictions have been put on production, but heavy protection is provided through compensation for reducing the area under cultivation or for skipping crops. Farmers, however, remain dissatisfied; and this dissatisfaction finds expression in the political pressure exerted by the agricultural cooperative associations and the continuing movement for further strengthening protective policies. The consequence of all this is that rice agriculture in Japan today, dependent on financial aid and receiving the protection of the government, is in a very weak state.

Third, there is the revolution in agricultural technology. Agriculture, particularly rice agriculture, now makes heavy use of fertilizers, machinery, and agricultural chemicals. The use of machinery to offset the labor shortage has extended from planting, harvesting, and threshing to the sowing of seeds, and is being promoted through the joint efforts of industries such as the machinery manufacturers and the agricultural cooperative associations.

Small individual farms work against the efficient use of these machines, but it would be difficult under the present circumstances to extend farmland in Japan. A new way of farming, therefore, is starting to develop: the owners of machines enter into contracts with the farmers and do the farm work themselves. The type of farmer who was completely immersed in the operation of his farm is giving way to a farmer who entrusts the operation of his farm to outside help and rented machinery. Enterprising farmers are specializing in commercially profitable products in order to increase the productivity of their land. They produce vegetables and flowers in all seasons in plastic hothouses or engage in large-scale poultry farming; these farmers, however, also have difficulty achieving a productivity competitive with other industries, and poultry farming and stock raising, moreover, are sources of pollution in densely built up areas. Their operation, therefore, is by no means economically stable.

Fourth, there is the change in the organization of the agricultural market. Direct, mechanized shipment from the area of production to individual consumer areas is becoming systematized, with the changeover from railway to truck transportation and the availability of full and immediate market information transmitted via the agricultural cooperative associations or the information network of distributors.

As a result, the regional organization of agriculture centered around the city has been destroyed, and the area of production of produce such as vegetables and fruits is determined not by the distance from the city but by the season. This is illustrated by the shift in the place of origin of watermelons during the period from spring to the end of summer, from south to north Japan. Thus the advantages of suburban agriculture are in large measure disappearing.

Fifth, there is the factor which has had the greatest impact on the conflict: the rise in land prices. The rapid concentration of population in the cities requires large areas of land for housing and factories. This situation is common to all countries, but the problem in Japan is that land is in extremely short supply, and moreover, there is no effective land policy to deal with this situation.

As a result, land prices have risen abnormally. The rise was accelerated in the 1960s and the 1970s, a time when the exchange rate favored the yen; the favorable balance of payments created large sums of available capital in the country which were then invested in real estate. At times prices rose 30 percent annually, and over the last 20 years they have risen on the average 15 percent annually.

In fact it was the capital gains from the rise in land prices that provided the huge capital necessary for the postwar growth of the Japanese economy. It would have been politically impossible to restrict and control the price rise. People used the rise in land prices as a hedge against inflation and attempted to acquire land as quickly as possible. In seeking cheaper prices, they moved progressively outward to the suburbs.

The rise in land prices was sharp, and the idea took hold that land prices would always continue to move upward. The ironical journalistic phrase "a nation of 100 million real estate dealers" was used to describe this phenomenon in which everyone seemed to be caught up.

The farmers in the suburbs, particularly those on the outskirts of the larger metropolises, are benefiting from tremendous capital gains without doing any work. This is radically changing the farmer's attitude that labor is virtuous, and together with the above-mentioned changes in agricultural operation it is producing farmers who are more affluent but also more negligent and detached from agricultural production.

These farmers consider arable land not a productive property but an asset for exchange. Yet they still resist changing the use of arable land on the pretext that they are practicing agriculture. In fact, as long as the rate of increase in land prices is high and it is more profitable to keep land than to invest money in something else, there will be no incentive to sell land. Thus the supply of developed land lags behind demand and further increases land prices. The irony is that land changes hands only when an owner dies and there is a need to pay off inheritance taxes.

The farmer who owns land is at an advantage in this game. This advantage, however, only serves to devastate suburban agriculture. When a balance in supply and demand is eventually restored and a change in the agricultural produce market has been effected, the farmer's position will have been undermined. At least that is the only outlook for an end to the present impasse.

The Destruction of the Ecological Balance

Throughout Japan's history as an agricultural society, projects in forest conservation, flood control, and development of new fields have been undertaken without upsetting the natural balance. As a result, an ecological equilibrium has been maintained in individual regions and in the country as a whole. To put it another way, human beings were much weaker than nature and could only use it to their advantage as best they could within the framework established by nature. It is a fact that rice-paddy farming is an excellent method of agriculture in that it effectively makes use of the water cycle and prevents soil erosion.

However, the rapid process of industrialization and urbanization after the Second World War destroyed the ecological system that had been built up over a long period of time. The power to change nature has vastly increased, and the technology to do so has also advanced. Because these have been applied to the creation of a different system—an urban system based on industrialization and urbanization—the ecological balance of the past has been upset, and Japan now is confronted by the serious consequences of that change.

Let us consider some actual instances of conflict. First, there is the retreat of the forests. This signifies a loss not only of recreational areas but also of forest conservation and flood control functions. Related to this is the serious problem of the confusion that exists in the system of water use. When water was primarily used for rice-paddy farming, it was used systematically. The water constantly circulated as it flowed down, irrigating the paddies, and eventually joined a river. With the advance of industrialization and urbanization, there was a growing use of water for hydroelectric power generation and urban (including factory) needs. The fight that developed between cities and rural areas over water is a classic confrontation.

These newer uses gradually came to employ water on a large scale, to the exclusion of other uses, until water use was no longer an integrated system. Various conflicts arose, including those over the contamination of irrigation water by sewage and the increased use of ground water for urban needs, which led to subsidence and greatly inconvenienced the farmers.

Recent urbanization has extended to both hilly and low, marshy areas that hitherto had been bypassed, and this has served to increase the confusion. The development of hill areas does damage not only by causing landslides through the carving up of stable, natural topography but also by bringing about floods through the construction of paved roads and buildings which cover the land and prevent the retention of water, thereby increasing the runoff.

The development of low, marshy areas, by changing surface conditions, also destroys the land's capacity to control water; moreover, the raising of the ground level and the prevention of water absorption causes the rainwater to run off and accumulate in the lower surrounding areas, thus passing the water problem off onto others. Aerial photos show many recent developments in unsuitable areas that have been filled in on a large scale; this is in sharp contrast to the villages of the past, which were often located on natural levees or in the hills where there was no danger of water damage.

That is not all. The fact that the land's capacity to retain water is low and the volume of runoff during rain is high means a precipitous drop in the volume of river flow in times of no rain. Because the volume of water flow in many urban rivers is so small, these rivers cannot adequately cleanse themselves and so become polluted. Needless to say, such confusion in the water system around cities greatly interferes with the agricultural use of water.

Such ecological changes make us wonder if we can maintain the traditional peaceful coexistence with nature (excepting, of course, calamities such as floods), or whether we will see an increase in the contradictions that presently exist and a continuation of the conflict. Although the future is undecided, the present-day situation in Japan leads us to the pessimistic conclusion that the latter is more likely.

In this age of urbanization, we must restore the harmonious relationship that once existed between mankind and nature. This is an important task, not only for Japan but for the whole world.

CONCLUSION

The conflict at the exploding urban fringe turns out to be an inevitable process of elimination of agricultural land use by urban uses, obliging the rural sector to retreat from the land it occupies. The issue raised in most of the cases in this process is that urbanization brings about a change in the natural environment and destroys necessary conditions for agricultural operations.

We would argue, however, that the social change that is brought about by urbanization erodes the basic structure of the rural community, which is the vital basis for healthy operation of the agricultural sector. These changes proceed hand in hand, but the social side should be considered more crucial; in fact, the rise in land prices plays the most critical role in this process.

In order to settle this conflict, a peaceful and orderly retreat of the rural sector should be insured. This is possible in the countries where there exist wide frontiers for agricultural development; however, it is difficult in countries such as Japan, where the land is intensively used all over the country. Perhaps the most reasonable way would be to reinforce agricultural productivity in areas beyond the direct influence of urbanization, with an aim to strengthening sound rural communities that can counteract urban influence. It should also be mentioned that in accordance with the decrease in agricultural population, land holdings per family can be enlarged, letting the farmers enjoy better-scale merit in agricultural production. In fact, recent trends in agricultural policy in Japan seem to aim in this direction. Such measures would be much more healthy than the usual salvage measures of distributing subsidies to the dwindling farm community on the urban fringe just to maintain the status quo. These can serve only as a transitory measure to save the present generation, whose way of life has always been agricultural, but will not attract the future generation, who will inevitably seek more gainful employment in the urban sectors.

In areas where urban influence is less, there is a possibility of solving the rural-urban conflict by creating a social environment in which both sectors can coexist. For example, there are cases in which agreement is reached within the community to close the factories during the peak days of agricultural operation, so that the whole work force can take part in agriculture.

In any case, it is important to create a system to suit the changing needs of the people who make up the community, and not to try to impose a preconceived system that takes no account of reality.

Chapter 9

The Urban-Rural Conflict

Jacques M. Kwak

Exploding cities and agricultural productivity, together with the conflicts at the urban fringe, cover such a wide range of issues for research and discussion that it is impossible to deal with them all in one congress. Besides, it is very difficult to talk about these issues in general terms, because the situation differs from country to country and from city to city. Still, I will try to give some material for discussion, and if necessary I will illustrate what I have to say with examples from my city, Amsterdam.

"EXPLODING" CITIES

Most of the exploding cities are to be found in the so-called Third World countries. In the affluent West, cities are not as "explosive" as they are in the developing countries.

The United Nations Conference on Human Settlements (UNCHS) paper on the Metropolis shows that in 1950 the number of these big cities (of more than 1 million inhabitants) in developing countries was 23; in 1975 it was 90. By the turn of the century, the report forecasts, there will be 40 cities of more than 5 million inhabitants each (of which some 15 will have more than 10 million inhabitants) in developing countries and only 13 in developed countries (of which five will have more than 10 million inhabitants). These figures show clearly where the problem lies.

Why are cities "exploding," and what does this mean? Although nearly all cities started as small settlements, some of them achieved enormous growth as regional or national centers for economic activities. Often they were food production centers located in the most fertile areas. In some developing countries they grew out of colonial settlements—for example in places where there were good harbors.

Urban economic activities usually involve a more profitable land use than rural activities. Moreover, they provide more jobs per acre, and those jobs are often better paying. When cities explode, they capture the surrounding fertile areas first, so that the balance of the areas for food production and human shelter is disturbed.

Although the countries in which this is happening often have a relatively low overall population density, the problem is that only a small part of the country is fertile enough for food production. If the food production is not increased by means of other methods like mechanization, chemicals, and breeding, this creates a problem. However, many countries are capable of producing more food than they do at the moment. Their reason for not doing so may be technical (lack of skills, for example), although it is more likely political.

AGRICULTURAL PRODUCTIVITY

An increasing world population needs more food. In Western society the first economic sector is agriculture. The most primitive societies are restricted to this sector. Within it each individual, or small group of individuals, is self-sufficient. The second economic sector, the industrial sector, arose in the last century, during the Industrial Revolution, pushing aside the old crafts. Industry causes specialization, creating a large group of people who must be provided for. One group takes care of food production, while the other takes care of industrial production. The third economic sector covers services like commerce and trade, causing still more specialization. The fourth sector, government facilities, completes the affluent society.

The extreme specialization and consequently the larger scale on which production has to take place has its impact on land use. Because of the fact that the agricultural sector is relatively less profitable than the industrial sector, a shift away from the agricultural sector has taken place. If no measures are taken, the need for food will grow faster than its production.

In the Netherlands the urban area doubled in the first half of this century. The total surface of arable land has been increased, by 25 percent, and the area of pasture land increased slightly. The horticultural area doubled in that period.

In 1950 the area of wasteland had diminished to roughly one-third the size it had been in 1900. The population doubled in that period, from 5 to 10 million people. In the year 2000 a population of 15 million is anticipated; the present figure is 14 million.

Although the population has, roughly speaking, tripled since the beginning of this century, food production has increased to such an extent that in 1982 the Dutch agrarian balance of trade showed a surplus of 8 billion guilders (US$3 billion), which is, roughly speaking, 40 percent of national agricultural consumption. The percentage of the population engaged in farming, however, decreased sharply. (In 1900, 30 percent of the population was engaged in agriculture, 32 percent in industry, and 38 percent in providing services. In 1950 the figures were 15, 40, and 45 percent, and in 1982 they were 5, 28, and 67 percent, respectively.)

The price of agricultural products has gone up, of course, but because of the higher income derived from other economic sectors, higher prices can be paid for a larger variety of luxury foodstuffs. These actual prices are higher but are still relatively low.

Unfortunately, this development in food production is not the same all over the world. The Western world is, generally speaking, capable of fulfilling all of its basic needs, whereas nearly half the world's population is underfed or otherwise malnourished. The primary economic sector deserves much political attention. A country that cannot take care of its own food production is dependent on others and thus economically and politically weak. A country that exports industrial products or other goods and services that other countries need is in an economic position to import food.

In doing so, however, such a country becomes vulnerable, especially when the world economy is in recession. In the poor countries, 60 to 80 percent of the population is engaged in farming, but their productivity is so low that it falls far short of feeding the population. Only when agricultural productivity per capita can be increased seriously is a change from agriculture to industry justified. Then a country can strengthen its economic and political position and raise its standard of living.

It is remarkable that even a country like the Soviet Union, with a closed economic system, has not been able to satisfy its own need for food. The Marxist tradition has always treated agricultural productivity as a stepchild, with all the consequences thereof. Forced collectivization of agriculture in order to supply the means for industrialization has failed. The result of the official agricultural policy is that 25 percent of national agricultural production comes from private land kept by farmers. In fact productivity on this private land is about ten times higher than on the official agricultural land.

Forced collectivization (not to be confused with public land ownership and cooperation) is no answer to the problem of food production, especially when the bureaucracy, without having expert knowledge, tells the farmers what to grow.

President Andropov tried to encourage agricultural productivity by letting smaller groups work on a parcel of land for a couple of years under their own responsibility. Years ago this system was rather successful because the production per acre was much higher, and so was the income per farmer. But this fact was considered contrary to the Socialist system, and was therefore abolished. If the Soviets are able to reintroduce this system, we may speak of a revolution. We may also expect an increase in agricultural production in the years to come.

Here we touch upon one of the most important elements of food production: the personal responsibility of the farmers. I am not saying that when farmers have that responsibility, all our problems will be solved. But when they don't have it, it will be very difficult to solve the problems.

I said that the primary economic sector deserves much political attention. Agricultural production, one of the basic needs of mankind, needs stimulating governmental support in the form of training, education, and research, but also financial support to start new developments like reallotment, breeding, and the use of fertilizers.

CONFLICTS AT THE URBAN FRINGE

What is happening at the urban fringe? Nowhere in the world does agriculture take the place of urban development. The process is always the other way around. Even when cities are not growing in terms of population, the need for urban land increases. The demand for more urban land results from the demand for bigger houses, fewer high-rise buildings, and a decreasing average dwelling occupancy.

In Amsterdam the average dwelling occupancy diminished from 3.34 persons in 1960 to 2.31 in 1982. The population decreased from 870,000 to 700,000, and the urban area increased in this period from 52 to 68 percent. The population decrease was caused mainly by the spillover policy, which forced many people to move to the suburbs and satellite communities. Part of the extra need for urban land during the last two decades has been due to the fact that the urban renewal policy was to demolish high-density housing blocks and to rebuild at a much lower density. Fortunately, the local authority has changed its urban renewal policy to one which lays emphasis on the preservation and rehabilitation of existing housing blocks with almost the same high urban density.

In cities that are growing, or exploding, the increasing need for urban land is even more evident. The greatest problem at the urban fringe is caused by the conflicting claims on land to satisfy basic human needs. This conflict urges political action. If no action is taken and land is merely considered an economic good, agriculture will surely lose.

Since the change from agricultural to urban land use is very profitable for the owners, this change will continue. Market mechanisms work only for short-term decisions and only for a certain sector. The land market is not concerned with agricultural production but only with the profits from the use of the land. The growth of cities and changes in land use should not be left to these market forces.

When the fertile area in a country is limited and the bigger human settlements are located in these areas, it is obvious that when these cities explode, the total agricultural land use is reduced, with severe consequences for food production. Unfortunately it happens every day, and we do not seem to be able to stop this process.

Another problem at the urban fringe is that of pollution versus preservation of the environment. The big cities produce a lot of air and water pollution which has to be eliminated by the rural areas. The ever-growing pressure on the environment reduces agricultural productivity. In the worst cases, pollution causes a complete halt to production when it makes a product dangerous for human consumption.

Preservation of the environment is also important for another basic need of mankind: leisure. In growing cities there isn't usually enough recreational land in the urban area. Normally only parks or similar smaller facilities are available. The more urban these cities are, the more their population will use the countryside for an escape on weekends and holidays. If the agricultural production is located in the adjacent areas of these cities, it will suffer.

Another conflict which appears at the urban fringe is the uncertainty for the farmers who work next to the growing cities. In fact I met this problem recently in Amsterdam. Since the local policy is to strengthen the city's function and to stop the spillover, we are searching for new building sites in and close to the city. Since horticulture can be considered to be the most "urban" form of agriculture, it is located near the city. It is the first to be resettled in order to make room for residential uses. The production of residential land is costly, and enormous subsidies are needed. That means that the final decision takes time. In the meantime, the farmers are not able to invest to improve their production. The uncertainty about future land use causes losses for horticultural production.

REFLECTIONS

The issue of the conflicts at the urban fringe is not an easy one. It is not easy to get a clear and complete view of what is happening, and it is even more difficult to give solutions for this problem. Still, I would like to offer a few reflections on this issue that, together with those of the other speakers, might help us solve parts of the problem.

Land can be described as a natural resource that has no cost of production and without which production is impossible. All human activities need land. There is, at least theoretically, enough land for the world's population. The total surface of our planet is more than 500 million square kilometers. That means a density of ten inhabitants per square kilometer. But if we leave the oceans out of this calculation, since they produce only 2 percent of our food, and because they cannot be considered a permanent residence, that leaves us with 150 million square kilometers, or a density of 30 inhabitants per square kilometer, which is roughly the population density in the United States.

Compared to that of other countries this is a low density. (In Europe the figure is 98, in China 100, in India 202, in the Netherlands 346.) Even leaving a lot of factors out of this calculation, like the fertility and climatological aspects for food production and human settlements, we can at least ascertain that the total figures are encouraging.

World food consumption can be divided into two categories. Whereas in the poorer countries the primary demand is for cereals, in the countries with a higher standard of living, cattle breeding is more important. This cattle breeding takes a lot of the food which can also be used for human consumption. In fact, only 40 percent of total cereal crops is used for direct human consumption. The rest is used for cattle breeding or is simply disposed of. If we talk in terms of calories, more than 80 percent of the production is used for cattle fodder.

If the world's population continues to grow as quickly as it has up till now, we will surely have bigger problems in only a few years if the policy is not changed. One of the main questions at this moment is whether explosive population growth can be stopped.

Another question is whether there is enough food for the world's population. If there is, do we have a distribution problem? In an earlier session of this Congress we talked about the problem of surplus and scarcity. I agree that we do not seem to be able to allocate food in a proper way. Statistically we might produce enough calories for the world's population, but if we are not able to make a fair distribution (or if we do not *want* to, which is probably the real reason), we will never solve the problem.

One of the other speakers told us that, because of the way we use or perhaps abuse our resources, our children will have to pay the bill in the form of higher prices. I hope that these high prices will be the only problem for our children! We are dealing with a moral problem, not an economic problem. Politics was once defined as the process of deciding who gets what, when, and how. For today's issue we could add "and where." In this process a world food bank could provide fair distribution of the world's food production.

The main cause of the urban-rural conflict is the growth of the city and the lack of fertile land for food production. Bigger cities generally have more and better facilities than smaller ones. But at a certain size there is enough basis for all facilities. When this size is exceeded, a multiplication of the same or similar facilities will take place without adding any quality to urban life. It is obvious that a city of 15 million inhabitants has many disadvantages compared to a city of, say, 1 million inhabitants. What I plead for is the development of several smaller cities instead of a few enormous concentrations of human activity. Of course I am sufficiently down to earth to realize that simply wishing will not make this happen, and that existing bigger cities will not be demolished.

The reason these cities have grown so enormous is mainly that their inhabitants expected to find better opportunities than in rural areas. To a certain extent this was true, but what we see now is that in the biggest cities unemployment, poverty, and famine are causing bitter grief. What we have to work on is the development of new centers for human activity instead of a system of *laissez-faire* growth. Let's bring our activities back to a more human scale. When individuals can play a role in society again, they will have a future.

The development of these new centers should be integral. That means that all of the economic sectors I described should be developed and well balanced. I know this is an enormous task, but in my own country there are encouraging examples. Smaller cities have many advantages—more efficient infrastructure and public transport, less pollution. They are more manageable and can be self-sufficient. The development of modern communications systems takes away a great deal of the need to live and work in huge concentrations.

Although planning is not holy to me, I believe in certain advantages of zoning, assisted by an active land policy. Urban and rural planning is a lot easier, and so is implementation, when the areas concerned are small instead of immense.

We face the challenge of using the earth for the benefit of all. Mankind is better off when people are less dependent on bigger groups, when they are self-sufficient, and when they have a future. I believe it is our task to work toward those ends.

Chapter 10

Prague: A Non-Exploding City

Blahomir Borovička

This paper on Prague has been included under the general heading of exploding cities, but in fact the city deviates quite distinctly from such common labels for most contemporary human agglomerations. To understand such an ambitious statement, one needs to look at the history of Prague, its urban development, and its role in the general settlement pattern of our country.

The entire history and territorial development of Prague is strongly influenced by natural conditions. The Prague settlement lies in gently undulating country typical of the entire landscape of Bohemia. To the southeast the town borders on a varied landscape which, despite considerable leisure-time pressure, has in many ways retained its original values. To the east, and mainly to the north, an area of fertile agricultural land borders on the city. In the west and especially the southwest we find dramatic formations close by—the protected Bohemian karst and the spurs of the Brdy Heights, which extend as far as the city itself.

The complex geology, further shaped by the effects of water, resulted in a terrain with considerable variations in altitude. The territory of the city varies 200 meters in height between the highest point, at 390 meters above sea level, and the 176-meter contour at the point where the Vltava River leaves the city. Around the Prague Basin, where the historic center lies, rise a number of hills, and in many cases it is possible to see from the city center to the remote environs, a distance of many kilometers.

The formation of the natural setting must be largely ascribed to the Vltava, forming a spatial axis for the entire city, which has spread since its foundation along both banks. The river runs through Prague over a length of 30 kilometers. It has shaped the Prague terrain over thousands of years into an effective composition of hills and lowlands. The terrain was further modeled by the numerous tributaries on both banks, which unfortunately today have mostly disappeared underground.

In addition to the terrain and water, the plant cover leaves a striking mark on the city, ranging from historic parks in the city center to new parklands and extensive woods on the outskirts.

Because of Prague's location in the center of the Bohemian Basin at a point where the river Vltava can easily be forded, this area has been settled from time immemorial. The true formation of today's Prague, however, did not begin until the arrival of the Slavs, the tribe of the Czechs, who by stages came to rule over the whole country. They arrived in the region of contemporary Czechoslovakia in about the fifth century A.D. and moved their main settlement center to the Prague area at the end of the ninth century.

By the twelfth century there existed in this area a considerable number of stone churches, monasteries, and convents, many surviving to this day, as well as Romanesque stone houses, of which over forty still exist. At that time the center of the settlement shifted from the left to the right bank of the Vltava, where the basic layout of today's Old Town began to take shape. The two mighty castles dominating the town served as residences of the Přemyslid rulers.

By the end of the fourteenth century, medieval Prague comprised two castles and four towns. With an area of over 800 hectares and roughly 50,000 inhabitants, it held a leading place among the big towns and important metropolises of Europe at the time. In 1348 a university was founded; the town harbored some 100 monasteries, convents, churches, and chapels; it had a new Gothic stone bridge across the river, a public water supply, several dozen large and small marketplaces; and it was the residential city of one of the most important European monarchs. The town proved its worth even under the monarchy of the Hapsburgs, who at the beginning of the seventeenth century transferred their imperial residence to Vienna.

Prague entered the nineteenth century as a city of 100,000 inhabitants which had still not spread beyond its medieval boundaries dating back to the middle of the fourteenth century. But signs of basic changes began to appear in the traditional urban body which were to convert Prague, in the course of that century, into a metropolis with half a million inhabitants and extensive residential and industrial suburbs, a network of railway lines leading to all parts of the country, and a rich cultural life that expressed the aspirations of the Czech nation for a national revival. The kingdom of Bohemia remained part of the Austro-Hungarian monarchy until the First World War, when Prague, despite its importance, was condemned to the role of a provincial city.

A new stage began when the country gained independence with the establishment of the Czechoslovak Republic, for which Prague was chosen as its natural capital. All former restrictions were lifted, and in 1920 it became possible to merge the historical city with all adjacent suburbs into Greater Prague, which then had over 670,000 inhabitants and covered an area of 174 square kilometers. A State Regulation Board was set up to plan the city, and the first overall plan of city development was completed in 1929. The function of the capital city encouraged extensive construction of industrial and public buildings and dwellings in all sectors of the city.

The end of the Second World War and the liberation of Czechoslovakia by the Soviet Army meant the onset of a new epoch for the whole country and its capital city. The first comprehensive town planning scheme for Prague was finished by 1948, showing the need for the systematic planning of the city. For that reason a Town Planning Office was set up in 1951. Its successor today is the City of Prague Planning Board.

The sixties and seventies added novel features to the planning of Prague, among them systematic attention to the entire city agglomeration, the enlargement of the administrative territory of the city to 300 and then to 500 square kilometers, and the decision to build an underground railway (the Metro). A project for the economic structure of the city was worked out, and the principles of its perspective development pattern were stabilized. In the midseventies a Master Plan of the City was approved, giving the basic directions of the social and economic development of the city; likewise a Regional Plan of the Prague Agglomeration covers the entire area up to the year 2010. These basic documents are being implemented and worked out in detail for each individual territorial unit and functional system of the city and the city region. At the same time they are continuously checked, reviewed, and updated.

The continuous process of updating the plan for Prague is strongly related to some of the questions raised by this Congress. The updating—as complex as it is—in reality makes its start from a rather restricted set of prerequisites. They are the demography, the stress on the economy of resources in both the development and the operation of the city, and the upgrading of the living environment of the inhabitants.

DEMOGRAPHY

At the present time roughly 1.2 million persons live in Prague, accounting for almost 8 percent of the total population of the Czechoslovak Socialist Republic. The demographic situation in the capital city has certain specific features that are due to urbanization processes in general. It could be stated that in our country the migration from the rural hinterlands to the biggest cities is over, and even the shift from smaller to bigger cities is not occurring anymore. This is evidently a very favorable indication that homogeneous good living conditions and job opportunities exist throughout the country, since people are not forced to move to urban centers in search of uncertain social promotion.

Thus in contrast to the great majority of big or capital cities in the world, migration presents no problem in Prague, and therefore there is no need to regulate this increment, which has proved beyond control in some world capitals. Efforts, on the contrary, are being made to stimulate the immigration of young persons of certain professions essential for the life of the city and its many functions. Since the midseventies population measures have led to a renewal of the natural increase of the population, which, together with the small migration into the town, provides a favorable demographic situation. It is assumed that even in the future the population of Prague will grow slowly and should reach 1.3 million only after the year 2000.

In conjunction with the projected increase of the number of inhabitants, it is essential to achieve a harmonious population structure and to create conditions for positive changes in the way of life, which increasingly includes an interest in education and culture, the growing demands on housing and the entire material environment of life, social activity, and an improving standard of living. The more or less stabilized number of inhabitants has its distinct implications in the sphere of work. Today about 10 percent of all economically active persons in Czechoslovakia live in the capital city, and Prague industry represents about 9 percent of the nationwide volume of industrial production, with the share rising to almost 16 percent in engineering and to over 30 percent in the printing industry. Even agriculture cannot be ignored, since more than 40 percent of all the land in the administrative territory of the city is used for agricultural purposes, and the soil is of such high quality that it contributes greatly to supplying the capital with agricultural and horticultural produce.

With scientific and technological progress and limited resources of manpower, it is impossible to count on extensive development of production. Certain sectors with high labor requirements and a large volume of freight transport do not find conditions suitable in the capital, and moreover they have a negative influence on the environment. The future lies in intensification, rationalization, and modernization of production, linked with preference for prospectively vital sectors.

The location of workplaces in the future foresees, apart from the reconstruction of the existing and traditional industrial districts and wards, the establishment of new localities in the vicinity of large residential areas, which would improve the relation between home and place of work and avoid the functional monotony of housing developments.

ECONOMY OF RESOURCES

It is not necessary to discuss the well-known fact that big cities and agglomerations are not just producers of many material and social goods but are at the same time insatiable consumers of every possible resource. Among them are raw materials, fuel, energy, manpower, and land. On the same list belongs also the entire environment—clean air, fresh water, trees, and even beauty.

Conservation and conscious management of resources is shifting today to one of the top priorities of contemporary urban planning. It relates to all its aspects, from the general settlement pattern of the country to the layout of residential areas and internal arrangement of buildings. It depends on the modal split of transportation means, networks of technical amenities, heating, water supply, and waste disposal. It influences heavily the entire investment policy and the effective use of existing urbanized areas.

High on the list of resources to be protected belongs agricultural land. In 1976 a strict law was adopted by the National Assembly, providing for every possible measure of protection of agricultural lands. The law protects completely all undeveloped land classified in the top two qualitative categories. Exceptions to just .5 hectares can be issued by regional councils; exceptions above this size can be made only at the discretion of the government. Every petition is accompanied by detailed analyses and complex evaluations of possible alternatives. A specific procedure has been introduced into the elaboration of urban plans whereby a special "agricultural supplement" is to be elaborated by the planning office and sanctioned by the Ministry of Agriculture. Planning permits for whatever functional use on undeveloped land cannot be issued without consensus on the above described procedures. Besides all this, the developer—be it industry, community, cooperative, or private individual—is obliged to recultivate the same amount of neglected or devastated land for agricultural purposes.

This sketchy description of the measures protecting agricultural land indicates the seriousness of the matter. It is obvious how substantially the whole urbanization policy is influenced. The concern turns the focus of development from exclusive new residential and industrial estates to the intensive modernization and conservation of the existing housing stock of inner cities, from lower to higher densities, from casual decisions to evaluation and quantification of options.

It is too early for a complex overview of all the outcomes of this rather severe land policy. However, the practice shows that hundreds of hectares of priceless agricultural land have been saved. In addition, in the extent to which this policy relates to the general tendency toward the economy of resources, it will eventually make our cities and settlements more compact, cheaper to build, and easier to keep up. Our task is not an easy one, but we are increasingly feeling its general positive effects.

ENVIRONMENT

The city of Prague inherited from the past its admirable buildings and its beauty, but also many problems which frustrate the life of its inhabitants. This includes old, unsuitable housing; a transport system that cannot cope with present-day needs; air and water pollution. Improvements to the environment require a deliberate and purposeful approach, divided into concrete stages for their accomplishment. Economic and cultural development involves increasing the stress on general quality, the level of the environment, the aesthetic and emotional impact of individual works of architecture and entire housing projects.

In the years of postwar recovery of building construction, the volume of housing construction in the capital grew gradually and its standard improved. In the period from 1945 to 1980 there was an increment of about 200,000 flats, and at the present time the annual volume of housing construction is approximately 10,000 flats and individual houses, with the standard rising all the time.

In the eighties, stress is being placed on the modernization and reconstruction of older residential quarters and on the regeneration of housing in the historic core of the city—which, among other things, relates to the policy of protecting agricultural lands.

The inhabitants of Prague have, on the whole, rather favorable conditions for leisure-time activities, thanks to the climate, the natural setting, and the greenbelts. Today the territory of the city provides per capita over 70 square meters of public green space; there exist 1,100 sports grounds and playing fields, 560 stadiums and gymnasiums, 14 covered and 19 open-air swimming pools, and 48 boathouses. Furthermore, Prague householders own over 60,000 weekend houses and cottages, to which over 40 percent of the population travels at least three times a month.

The present state of social services cannot be considered satisfactory, and the development plan, therefore, foresees further improvements, which are to take the form of an extension of the greenbelts, more sports grounds, and systematic attention to the leisure-time aspects of the environs. It is not a matter of establishing individual large facilities but of creating an evenly spaced network throughout the city, and in particular in the older parts of the center where there is a shortage of leisure-time facilities.

Of particular importance are the green areas which penetrate from the suburbs into the city center. Their importance rests not only in their function in the overall layout of the city but in the fact that the high quality of the agricultural land prevents the establishment of a continuous greenbelt around the outskirts for leisure-time activities. These green wedges, to which most sports grounds are linked, should therefore be carefully protected and should be renewed in places where they have in the past been damaged.

The large area, complex terrain, and building configuration of the city make exceptional claims on transport services. Daily over 2.5 million journeys are undertaken by the resident population and visitors, covering an average distance of over seven kilometers. In addition, over 60 million tons of material are moved across the city annually in the course of work and in the form of delivery of supplies.

The public transport system of the city comprises the Metro, trams, and buses, and provides transportation for more than 78 percent of all travelers. Twenty percent use private cars, of which over a quarter of a million are today registered in the city. In the future, the Metro is expected to take 40 percent of the total volume of public transport. Furthermore, the number of private cars is likely to double, making additional demands on road communications and parking places. Account needs likewise to be taken of the railway network, with its considerable claims on land, and of air transport, where air corridors influence the developmental possibilities of the city.

The most important transport construction site in Prague at present is undeniably the Metro, which at the beginning of the eighties had 20 kilometers of lines and will by stages extend to over 93 kilometers with approximately 100 stations. The main system of roads is at present also developing rapidly and is to take the form of circular and radial roads with a total length of 240 kilometers. These are to be modern highways with overpasses and underpasses laid out so as to influence least negatively the buildings in the vicinity and, at the same time, to draw off maximum road transport, which today causes so many difficulties in the network of streets where adaptation to the growing demands is out of the question.

The plans for the future city transport system deal with one aspect of the overall perspective plans for the construction and reconstruction of Prague, and at the same time they aim at the maximum integration of services for the town and influences on the environment, on which transport has a considerable effect in a positive and negative sense.

Life in present-day Prague would be unthinkable for its inhabitants without the complex system of technical mains, equipment to provide drinking water, drain off waste and rainwater, remove and clean sewage, supply thermal and electric energy, and organize refuse collection.

The recently built Želivka reservoir provides drinking water for present needs and the immediate future—a volume of 500 liters per capita daily. By the end of the century this volume is expected to be no less than 700 liters, which makes the building of a further high-capacity source of drinking water a most urgent task, and all perspective plans provide for this.

To deal with waste a new network of sewers is being built. A recent investment is the K main sewer, 11 kilometers in length and costing thousands of millions of crowns. An urgent task that remains is to build a new water recycling plant, to be situated north of the city, since the cleaning plant at Troja, built immediately after the war, cannot cope with the growing needs of the city despite costly reconstruction.

Among other systems special importance must be attached to the provision of heat as related to the improved standards of the flats and the urgent need to clean the air, which is already heavily polluted by motor vehicle transport and by small heating plants using imperfect technology and inferior quality fuel. City authorities are devoting increased attention to this problem, even though the solution depends on the effective application of a nationwide fuel and power base.

CONCLUSION

The intention of this short paper on the urban development of Prague has been to portray a city coping with some of the general problems of the man-made environment and to offer some experiences toward the urgent task of formulating a new approach to land protection policy. Its aim would be more than attained if it evokes any new insights and revelations.

Chapter 11

Land Utilization in Zimbabwe

Robbie Matongo Mupawose

Zimbabwe is a landlocked country bounded by Zambia and Mozambique to the north and east, Botswana to the west, and apartheid South Africa to the south. It occupies an area of 39,075,700 hectares and is part of the great plateau which is a major feature of the geography of southern Africa. Almost the whole of the country lies above 300 meters and more than 80 percent above 600 meters, but less than 5 percent is above 1,500 meters, including some points in the eastern border mountains near Inyanga above 2,600 meters.

The area is drained by three major river systems: the Zambezi to the north and northwest, and the Limpopo and Sabi rivers to the south and southeast, respectively. The Makgadikgadi drainage basin of Botswana extends into the southwestern area.

An outstanding feature is a broad ridge or watershed running across the entire country, from which emerges a belt of high plateau about 640 kilometers long by 80 kilometers wide. This watershed, which averages 1,400 meters above sea level, traverses the country in a northeasterly direction. The drainage system originates from this watershed.

The vegetation varies from semidesert in parts of the Wankie Game Reserve to open grasslands, woodland savannah along the watershed, forests in the eastern highlands, and tropical forests in the well-watered areas.

The topography, soils, and climate are not conducive to intensive agricultural production. It is estimated that 75 percent of the land mass is subject to conditions that make dry-land crop production a risky venture. Most of the country receives between 300 and 1,000 millimeters of rainfall annually, mainly in thunderstorms, with a small area in the eastern highlands receiving over 1,500 millimeters.

Current measures being taken by the government of Zimbabwe to address problems associated with land utilization and demographic factors are centered around two major issues. These are (1) the rural-urban demographic pattern, and (2) the relationship between agricultural productivity and the land question.

Important questions confront policymakers shaping land policies. Does a relationship exist between changes in agricultural productivity and movements of population from rural to urban areas? What policy measures should be employed to exploit the potential productive capacity of rural areas to levels that will contain population increases, maintain satisfactory living standards, and prevent urban drift?

At present, the problems of developing nations are not so much those of urban areas expanding into and encroaching on farmland as of the uncontrollable movement of able-bodied rural people flocking to crowded urban areas either in search of employment or in response to declining agricultural productivity. An understanding of the causes of rural-urban migration and of the relationship between relative economic opportunities in rural and urban areas is crucial to the implementation of suitable land policies.

Agrarian reform and the question of land are central to the future development of Zimbabwe, mainly because the country's struggle for liberation was centered on land. Like most African countries, Zimbabwe faces the problems of declining agricultural productivity, particularly in the peasant sector, massive rural-to-urban population movements and migratory labor systems, and growing urban unemployment and underemployment.

RURAL-URBAN MIGRATION

Structurally, substantial urban-rural and rural-urban flows of persons, goods, and services seem to be firmly built into the Zimbabwean economy.

It is estimated that 21 percent (1.2 million) of the black population live in towns, 22 percent (1.3 million) live in the large-scale farming areas, about 54 percent (4.2 million) are in the communal areas, and 3 percent live in the small-scale farming areas and in national parks. This brings to over 70 percent the total population directly dependent on farming. (Total 1980 population was estimated at 7,480 million, and the total land area is 39,072 million hectares.) Tables 11-1 and 11-2 further illustrate these figures.

Within the urban areas, the demographic profile of the black population shows an uncomfortable distortion, with a preponderance of single males in the 15-to-34 age group. Migrants comprise the majority of the urban labor force. It is surprising that masses of able-bodied men continue to migrate from rural areas into congested cities in spite of high and rising levels of urban unemployment.

Urban population growth rates in 33 sub-Saharan capitals are currently averaging 8.5 percent, against national population growth rates on the order of 3 to 4 percent in most of the countries. According to various studies, 70 percent of the growth in urban population is caused by the migration of rural people, while the other 30 percent is due to natural population increase.

Growth in cities is accompanied by a serious deterioration in the general conditions of life. Population figures in these cities quickly reach the point at which the balance of urban living begins to tip in one direction—that is, the disadvantages of city life start to outweigh the benefits in terms of quality of life and income. Urban squalor, slums, and crime rates, in the absence of strict control, become the order of the day.

There is a general tendency for people in Africa, and elsewhere, to associate cities with a better life, better jobs, bright lights, and a higher standard of living. Migration to cities is also speeded up by advances in mass communication, recreation, and transportation, which artificially raise the aspirations of rural folk.

Among the many causes of urban migration is the observation in Zimbabwe that one of the best investments a peasant farmer can make is to educate his family so that they can obtain urban employment and help support the farmer, especially when he gets old. Usually when these children complete school, they are forced to flock into cities in search of white-collar jobs. The farmer, in order to pay for the education of his children, must also seek work as a wage earner in the city or on commercial farms. In so doing, he

Table 11-1. Population Estimates (1980, 1990, and 2000) by Land Classification

Land Classification	Population Percentage by Year					
	1980		1990		2000	
	N^a	%	N^a	%	N^a	%
Communal	4,050	54.1	4,218	39.6	5,828	38.4
Resettlement	0	0	1,377	12.9	1,902	12.5
Large Scale	1,680	22.5	2,321	21.8	3,207	21.4
Urban	1,645	22.0	2,588	24.3	4,024	26.5
National	105	1.4	149	1.4	212	1.4
Total	7,480	100	10,653	100	15,173	100

Source: Department of Land Management, University of Zimbabwe.
^{a} N =number in millions.

leaves behind a family with limited resources and a limited capability of increasing agricultural production and making money.

Migrant labor as a result becomes a major phenomenon among rural families firmly enmeshed in agricultural production and the employment decisions of peasant households. Three theories have been put forward by socioeconomists in an attempt to explain the causes of rural-urban migration:

1. *The "pull" theory* explains a worldwide phenomenon, the attraction of bright lights, which leads people to drift to towns in search of higher wages and a better life.

2. *The "push" theory* holds that the lack of employment opportunities, declining agricultural productivity, and the failure of farm production to sustain families combine to push people out of rural areas.

3. *The "push back" theory* asserts that rising urban unemployment, difficult living conditions, and frustration push people back to the rural areas to retire or to start a new life. War and drought have at times speeded up such movements in Zimbabwe.

Without suitable policies and reasonable economic and social incentives, it becomes unrealistic to expect husbandry and farming practices to improve in the absence of able-bodied young men. And it is equally unrealistic to expect young people to remain in rural areas, especially in remote ones, to face a harsh and cruel life devoid of modern amenities and comforts.

Table 11-2. Land Classification, Population, and Agricultural Output, 1980

Land Classification	Land Area		Population		Gross Agricultural Output (Crops and Livestock)		Sales of Principal Crops and Livestock	
	Hectares	%	Number	%	$ Million	%	$ Million	%
Communal Areas	16,355,000	41.9	4,050,000	54.1	147.4	19.5	27.2	5.5
Resettlement Areas[a]	2,142,712	5.5	0	0	0	0	0	0
Small-scale Farming Areas	1,477,081	3.8	110,000	1.5	0	0	0	0
Large-scale Farming Areas	13,026,892	33.3	1,570,000	21.0	607.4	80.5	465.6	94.5
Urban Land	193,315	0.5	1,645,000	22.0	0	0	0	0
National Land	5,877,000	15.0	105,000	1.4	0	0	0	0
Total	39,072,000	100.0	7,480,000	100.0	754.8	100.0	492.8	100.0

Source: Ministry of Lands, Resettlement, and Rural Development, Zimbabwe.
[a] This figure indicates the total area of farmland committed for resettlement by the Ministry of Lands, Resettlement, and Rural Development as of February 1983.

It appears that the major cause of urban migration is that the profitability of peasant agriculture has not been sufficient to attract and maintain young and enthusiastic farmers. Agriculture, in addition, tends to be regarded as an inferior occupation by the educated young, partly reflecting a shortcoming in past educational systems.

In the case of the aged and the urban unemployed, in the absence of sound urban policies which provide lifelong social security, such as insurance and housing plans, these people are forced to drift back to rural areas.

Policies should therefore be geared to enabling those who have a stake in both modern and peasant sectors to choose to live, and permanently earn a living, in either the modern or the peasant sector.

Before suitable land policy measures can be instituted, it is important to examine the relationship between agricultural productivity, land ownership, and population movements between rural and urban areas. Let us briefly do so in the context of developing countries.

AGRICULTURAL PRODUCTIVITY
AND THE LAND QUESTION

Agriculture in Zimbabwe plays an important role in the overall economy of the country. More than 70 percent of the population depends on agriculture for their livelihood. More than 32 percent of persons in formal wage employment are engaged in agriculture, thus making it the largest employing sector. In 1980 its share of the GDP was 14 percent, placing it second to manufacturing.

Nationally Zimbabwe produces all her food requirements (except in periods of drought) and a surplus for export. The government's policy is for self-sufficiency in food. There are many agricultural commodities produced in the country, both edible and nonedible crops. The Ministry of Agriculture keeps an accurate account of marketed crops of the so-called controlled products—those that enter the market economy. Among these, using as an example the 1981-82 intake year, are the edible crops shown in the table at the top of the next page. The controlled products group also includes beef and dairy products.

Among uncontrolled crops are tea, barley, sugar cane, potatoes, fruits and vegetables, and of course tobacco. There are also large

Crop	Intake	Local Sales
Maize	2,013,843	664,912
Sorghum	30,392	18,438
Soybeans	65,326	74,105
Groundnuts (unshelled)	19,159	0
Wheat	200,912	222,990
Seed cotton (for oil)	199,516	0
Sunflowers	8,674	8,674
Coffee	4,903	601

quantities of other uncontrolled commodities grown as food for individual families or for local sale, including millet, beans, rice, nyimo (*Voanzeia substeiranea*), and sesame. Apart from beef, there are animal products from sheep, goats, pigs, rabbits, poultry, and fish.

The role of agriculture in the economy of a developing country needs to be reassessed. Conventionally, agriculture has been a source of industrial labor and investable savings. According to development theories, as agricultural productivity improves through the adoption of new technology, labor and other resources are released.

In low-income countries, the theory states, a large percentage of the population is engaged in agriculture during the early stages of development largely because of low levels of productivity, and because of the need to produce food for subsistence. The more developed and industrialized a country, the smaller is the proportion of its population engaged in agriculture and the less significant is the role of land in the economy.

Experience has shown, however, that the potential of industry in Africa to absorb surplus rural labor is highly limited. The modern sector has failed to create sufficient employment opportunities due to limited technology, inadequate demand for manufactured products, and heavy competition from industrialized nations. The developed countries demand raw materials at their own set prices to provide for their industries, and export the finished product back to the developing countries.

Events today point to the need for creating employment as a major economic and social objective, and the need to maintain a productive and labor-intensive agricultural industry. The role of agriculture in national development should be not to release labor but to create employment opportunities.

There are disquieting trends toward declining productivity in African agriculture and increasing dependence on the importation of foodstuffs. Food production per person in Africa fell by 7 percent in the 1960s and by a staggering 15 percent in the 1970s. From 1975 to 1981 the level of food aid to Africa rose by 125 percent, from 800,000 tons to 1.8 million tons.

Attempts to derive a higher proportion of subsistence from the land without the adoption of good farming practices, including the use of purchased inputs such as hybrid seed and fertilizers, together with rising human and livestock populations, have resulted in serious land and ecological degradation in the peasant sectors of most African countries, and a continuous decline in productivity. Agricultural productivity is defined as technical or economic efficiency in the use of resources, and it measures output per dollar of input. Farmers, soil, and water alone cannot ensure successful agriculture. For agriculture to be successful, there is a need to ensure the availability of supporting services and infrastructure—roads, input and marketing outlets, credit facilities, promotion of appropriate research and motivated extension, and equitable prices.

Land productivity refers to output per hectare. Land cannot continually absorb high rates of population growth and sustain intensive utilization. New technology, better farm management, economic incentives, and high levels of investment are necessary to maintain productivity and to increase output per hectare. Labor productivity, with fixed land area, refers to output per man. Improved labor productivity results from an increase in hours worked per man per day, and from greater output stemming from changed management practices.

Increases in productivity are closely linked to capital formation, because investing in capital increases the productivity of land and labor. If the labor force is growing, some increases in the use of capital and new farming techniques are necessary just to keep pace—that is, to avoid diminishing marginal and average returns per person. More rapid growth of capital inputs and technological innovations will bring about an increase in marginal and average products per unit of labor and hence an increase in family income for those engaged in farming.

In some countries, particularly industrialized countries, there has been a trend towards labor substitution by mechanization as a direct consequence of increasing farm productivity, rising labor wages, and increasing employment opportunities in nonfarm sectors. Where large-scale farms exist, this trend is inevitable due to economies of scale.

In most parts of Africa, the land area devoted to agriculture has not been made to yield more as human population increases. In some cases there has been an expansion of the land for farming, but the total yield has not increased. The matching of appropriate varieties to suitable agro-ecological areas has not been done. In other cases, those crops better suited to arid and semi-arid areas have not been emphasized by imported food types, or the import demands of foreign markets have dictated the agricultural patterns.

The development of appropriate technology which can be serviced in the locality of the farmer at a cost he can afford can change the levels of productivity of the peasant farmers. It cannot be overemphasized that for Africa to be able to feed herself, she must improve the level of productivity of the small farmer.

SMALL VERSUS BIG

An issue of great importance in less developed countries is the relationship between farm size and the productivity of agriculture. This stems from the fact that there has been a recent heightening of concern to satisfy the basic needs of the rural poor and landless through land reform and redistribution. Lack of alternative employment opportunities has meant that land is looked upon as the main source of subsistence, shelter, security, and wealth.

In many such countries, only comparatively wealthy large farmers could afford to take advantage of new hybrid seeds, fertilizers, farm machinery, and irrigation techniques to improve productivity, produce more food and marketable surplus, earn more money—and, in places, push out the poor small farmer.

Smallholder agriculture can provide the most intensive use of land. Small farms make better use of available land than large farms through applying high levels of family labor input per unit of land. However, the concept of family units can be misleading in that often family labor is not available at peak demand periods: because of free education, children are at school.

The contrast between large-scale and small-scale farms can best be demonstrated by looking at the present and historical features of the agricultural industry in Zimbabwe.

An unbalanced agricultural sector evolved under previous colonial administrations through the use of institutional structures which formalized various means of control affecting the relationship between categories of land uses, accessibility of external institutions, infrastructure, markets, and service in favor of one sector.

Since the Second World War the country has thus developed a substantial and responsive export-oriented large-scale agricultural industry made up of farms, normally with freehold titles (this comprises the former white farming areas). This industry is supported by a high-quality infrastructure of marketing organizations and other allied services and input industries, including advanced agricultural research. It occupies the best agricultural land, and its sales of principal crops and livestock amount to 94.5 percent of total agricultural output (1980 figures). The yield and quality of production compares well with that of the developed countries. (See Tables 11-3, 11-4, and 11-5.)

However, the communal sector, made up of farms held under various forms of traditional and communal ownership, has become increasingly disadvantaged over the same period, and has contributed a relatively small proportion of marketable surplus. Low productivity, high cost of inputs, lack of satisfactory marketing arrangements, transport problems, and labor shortages at critical production periods characterize this subsector. Sixty percent of the communal lands fall into areas of poor or very poor agricultural potential, and in these areas human and livestock populations exceed carrying capacity.

There is a need to rehabilitate the communal lands (as stated in the country's Transitional Development Plan, 1982) by using the same programs which led to the success of the large-scale farmers— disregarding one widely held but ill-founded myth that the communal farmer is unresponsive to the economic incentives which have stimulated production in the large-farm sector. Various studies have been made which refute this myth.

SUGGESTED MEASURES FOR TACKLING THE LAND QUESTION

The solution to the problem of underdevelopment lies with the small-farm sector. Continued reliance on the rural base is essential in view of the notorious flow of rural population to urban areas and the resultant high rates of urban unemployment and related problems.

The key lies in increasing the productivity of smallholder farms, and in implementing measures which make it economically and socially attractive to live in rural areas. Efforts should be made to achieve productivity increases large enough to enable communal

Table 11-3. Agricultural Commodities: Intake, Domestic Consumption, and Exports

Commodity	1981 tons[a]			1982 tons[a]		
	Intake	Domestic Sales	Exports	Intake	Domestic Sales	Exports
Maize	2,108.5	634.2	238 (Z$34,737,000)	1,396	947	356 (Z$42,368,000)
Soybeans	65.7	83.6	.651 (Z$202,000)	84.371	82.67	—
Groundnuts	13.0	8.8	2.678 (Z$202,000)	9.839	8.36	4.369 (Z$2,806,000)
Sorghum	30.3	17.7	—[b]	19.254	22.742	2.5 (Z$322,000)
Wheat	201.2	219.8	1.765 (Z$282,000)	213.45	226.792	
Virginia tobacco	58.6	3.4	126.970 (Z$214,269,000)	80.948	3.183	80.18 (Z$176,396,000)
Burley tobacco	1.754	.173	1.435 (Z$3,980,000)	2.534	.034	1.374 (Z$2,751,000)
Beef	76	70	2.672 (Z$4,526,000)	101.25	90.97	4 (Z$6,000,000)
Cotton (lint)	69.8	11.8	53.50 (Z$60,298,000)	55.8	12.022	58.133 (Z$64,725,000)
Coffee (green)	5	.5	5.276 (Z$9,915,000)	6.653	.507	6.378 (Z$10,079,000)

[a] Measured in thousands.
[b] Negligible.

Table 11-4. Agricultural Imports and Exports[a]

	Exports		Imports	
Product	1980	1981	1980	1981
Food and Live Animals	102,895	130,905	28,021	15,308
Beverages and Tobacco	123,004	224,574	3,697	2,193
Animal and Vegetable Oils and Fats	2,163	1,035	6,615	8,504
Fertilizers	0	0	9,695	22,608
Pesticides	0	0	15,893	18,484
Grain Bags (hessian and jute)	0	0	4,109	2,037
Machinery	0	0	17,353	18,677
Petroleum Products	0	0	27,516	19,868

Source: Statement of External Trade CSO.
[a] In thousands of dollars.

Table 11-5. Input-Output Accounts: Commercial and Communal Farm Sectors 1974-1980[a]

Year	Total Outputs	Total Inputs	Total Value Added	Total Outputs	Total Inputs	Total Value Added
1974	369	145	224	108	7	101
1975	385	165	220	106	8	98
1976	415	178	237	107	8	99
1977	404	197	207	108	9	99
1978	430	210	220	75	8	67
1979	452	231	221	104	8	96
1980	607	298	309	147	11	136
Average	437	203	234	108	8	99

Source: Ministry of Agriculture, Zimbabwe.
[a] Excluding labor (reliable estimates on communal area labor inputs are unavailable).

areas to support their inhabitants and make a net contribution to the economy.

Unless the young and able-bodied can be persuaded to stay on the land, productivity can never improve. It is important to make rural work economically competitive, and to encourage full-time farming. Labor policies and wage policies should avoid urban biases and strive to minimize the imbalance between rural and urban wages. High urban wages frequently result in increases in farm costs, and this, added to the fact that urban food is heavily subsidized and the fact that average income derived from agriculture is generally low and highly variable, further widens the income gap between urban and rural inhabitants.

Education policies should avoid excessive bias in educational programs geared to produce white-collar job seekers, but instead should have an agricultural bias. At the same time, sound urban policies should be used to create life-time security for urban dwellers by means of insurance and housing plans, thereby preventing elderly, less productive people from drifting back to rural areas.

As farm families gain greater disposable income through increased agricultural profits, they purchase goods and services and other products of urban industry. Employment rises not only on farms but in rural trade centers and service centers. Further opportunities for employment are provided by several industries and infrastructures which are built around agriculture.

It is official policy to encourage the growth of independent small-scale manufacturing and distribution industries at selected growth points. The government is also encouraging decentralization of industrial development.

Rural Service Centers are being constructed with the aim of forging linkages with the national economy and stimulating the development of local markets, with regional specialization where possible, and a multitude of associated informal employment opportunities.

The creation of rural service centers and improvements in rural infrastructure are seen as measures to create a favorable environment for future manufacturing industries and, above all, for bringing facilities to rural areas. Rural people are entitled to the comforts taken for granted in the urban areas. It must also be realized that not all people living in the rural areas are farmers. Some only till the soil to eke out a living because there are no other nonfarm occupations. If there were, these people would opt for other occupations and release land to real farmers.

The ultimate aim is to enable, through the multiplier effect, as much money as possible to circulate within the rural areas, instead of having it invested in urban areas. This will lead to an improvement in the quality of life of the rural people.

RESETTLEMENT

The war for independence in Zimbabwe came about in the main because of the inequitable distribution of land. Table 11-6

Table 11-6. Land Classification by Natural Region[a]

Natural Region	Communal Areas	Parks and Wildlife Areas	Forest Areas	Small- and Large-scale Farming Areas	Totals
I	135,000	50,000	70,000	450,000	705,000
II	1,270,000	25,000	2,000	4,560,000	5,857,000
III	2,820,000	545,000	145,000	3,780,000	7,290,000
IV	7,340,000	2,510,000	620,000	4,300,000	14,770,000
V	4,790,000	1,840,000	70,000	3,750,000	10,450,000
Total	16,355,000	4,970,000	907,000	16,840,000	39,072,000

Source: Natural Resources Board, Zimbabwe.

[a] The land, measured here in hectares, is divided into five natural regions according to ecological features and agricultural potential, with regions II and III best suited for intensive crop production.

illustrates the land classification scheme. The high population densities in communal areas compared to commercial areas and the greater percentage of inherently more productive regions in the commercial sector presented imbalances unacceptable to the government.

Soon after independence in 1980, the government embarked on a massive land redistribution policy. Land had to be acquired from the commercial areas (owned by whites) and reallocated to resettlement schemes (for blacks). However, the government's plans were fettered by the Independence Lancaster House Constitution, which required land acquisition by the government for resettlement to be on a willing-seller/willing-buyer basis, with prices negotiated between the parties.

To resolve the political contradictions in production, any redistribution policy had to strike a balance between the vested interests of the landed commercial farmers and the landless peasants. It also had to strike an economic balance between the two extreme policy options of either radically redistributing all commercial land, which might disrupt production, especially in the short run, or of adopting a more cautious and pragmatic redistribution policy, which might not immediately satisfy all the existing demand for land.

This contradiction presents the most difficult choice for the government when it resolves itself into its most naked form and becomes simply a question of food and foreign exchange versus the people's hunger for land. Moreover, the formulation of a land redistribution policy is further complicated by the fact that the connection between land and agricultural production is not clear. Numerous factors other than land are involved in agricultural production.

It cannot be said that the mere transfer of land to the people who need it will automatically lead to successful agricultural production. Therefore, to redress the imbalances of the previous production structure and, hence, the relative importance of the commercial and peasant sectors, reliance should not be placed on land redistribution alone as the total answer but rather on a much more thorough analysis of the mechanisms and operations of state aid, and the role of inputs such as extension, management, and credit.

The Ministry of Lands, Resettlement, and Rural Development is charged with the responsibility of administering the government's land redistribution policy. As the name of the ministry implies, it performs three main functions: (1) the transfer of land from the commercial sector to the peasant sector; (2) the resettlement of people on an orderly basis upon the newly acquired land; and (3) the development of all the communal and resettlement areas.

LAND ACQUISITION

The Ministry of Lands has been acquiring land from the commercial areas in all the natural regions of the country. Land has been purchased from its holders on a willing-seller/willing-buyer basis. There has been no forceful seizure of private land.

A Land Selection Committee, acting on the advice of government land valuation and extension officers, has been deciding what land the ministry should purchase. The government has particularly wished to acquire all underutilized, abandoned, and derelict land. Those commercial farmers who have been fully utilizing their land have been left to make their own contribution through production for food and exports.

By February 1983 the government had purchased 2,142,712 hectares of land, with 1,657,000 hectares developed and 33,880 families actually settled.

INTENSIVE RESETTLEMENT

Once land has been acquired, it is surveyed, planned, and demarcated, and its carrying capacity is determined. When this is done, essential infrastructure is built, including access roads, dip tanks, boreholes, clinics, schools, and service centers. At the same time the infrastructure is being laid out, settlers are selected on the basis of established criteria which emphasize the need for land. The selection is made from the refugee, displaced, and landless peasant population who show a willingness to settle down as farmers. After their selection, these people are resettled according to certain models of resettlement.

The first model calls for intensive village settlements with individual arable allocations and communal grazing areas. The second model is an intensive settlement with communal living and cooperative farming. A third model calls for the formation of an intensive settlement such as in the first model but combined with a centralized core estate.

In each case the amount of grazing and arable land allocated per family is determined by the potential of the area in question and varies greatly from one natural agro-ecological region to another. The department responsible for conservation and extension determines the agricultural potential of each region and advises on the most appropriate cropping and livestock system.

The second model—that of cooperative farming—is intended for those groups of people who are well motivated and have a heightened ideological consciousness. In the long run this model will become the basis of implementing the government's policy of socialist transformation of peasant agriculture. People are not compelled to join cooperatives against their will or before they understand the merits of cooperative agriculture.

In the drier livestock areas new modifications of models are currently being evolved. In many cases the government gives initial assistance to genuine cooperative groups to help them establish themselves; otherwise the government insists on the principle of self-reliance. The assistance offered is usually in the form of agricultural inputs such as fertilizer, seed, credit, draft oxen, tractor implements, vehicles, and dip tanks.

The largest component of assistance is, however, the provision of infrastructure in the form of transport and service centers, roads, dip tanks and water supplies. Recently the ministry embarked on an emergence program of accelerated intensive resettlement. Under this program the ministry tries to resettle as many people as possible in the shortest possible time by putting them on resettlement land before roads and other elements of the infrastructure are built. It is assumed that the settlers would in this case use the infrastructure available in adjacent communal areas. The government plans to resettle 162,000 families in three years.

LAND TENURE

The government has not yet evolved a national system of land tenure. This is a complex exercise whose analysis would have to take into account the desired socioeconomic transformation as well as the likely impact on production. However, in the meantime the settlers on different resettlement models are occupying their holdings under a variety of permits.

Model A

According to this model, settlers are issued the following permits:
1. Permit to reside, which covers the residential plot in the village.
2. Permit to cultivate, which covers the arable land.
3. Permit to depasture stock, which covers the right to graze a given number of livestock units.
4. Temporary permit to cultivate, which covers the half-hectare of land plowed for the settler when he first moves onto his holding.

Model B

Permits are also issued in respect of those farms run on cooperatives by organizations registered with the Registrar of Cooperatives Societies.

All the permits emphasize and encourage the practice of proper and sound land husbandry methods by the settler. Those settlers who simply reside on the land or who fail to make the land productive are liable to be evicted.

CONCLUSION

This paper has attempted to demonstrate that land policy as an improvement component of rural and urban development should be considered in conjunction with a complex mix of policy measures designed to maintain productive populations in rural areas and to curb urban migration. These policies include urban policy, population policy, land reform policy, credit policy, producer pricing policy, educational and social policy, and wage and labor policies.

A package for agricultural development targeted for the small-farm sector and emphasizing provision of credit, inputs, extension services, accessible marketing facilities, attractive producer prices, storage depots, and distribution centers forms the cornerstone of successful land policies.

REFERENCES

Chambers, R. 1978. *Managing Rural Development: Ideas and Experience from East Africa*.

Economic Impact no. 39. 1982-83. *Quarterly Review of World Economics: Improving Agricultural Productivity*.

Jackson, J.; Blackie, M. J.; and de Swart, L. 1983. *Human and Economic Conditions in the Communal Lands of Zimbabwe*. Department of Land Management, University of Zimbabwe.

Levil, I., and Havinden, M. 1982. *Economics of African Agriculture*. London: Longman.

Mellor, John W. 1966. *The Economics of Agricultural Development*.

Todaro, Michael P. 1977. *Economics for a Developing World*.

Upton, M. 1973. *Farm Management in Africa: The Principles of Production and Planning*. London: Oxford University Press.

World Bank. 1975. "Sector Policy Paper: Land Reform." Washington, D.C.: World Bank.

Chapter 12

Conflicts Between Land for Agricultural and Urban Use: The Case of Veszprém City

Eta Daróczi

IMPORTANCE OF LAND PROTECTION

Demographic explosion, radical changes in the quantitative and qualitative aspects of production, degradation of the conditions of biological existence, and, most directly, the energy crisis have amplified our concern over vulnerable, exhaustible natural resources throughout the world. Agricultural land in particular deserves protection, not only so that we may ensure vital conditions for renewing vegetation—food, fiber, energy—but because it is a finite resource itself.

In Hungary long-standing efforts to make good use of existing natural resources in a rational way and to develop an economic structure which squares with national endowments, as well as with the strategic importance of food, and the keen demand for goods made of genuine components in natural circumstances, have recently focused attention on land protection. The need had already been formulated in the Land Protection Act of 1961, but important progress was made only after the Eleventh Congress of the Hungarian Socialist Workers' Party in 1975, which stated in a program declaration, "Land in the Hungarian People's Republic—irrespective of the form of ownership—represents national wealth."

Delay in acting is not justified but can be partly explained by the undervaluation of productive lands stemming from socioeconomic policies predominant in Hungary until the late 1970s, characterized by favoring industries and urban developments over agriculture and rural settlements. The fortunate fact of relative abundance of land delayed recognition of the damage caused by wasteful land management. In spite of significant losses of cultivated areas and the important changes in land use structure, land can still be regarded as in favorable supply. According to *The Statistical Pocket Book of Hungary, 1981*, in 1981, 70.9 percent of the total national territory was used for agricultural cultivation. In Europe, Hungary ranks second after Denmark with regard to the proportion of intensive farming. Out of the total area of the country, 50.4 percent is arable land, 3.7 percent garden, 3 percent orchards and vineyards, and 13.8 percent is meadow and pasture. The population density is only 1.6 persons per one hectare of agricultural area.

Only a small portion of the land is of excellent quality; most of it has mediocre fertility, and about one-third is poor soil requiring amelioration. Nevertheless, due to the mutually reinforcing effects of relatively advantageous relief and climatic conditions and high standards of farming, Hungarian agriculture has been successfully developing in both yield and quality. According to the same source, the economic importance of this sector is shown by the fact that in 1981, one-quarter of the total value of exports and one-third of exports in convertible currency were agricultural and food industrial products. According to certain estimates, it will be possible in the long run to export one-third of Hungary's total food production.

The achieved results are particularly valuable considering the fact that, traditionally, agriculture has been the least profitable productive sector. After the country corrected the serious agropolitical mistakes of the 1950s, it took important steps toward strengthening the self-management of cooperative farms and widening the range of their activities. But even now, agriculture is at a disadvantage in the system of state taxation and subsidies because of the extensive application of fixed and maximized prices for sociopolitical considerations for the purpose of maintaining export marketability and in response to the widening gap between industrial and agricultural prices. An overcentralization of food foreign trade also plays a negative role.

At the same time, there has been a growing demand for urban areas resulting from vigorous population growth in cities and towns and the centralization of production and service activities. There are several reasons for this urbanization. Immigrants were settled mainly in urban peripheries in new housing estates of medium- and high-rise buildings. These town dwellers wedged in man-made environments and surrounded by walls have felt an increasing need for green areas for daily and weekly recreation. Furthermore, the low price of industrial, commercial, and institutional land has not encouraged investors to economize. Master planners consider primarily precautionary measures (safety, health protection) when deciding on the location of incompatible urban uses and various structures. They are bound more by compulsory "minimal distances," immediate cost factors, and the possibility of rapid completion than by the requirements of rationally compact (not crowded) urban planning, the need for reconstruction, and the necessity of exploring, planting, or building up derelict urban plots.

In Hungary up to 1923 the expansion of agricultural areas through deforestation, drainage, and so on surpassed contraction owing to urbanization. For a while the positive and negative changes were more or less equal. Since the Second World War, however, agricultural areas have been rapidly decreasing: up till now 500,000 hectares were used for afforestation, and 370,000 hectares were taken out of production. Following the introduction of the Land Protection Act, the loss of cultivated land slowed down temporarily, but the process intensified during the 1970s. There was an urgent need for amplifying and improving legislation to protect the land.

LEGAL FRAMEWORK OF LAND PROTECTION

The economic benefits of environment, including land, usually show up in the long run, and not necessarily, or not only, for the owner-user. In the absence of direct and strong economic interest of farmers, and due to strict restrictions concerning the marketing of land as a means of production, legislation plays an outstanding role in land protection in Hungary.

The Land Protection Act of 1961 contains provisions for agricultural land use, soil protection, increasing fertility, and land conversion. The act was conceived in a progressive spirit, but for a long time it served mainly as a guiding principle. Since its introduction several modifications have been made concerning some details, but the first comprehensive enabling clauses appeared only in 1977. It is symptomatic that sanctions against converting land from agricultural to urban uses were much more rigorous in 1977 than more recently. At present, one cannot yet speak of coordinated, comprehensive legislation embracing all aspects of the protection, use, ownership, and marketing of land, including regulations for both agricultural and urban uses. But preparations are being made at various institutions for a new, integrated Land Codex and an Urban Development Act, and related issues are being widely debated at conferences and in professional publications.

Of the land control regulations, I will discuss only those that are directly connected with settlement development—namely, legislation concerning the expansion of areas to be urbanized and land conversion.

Administrative areas of all Hungarian settlements are divided into inner and outer areas and some closed gardens. Distinctions are made according to specific functions. Consequently, regulations concerning land use (cultivation, construction), the modes of property acquisition, and alienation vary by locality in inner or outer areas or in closed gardens. In inner areas purchase or expropriation price is defined by the marketing of plots in personal ownership; in outer areas it is fixed according to the agricultural value of the land.

The *inner area* is designed for settlement (urban development). It is managed by the local council, which fixes its boundaries and decides upon its use. Modifications are made when the master plan is prepared, and then continuously as the realization of the plan advances, usually by five-year periods.

The *outer area* in practical terms is the land between the inner areas and the administrative borders of a settlement. Its function depends on local endowments and needs: large-scale farming and silviculture, wildlife, industry, infrastructure, tourism, recreation, special state use, and so on.

The *closed garden* is a part of the outer area, traditionally orchards and vineyards, usually in hilly areas, where large-scale farming is not economical. In order to maintain farming, these areas were designated for individual ownership. The primary function of closed gardens is production—however small, the land has to be cultivated—but it also serves recreational purposes. The personal right to agricultural land was recognized in 1967 with the introduction of a new economic mechanism. Subsequently, closed gardens were delimited by committees created in each of the 19 counties of Hungary.

Lands for agricultural use are defined in the Land Protection Act as arable lands, vineyards, gardens, orchards, grasslands, reeds, and fishponds located in outer areas and in closed gardens of settlements (the capital, cities, towns, and villages), and any other uncultivated land which justifies restoration. Land control regulations are enforced in inner areas as well where there is land of more than 1,500 square meters which is suitable for agriculture.

Lands for non-agricultural use are those located in inner areas of settlements, all lands which were withdrawn from agricultural use, and those for which such permission has been given.

Both the expansion of inner areas and land conversion from agricultural to other uses are subject to previous permission. According to the regulations introduced in 1977, land offices were given sole authority, replacing their earlier advisory role, to permit appropriation of agricultural lands. Applications are submitted to the lowest-level (town and non-urban district) land offices. For parcels up to three hectares, they decide in their own capacity; for between three and ten hectares, the consent of the county land office is required; above ten hectares, the consent of the Ministry for Agriculture and Alimentation is needed. Town and district land offices must not refuse to give permission if a higher-ranking institution has consented. Unfortunately, this may restrict land protection, because applicants with high-level connections may wangle extra favors. These rules also relate to areas designated in master plans for building. Thus at present the right of control over urban sprawl lies with land offices.

The National Building Code stipulates that land use categories—excepting agricultural and silvicultural lands—are to be designated so that first those lands should be used which are inadequate for agricultural production or which are of poor quality. Designations should be limited to the smallest possible areas satisfying these needs. These regulations provide guidelines but do not stimulate the planner to manage the area of a settlement in a rational, thrifty way.

The fact that inner areas have been underutilized for urban purposes is reflected by legal measures taken in 1977 (the enabling clauses of the Land Protection Act) and in 1980 (instructions of the Minister for Building and Urban Development) that ordered a revision of inner-area boundaries of all Hungarian settlements. The aim was to provide increased protection for land cultivated by large-scale farms and the urbanization of which is not expected within five years, by reclassifying them from inner to outer areas.

In the case of land conversion from agricultural to other uses, with certain exceptions, an *indemnity* is levied, irrespective of the compensation paid for the acquisition of the ownership or the use of the land. This is an essential new feature of the Land Protection Act embodied in 1977 which stresses the importance of land control by making cultivated land more expensive.

In Hungary lands are grouped into eight classes within each agricultural land use, the best lands being first class. According to the regulations of 1977, indemnity was to be paid only for the conversion of lands in classes one to five and the tax rates were graduated depending upon the quality of land: for example, the tax rate for first-class arable land was double that of fifth class. The taxable property value—until the introduction of a new land value system under preparation—is the net income of lands as it was established at the end of the last century and revised in 1909.

Regulations valid from 1982 stipulate that an indemnity must be paid for the conversion of lands in all eight classes. The tax rates increase as follows: in class five tax rates increase by a factor of 3.25, in class four by 3.6, in class three by 3 5/6, in class two by 4, and in the first class by 4 1/8.

Indemnity is not levied if the interested party recultivates in a value equivalent to the sum otherwise charged, provided the investment concerned serves soil protection or provides an irrigation canal. It is important for urban development that the conversion of agricultural lands in inner areas into public parks be tax free, with half the indemnity to be paid if land conversion serves housing. In the incidence of unpermitted withdrawal, triple the usual indemnity is charged.

Until 1982 the sum of indemnities sat in the development funds of county councils which decided on its use within its regular budgetary planning. The people most concerned—the taxpayers, the former farmers, and those who knew the situation best, the local councils and land offices—could not influence the use of this money.

According to present regulations, half the receipts from such indemnities go toward increasing the development fund of county councils; from the other half a Land Protection Fund is to be created, which may have other sources as well. It would be expedient, however, to collect all indemnities as well as all taxes and fees related to land use in this fund, which would then fulfill the requirement that all secondary revenues derived from land should be put toward its amelioration and reclamation. The Land Protection Fund is used for recultivation of derelict and fallow lands. Subsidies are allocated by county councils upon application of state and cooperative organizations.

In the county of Veszprém during the years 1980 and 1981,

respectively, the total sum of indemnities levied came to 12.8 and 9.5 million forints: 1.1 percent of the development fund of the County Council on the average.

In 1980, 93 permissions were given for the withdrawal of 355 hectares of land from agricultural use. Apart from 12 claims for afforestation, affecting 147 hectares, 19 cases affecting 68 hectares were tax free. No application was refused.

In 1981, 106 permissions were given on 1,136 hectares, 19 applications for afforestation on 753 hectares, and 12 cases on 90 hectares were tax free. Five applications relating to 189 hectares were refused.

In Veszprém County alone, the size of the Land Protection Fund was estimated at 6 million forints for the year 1982. This amount is sufficient to cover the reclamation costs of 500 to 600 hectares of land.

These rulings include urban fringes as well; no specific measures were taken. It is expected that legislation introduced as of 1982 would encourage the reutilization of agricultural lands and would curb their decrease—particularly that of arable lands and good-quality soils.

In 1981 agricultural lands decreased by 19,022 hectares (-0.3 percent) in Hungary. At the same time 7,418 hectares of forest, reed, or unused areas were recultivated. The area of land withdrawn from agricultural use increased by 18,010 hectares, from among which 2,157 hectares were withdrawn without permission. Out of this increase, 30.5 percent was taken out of arable lands, 30.6 percent from gardens, and 21.4 percent from forests; 21.4 percent of the newly withdrawn lands was taken out of areas of good soil qualities. The proportion of classes one through three among withdrawn arable lands was even higher: 32.6 percent.

Effects of the latest measures cannot yet be evaluated. Lasting results, however, can be achieved only if the social interest in maintaining cultivation and in protecting lands is directly expressed in the financial interests of the agricultural employers—the farmers themselves as well as urban land users. This should be promoted by increased state subsidies differentiated by regions and products.

Nevertheless, these restrictive and incentive measures can be effective only if they are based on reasonable land values. A new evaluation system of productive lands is already under preparation. It would be tremendously useful to evaluate urban areas as well, because at present rational urban land use is not backed by any system of principles, even though this is an important factor which also influences the extent to which the non-agricultural use of lands can be limited.

VESZPRÉM CITY

Veszprém City is situated in Transdanubia, between the Bakony Mountains and Lake Balaton on a low plateau the surface of which is articulated by seven hills and narrow valleys. North-south fractures are dominant, marked by a hairpin bend in the course of the river Séd.

The development of this historic city was determined in the past by a series of functions; it served as a royal seat, a county seat, a religious and military center, and it was the site of crown and church estates and a center for crafts and trade. During the twentieth century the royal character has of course disappeared, the role of the church has diminished significantly, and craftsmanship has wasted away. But the other functions have been transformed and strengthened, and the city has taken on important new roles.

During the past decades there have been developments in production, administration, education, science, and tourism. The city was already surrounded by large industrial centers (mainly chemical industries) when significant industrialization occurred in the 1960s. In spite of her function as an administrative center, of the 39 state and cooperative industrial plants located in the city, only 15 have headquarters there. This is unfavorable from the point of view of urban development, because it is difficult for local organizations to cooperate with enterprises which are controlled from a distance. Local influence on them is far less effective than on locally managed institutes and factories, and the latter care more about development.

The historically developed radial road network was unchanged until recently, in spite of extensive sprawl of the city. The relatively even concentric development could continue for so long because the railway was far from the center to the north, and big industries were only recently located in peripheral areas, close to the railway.

During the last two decades the population increase in Veszprém has been extremely dynamic in comparison with average urban population growth in Hungary. Within the present administrative boundaries, the number of inhabitants grew from 22,000 in 1941 to 38,000 in 1970 and to 57,000 in 1982. Unprecedented developments rendered all master plans antiquated before they were due. A constant race to address needs, mainly in housing, has transformed the traditional city structure.

Two forms of urban growth are increased population density and spatial expansion. In the city center of Veszprém, population density could be increased only to the detriment of a valuable historic area. In the Séd Valley a certain amount of increase was possible, but only within a limited area requiring slum clearance. However, increased population requires the construction of public utilities, and this would be very expensive in some parts of the city due to the dolomite rocky surface.

In order to speed up housing construction, and for technological and other reasons, new districts were built, as in most Hungarian towns, on the peripheries from the 1960s, as a result of which the urban area of Veszprém expanded in a north-south direction.

Increased inner-city and transit traffic overburdened the only main road that secures east-west communication to such an extent that acute traffic congestion in the center formed a constant obstacle to the normal functioning of the city. Traffic surveys made during 1974 established a 22 to 23 kilometer per hour travel speed and 1,160 vehicles per hour average traffic on the main road in the city center. Another problem was the diversion of truck traffic, because a weight limit imposed on the historic viaduct could not be lifted. It thus became essential to construct a ring road. This road took on an important role in the planning of the spatial expansion of the city as well.

The latest master plan for Veszprém City was approved by the local council in November 1982, after several years of preparation. The plan could not disregard land protection requirements; it had to take into consideration the quality of land on the urban fringes, where there is some extremely fertile soil, a precious resource in a region where good lands are not abundant. The plan calls for the following:

1. To the south and southeast of the center, along about 40 percent of the perimeter of an imaginary circle drawn around the built-up area, there is a contiguous zone of Ramann's brown forest soil, the best of the urban area, and some second- and third-class arable land as well. This area is located between the city and Lake Balaton, an area very attractive to developers, not only for its privileged geographical situation but also because construction here is relatively easy and cheap.

2. At each end of the above-mentioned area, accounting for about ten percent of the circle, there exists soil of the second-best quality— brown forest soil with eluvial clay.

3. To the north of those regions, predominantly to the northwest, and occupying about 30 percent of the circle, the poorest soils of the city, Rendzina soils, are found.

4. Finally, to the north of the city center, beyond the railroad, along the remaining 20 percent of the ring, as well as in the valley of the river Séd, wet alluvial soils are predominant. About two-fifths of the last two sections are covered, in effect, by bare dolomite.

Urban expansion in the section where the soil is poor is limited by the presence of industry, the railway, and the military. Thus the areas where the land is of the best quality are under the greatest pressure, and are the most directly threatened urban fringes.

AGRICULTURAL VS. URBAN
LAND USE

At the beginning of the 1970s the future economic difficulties and the slow-down of demographic processes were not yet perceptible. Policymakers of both the county and city of Veszprém had ambitious expectations: the number of inhabitants in Veszprém City would reach 100,000 by the turn of the century; the city would develop into an important industrial center; tourism would thrive at Lake Balaton. Money was concentrated on developing the city as the county seat. Several housing estates were built, and some spectacular projects were realized to increase the prestige of the city, but no mature strategic plan was elaborated to coordinate these developments. Deficiencies in technical and social infrastructure caused intolerable tensions. There was a call for a new master plan, and preparations began in 1974. Various and sometimes conflicting interests were expressed during the planning process. Thus the approved plan reflects a compromise which was reached through consultation and debate. It also reflects the modified socioeconomic circumstances and priorities.

The limits of urban expansion are practically determined in the master plan by defining the size of the inner areas. Earlier aspirations of the city are expressed in the fact that the village of Kádárta was annexed to Veszprém in 1973; then inner areas of the city were enlarged from 920 hectares to 2,246 hectares in 1976. Later, with regard to the changed economic situation and the need for land protection, when inner-area boundaries had to be revised, 246 hectares were reannexed to outer areas to the north and south. Most of the areas slated for urbanization have been adjusted to the bypass ring road. The original plan, according to which the inner area would have surpassed the south arc of the road by 600 hectares, was rejected by the Ministry for Agriculture and Alimentation. Permission was given for the withdrawal of only 65 hectares of agricultural land for housing purposes. But even this smaller area may not actually be converted. Frequent modifications of inner areas and delays in registering changes have led to misunderstandings and litigation. The owners whose lands are to be appropriated are demanding the market price for construction sites, while those who have to pay are attempting to prove that the land has been in agricultural use.

Gross losses of agricultural land within the total administrative area of Veszprém City (7,945 hectares) are shown in Table 12-1, broken down by purpose of conversion, for the period 1972-1981.

In spite of considerable decreases, in 1982 one-third of the reduced inner area (1,989 hectares) was still used for agriculture, the proportion of forest was 5 percent and the remaining 62 percent represented other uses. A large part of this withdrawn area could not be used by the city (derelict sand and gravel mines, industrial or military sites). This fact has been cited by opponents of inner-area expansion, who feel that reserves of land within the boundaries should be used first. Developers, however, allege technical difficulties, environmental constraints, and high cost as reasons for not using this land. The conflict has been resolved in a way by circumstance: as the pace of urban growth has diminished in Veszprém, the period of new industrial investment has ended, urban reconstruction and qualitative improvement have gained ground, and rigorous land protection regulations have been introduced.

In 1980-81 most of the agricultural land (26.43 hectares) converted for urban uses (see Table 12-1) was located in the inner areas of Veszprém City. Indemnities were levied for all conversions—occasionally very high sums, reaching 100,000 to 150,000 forints per hectare. And this financial burden was increased in 1982. The local council has been particularly affected. In spite of the allowances, it has been unable to cover indemnity payments for the withdrawal of agricultural lands for housing from its regular budget. Future residents will be charged with these expenditures, within the limits of construction site market prices.

The largest consumer of good land in the city is the local Public Roads Management, which is responsible for the construction and maintenance of the ring road. The construction started in 1977, connecting with road reconstructions carried out in 1974-1976. Its total length will be 16 kilometers, of which 11.8 kilometers were

Table 12-1. Withdrawal of Agricultural Lands for Other Uses in Veszprém City, 1972-1981

Land Area (in Hectares) by Use

Year	Construction Industry	Mfg.	Roads	Warehouses	Municipal Services	Housing, Garages	Consumer Services	Medical, Cultural	Parks	Urban Subtotal	Mining	Forest	Other State Use	State Subtotal	Total
1972-73	0	3.84	0.37	0	0.08	7.32	0	0	0	11.61	16.19	20.09	0	36.28	47.89
1974-75	11.90	51.33	10.70	21.56	5.88	7.65	0	2.76	11.50	123.28	0	23.04	0	23.04	146.32
1976-77	15.14	0	6.79	3.18	0.05	86.39	3.19	0	0	114.74	0	140.52	0.25	140.77	255.51
1978-79	0	3.70	0.43	0	1.61	1.36	0	0	0	7.10	0	18.24	0	18.24	25.34
1980-81	0	7.21	10.91	0	3.33	4.98	0	0	0	26.43	0	0	420.38	420.38	446.81
Total	27.04	66.08	29.20	24.74	10.95	107.70	3.19	2.76	11.50	283.16	16.19	201.89	420.63	638.71	921.87
% of Subtotal	9.6	23.3	10.3	8.7	3.9	38.0	1.1	1.0	4.1	100.00	0	0	0	0	0
% of Total	2.9	7.2	3.2	2.7	1.2	11.7	0.3	0.3	1.2	30.7	1.8	21.9	45.6	69.3	100.00

Source: Emil Sebestyén, Veszprém County Land Office.
Note: All data are estimated figures.

opened in 1982. So far 55 hectares of land have been appropriated; this was mainly productive land, most of it taken prior to 1978, when indemnity payments were enforced.

Up to now, about 6 million forints have been spent on the acquisition of land. Most of this sum includes only the appropriation or purchase price and compensation for green damages. Still, this amount of money runs to almost 3 percent of the total investment cost of the finished sections. The proportion of land costs is expected to increase, not only because of the enforcement and augmentation of indemnities but also because state-owned lands were exchanged free of charge before 1978, but since then it has been permissible to charge for the transfer of the use of land. The Veszprém City Council has not exercised this right, but the Veszprém State Farm has done so. Furthermore, extra expense is created by delays in the land office.

The largest part of agricultural land in Veszprém City is owned by Dózsa Agricultural Cooperative; thus, conversion to urban uses mainly affects their lands. The total area of the co-op covers 6,000 hectares. The co-op has 800 members and employs 1,200, including 900 persons engaged in industrial activities.

Dr. Zoltán Varga, the president of the cooperative, was a successful speculator. As soon as it became possible in 1968, the co-op bought up all state-owned lands which they had cultivated. Because they used some of those lands for non-agricultural purposes, a lot of money had to be paid for the expropriation. Serious charges were brought against the cooperative and its president. For the first time agriculture was seen to profit from the difference in land use value.

From 1968 onwards, 200 to 300 hectares of arable co-op land and around 600 hectares of other areas (forest included) were expropriated for about 15 million and 20 million forints, respectively. During the same period the co-op had invested about 200 million forints. The contribution of compensation payments to this sum is therefore considerable. It is also true that the co-op has given up its poor land willingly but is, however, keen to preserve a relatively low average land value in order not to lose state subsidies.

In Dr. Varga's perception, the most serious problem arising from their location on the urban fringes is that construction and other operations carried out on cultivated lands very much disturb agricultural production. The bypass road touches their best lands, cutting out 10- to 20- to 30-hectare pieces of 200- to 300-hectare fields on which their giant agricultural machines can now hardly move. The same machines must also move around 500 electric poles. The co-op also has to tolerate the use of its lands for laying down and servicing wires, pipelines, and so on. Though the users have to compensate the co-op for damages, they can usually charge others to cover the expenses and are therefore uninterested in diminishing them. Besides personal persuasion, the cooperative has no means to decrease damages through proper timing of outside works. They can come to terms with the City Council and local enterprises, but they find it hard to negotiate with institutions controlled from other countries, and particularly from Budapest.

CONCLUSIONS

The protection of irreplaceable agricultural lands which represent increasing value is a national cause. This would best be accomplished by rendering agricultural production more profitable. In the present situation, it is very difficult to change public opinion as to which losses of cultivated lands are normal and inevitable. Improved legislation is needed, but it cannot replace economic regulators. Present legal frameworks provide more for financial recompensation of losses than for preventing them in the first place.

According to Dr. Varga, "The most important [thing] would be, however, that instead of a simple money flow, the land be esteemed and respected—if the Land Protection Act would become a matter of common knowledge like the red light in traffic."

Land protection should cover not only cultivated lands but also those which have been withdrawn from agriculture. This requires the elaboration of basic principles of rational urban land use. For the moment, one must remain satisfied that the requirements of land protection are considered in master planning as constraints. Thus it has become significantly harder to use unreasonably large parcels or particularly good quality agricultural lands for urban use.

Finally, qualitative improvements are needed in the activities of institutions that professionally deal with land control. It is not the case that a higher-level decision maker will take national interests into account more than a local one. It would therefore be advisable to invest more power in local authorities for the sake of the land.

REFERENCES

Andorka, Rudolf. 1982. "Az életmód területi különbségei az időmérleg-felvétel alapján" (Spatial Differences in the Way of Life Based on Time-Budget Surveys). *Területi Statisztika* 32, no. 4: 344-358.

Baráth, Etele. 1981. "Az országos területrendezési tervkoncepció" (The National Strategic Physical Plan). *Városépítés* no. 2: 5-18.

Barta, Barnabás. 1982. "Az urbanizációs folyamat társadalmi és környezeti vonatkozásai" (Social and Environmental Aspects of the Urbanization Process). *Területi Statisztika* 32, no. 4: 313-329.

Berényi, István. 1980. "Die geographischen Typen der Brache in Ungarn" (Geographical Types of Fallow in Hungary). *Erdkunde* 34, no. 1: 36-46.

————. 1980. "A területhasznosítás átalakulásának főbb irányai az Alföldön" (Main Tendencies of Land Use Transformation in Alföld). *Alföldi Tanulmányok* 4: 63-84.

Bernát, Tivadar, ed. 1981. *Magyarország Gazdaságföldrajza* (Economic Geography of Hungary). Budapest: Tankönyvkiadó.

Bunyevácz, József. 1981. "A települési környezet építésének, alakításának környezetvédelmi szempontjai" (Environmental Aspects of Building and Shaping Settlement Environment). *Városépítés* no. 1: 21-15.

Daróczi, Eta. 1982. "Suburban Land Economy. A Case Study in Veszprém Functional Urban Region." In *Development of Rural Areas.* Proceedings of the Fourth Hungarian-Polish Seminar, Godap, Poland, May 20-30, 1980, edited by Jerzy Kostrowicki and Wadiysawa Stola.

Egri, Antal. 1982. "Gondolatok: 'A jog szerepe termőföldjaink megóvásában cimü tanulmányhoz' " (Comments on the Study "The Role of Legislation in Land Protection"). *Tudomány és Mezögazdaság* 20, no. 5: 28-31.

Enyedi, György, ed. 1976. *Rural Transformation in Hungary.* Budapest: Akadémiai Kiadó.

————. 1982. "Industrial Activities in Large-Scale Farms." In *Development of Rural Areas.* Proceedings of the Fourth Hungarian-Polish Seminar, Godap, Poland, May 20-30, 1980, edited by Jerzy Kostrowicki and Wadisawa Stola.

Hoffer, István. 1982. "A nemzeti kincs megőrzése" (Preserving the National Wealth). *Figyelö* 26 (February 3).

Jantner, Antal. 1982. "A települési környezetvédelem koncepciója és követelményrendszere" (The Concept and the System of Norms in Settlement Environment Protection). *Városépítés* no. 1: 1-2.

Katona, Sándor. 1981. "A települések környezetre gyakorolt hatásának értékelése" (Evaluation of Settlement Influence on Environment). *Földrajzi Értesitö* 30, no. 1: 123-132.

Kálnoki Kis, Sándor. 1982. "A városfejlesztés-településfejlesztés új tendenciái" (New Tendencies in Town and Settlement Development). *Társadalmi Szemle* 37, no. 5: 63-71.

Koronczay, Miklós. 1982. "A Termőföld hasznosítását elösegitő jogi eszközök" (Legal Means Promoting the Use of Productive Land). *Állam és Igazgatás* 32, no. 5: 411-417.

Láng, István. 1982. "A hazai környezetvédelmi kutatások eredményei és további feladatai" (Results and Tasks of Environmental Research in Hungary). *Magyar Tudomány* 27, no. 12: 894-903.

Lukács, Béla. 1982. "A termőföld védelmének időszerü kérdései" (Current Issues in Land Protection). *Geodézia és Kartográfia* 34, no. 6: 402-406.

A Magyar Szocialista Munkáspárt XI. Kongresszusa (The 11th Congress of the Hungarian Socialist Workers' Party). 1975. Budapest: Kossuth Könyvkiadó.

Mezőgazdasági és Élelmezésügyi Értesitő (Bulletin of the Ministry for Agriculture and Alimentation). 1982. Vol. 33, no. 10 (April 30): 526-596.

Molnár, István. 1982. "Miért nem nő a mezőgazdaság nemzeti jövedelemhez való hozzájárulása?" (Why Does the Contribution of Agriculture Not Grow in National Income?). *Közgazdasági Szemle* 29, no. 2: 172-179.

Nagy, László. 1982. "A földtulajdon és a földhasználat szabályozásáról de lege ferenda" (On the Regulation of Land Ownership and Land Use in Lege Ferenda). *Állam és Igazgatás* 32, no. 8: 686-695.

Országos Épitésügyi Szabályzat (National Building Codex). 1974. Budapest: Épitésügyi Tájékoztatási Központ.

Romány, Pál. 1982. "A szocialista agrárátalakulás és a falu változásai" (Socialist Agrarian Transformation and Changes in Villages). *Társadalmi Szemle* 37, no. 4: 39-52.

Sárándi, Imre. 1982. "A jog szerepe termőföldjeink megóvásában" (The Role of Law in Land Protection). *Tudomány és Mezőgazdaság* 20, no. 5: 24-27.

Soós, Gábor. 1982. "A termőföld a mezőgazdasági termelésben" (Productive Land in Agricultural Use). *Tudomány és Mezőgazdaság* 20, no. 5: 9-12.

Statistical Pocket Book of Hungary, 1981. 1982. Budapest: Statistical Publishing House.

Stefanovits, Pál. 1982. "A termőföld megismerése, használata és védelme" (Knowing, Using, and Protecting Productive Land). *Tudomány és Mezőgazdaság* 20, no. 5: 3-8.

Thiery, Árpád. 1981. *Királynék városa* (Town of Queens). Budapest: Szépirodalmi Könyvkiadó.

Tóth, József. 1981. "A településhálózat és a környezet kölcsönhatásának néhány elméleti és gyakorlati kérdése" (Some Theoretical and Practical Problems of the Interrelationship between the Settlement Network and the Environment). *Földrajzi Értesitő* 30, nos. 2-3: 267-292.

Veszprémi településcsoport általános rendezési terve (Master Plan of Veszprém Functional Urban Region). 1982. Budapest: Városépitési Tudományos és Tervező Intézet.

Zsuffa, Ervin. 1982. "A mezőgazdasági nagyüzemek differenciált fejlődése" (Differentiated Development of Large-Scale Farms). *Társadalmi Szemle* 37, no. 4: 3-19.

In addition the author has relied on unpublished materials provided by László Balassa and Zoltánné Takács, Veszprém City Council; Dr. János Földy, Jenő Holczhauser, Dr. Sándor Palatinus, and Márton Zachariás, Veszprém County Land Office; Dr. Lajos Gáncs, Veszprém County

Council; Szilveszter Bordács and Dr. László Szentmiklóssy, Veszprém Public Road Management; Dr. Gábor Ortutay, László Posta, and Dr. Zoltán Varga, President, Dózsa Agricultural Cooperative, Veszprém; and Lajos Koszorú, Institute for Town Planning and Architecture, Budapest. The author has also relied on unpublished materials and data from László Pinczés, Computer Center of the Ministry for Agriculture and Alimentation; Tamás Erős, Emil Sebestyén, and Judit Táboriné Végh, Veszprém County Land Office; Árpád Balogh, Veszprém Town and Nonurban District Land Office; and Dr. Béláné Sebestyén, Veszprém County Council.

Chapter 13

A Design for Implementing an Ethical Land Policy

Ann L. Strong

I assume that those of us gathered here—whether we come from developed or developing countries and whether we are liberal or conservative in our political orientation—share a common sense of what constitutes an ethical land policy. I will test this assumption by offering you two definitions of an ethical land policy—my own and the more eloquently stated one of Aldo Leopold in that bible of American conservationists, *A Sand County Almanac.*[1]

From my perspective, an ethical view is holistic and long-term. It sees man as one part of an ecosystem whose components have a natural fit or balance, shaped by eons of interactions between earth, air, fire, water, and living matter. It assumes that the health of any component of the ecosystem is dependent on the health of all other components. Its concern is for the future as much as for the present. The obvious implication of such an ethic is that man does not act to maximize his own immediate return from the land, for if he does, other parts of his ecosystem will suffer.

Aldo Leopold put it as follows:

An ethic, ecologically, is a limitation on freedom of action in the struggle for existence. An ethic, philosophically, is a differentiation of social from anti-social conduct. These are two definitions of one thing.

The thing has its origin in the tendency of interdependent individuals or groups to evolve modes of cooperation. The ecologist calls these symbioses ... The first ethics dealt with the relation between individuals ... Later accretions dealt with the relation between the individual and society ... There is as yet no ethic dealing with man's relation to land and to the animals and plants which grow upon it ... The land relation is still strictly economic, entailing privileges but not obligations. The extension of ethics to this third element in human environment is, if I read the evidence correctly, an evolutionary possibility and an ecological necessity ... All ethics so far evolved rest upon a single premise: that the individual is a member of a community of interdependent parts ... The land ethic simply enlarges the boundaries of the community to include soils, waters, plants, and animals, or collectively: the land ... In short, a land ethic changes the role of Homo sapiens from conqueror of the land-community to plain member and citizen of it. It implies respect for his fellow members, and also respect for the community as such.

Leopold concludes his discussion of ethics by saying: "Examine each question in terms of what is ethically and aesthetically right, as well as what is economically expedient. A thing is right when it tends to preserve the integrity, stability, and beauty of the biotic community. It is wrong when it tends otherwise."[2]

Man today has vast knowledge about the global interactions of climate, soils, water, people, and crops. It is possible to employ this knowledge to design a land policy which is in harmony with natural forces and which assures continuing fertility and productivity. Many of us have in fact designed such policies, and many of us have in common a frustration over our inability to move from policy design to policy implementation.

Aldo Leopold's call to renounce the concept of land as a commodity and to embrace land as a part of the community to which we belong has been answered in some measure in his home state, Wisconsin. The policy there of limiting use of shore lands and marshes to protect them and bordering waterways has been justified on the ground that the state has a public trust obligation to protect resources for those here now and those as yet unborn. It is this sense of a public trust, extended to embrace the land community, which must become pervasive before we can implement ethical land policies.

I set out recently, with what now is evident as a considerable measure of hubris, to analyze successful examples of ethical land policies with the intent of determining common catalytic elements. I speculated that the critical elements might vary between situations in which the threat to a resource was tangible or imminent and situations in which it was remote. I speculated as well that the critical elements might vary between developed nations, with all manner of networks and communication systems, and developing nations, with less complex interactions. With this four-cell matrix— threatened/non-threatened resource, developed/developing nation —in mind, I began to contact many people for descriptions of active, successful programs which manage food or fiber production so as to maintain or enhance the land's potential for continuing fertility. Since I believe that my question was a proper one, the frequency with which eminent, knowledgeable people, including some of you present today, told me that they did not know of a single successful program has led me to believe that we at this Congress should concentrate our thoughts on ways to persuade people and governments that only a holistic, long-term land policy is acceptable. Our problem, as I see it, is not to design such policies but to design a program which will result in their implementation. I will first state briefly the evidence that persuades me that this issue is critical, and I will then propose a design for carrying out ethical land policies.

THE SCALE OF THE PROBLEM

There are those, exemplified by the Heritage Foundation's *Global 2000 Revised* report, who see little cause for alarm. There are others, including Roger Sedjo and Marion Clawson of Resources for the Future,[3] whom I would describe as guardedly optimistic, viewing the world's food and fiber resource base as adequate, provided that we can achieve a more equitable distribution system. And then there are those who, like the Carter Administration's *Global 2000 Report*, see the trend toward a world which is more crowded, more polluted, less stable ecologically.

My perception is that the Sedjo and Clawson view of the resource base is probably correct, but that given our past inability to manage this resource base either wisely from an ecological perspective or equitably from a human perspective, the original *Global 2000* projection is all too likely to occur. We are among the people who have the responsibility to see that it does not.

Why am I pessimistic? Let's look at United States farm production as an example. You will recall that our Great Plains suffered devastating drought, dust storms, and erosion in the 1930s. As Marion Clawson has pointed out, this area had not been prone to erosion until white settlers stripped the prairie, plowed, and planted. In response to the Dust Bowl, the Roosevelt Administration instituted a nationwide soil conservation program. At the time that the Soil Conservation Service was established, there was considerable debate as to whether farmers should be cajoled or required to institute what the government thought to be sound land management practices. The voluntary approach won, and we created a corps of county agents who visited farmers to advise them on crop rotation, contour plowing, irrigation, drainage, and soil suitability. The advice was often accompanied by financial incentives in the form of cost sharing. Now, after almost fifty years' effort, what have we achieved? In judging whether erosion is reasonable or excessive, the United States applies "T" values. "T" is defined as tons of soil lost per acre per year. The "T" value is the maximum loss which can occur while maintaining soil productivity over time through formation of new topsoil. "T" values, depending on soil type, vary from 2 to 5. A 1977 national study[4] found that water erosion on crop land averaged 4.7 tons per acre, or 1.9 billion tons per year. Wind erosion in the 10 Great Plains states averaged 5.3 tons per acre. Overall, the study concluded that 60 percent of crop land, 71 percent of pasture land and range land, and 67 percent of forest land needed conservation treatment. Looked at from the perspective of the individual farm, 84 percent of farms had erosion in excess of the applicable "T" limits.

Why are we continuing to have such severe erosion? Partly because federal farm export policies led farmers to bring marginal lands back into production, partly because of the loss of hedgerows and windbreaks as bigger tracts and bigger machines produced a higher return. However, erosion continues in large part because farmers, including the huge conglomerates which own so much land, are more concerned with obtaining maximum short-term return than with the future fertility of the land. "Après moi, le déluge."

Iowa, one of our most productive corn-growing states, has moved beyond the voluntary approach, having seen its topsoil decline from an average depth of 15 inches to an average depth of 7 inches. The state since 1971 has required soil conservation districts to set soil-loss limits. The state's Supreme Court upheld this mandate for local regulation, saying: "The state has a vital interest in protecting its soils as the greatest of its natural resources, and it has a right to do so."[5] However, a recent study by Robert Coughlin, a colleague of mine at the University of Pennsylvania, shows that establishing soil-loss limits hasn't had much impact on erosion because of limited enforcement. Since 1980 the local districts have been authorized to inspect a farmer's land for violation of the "T" limits and to require the farmer to spend up to $10 per acre a year to reduce the erosion. Because there have been few complaints and little exercise of initiative by the districts, this enforcement power has had little effect so far.[6]

We continue to plant wheat on lands suited to grass, to cut delta bottomland hardwoods to grow soybeans, to mine groundwater in the arid Southwest for crop irrigation. Our 1983 winter wheat crop, despite federal incentives to reduce the area planted by 19 percent, is expected to average a record 40.1 bushels per acre, compared to the 1982 yield of 36.1 bushels per acre, partly thanks to good weather, but also partly because of very high levels of fertilization. Our farm subsidy program, intended to reduce surplus production, is estimated to have cost $21 billion in 1983, compared with $4 billion in 1981.[7]

Farmers here are responding to economic imperatives; farmers in other nations, such as those in the Sahel facing famine, are responding to the imperative of survival. Their response—cultivating sub-marginal lands—like our response, leads to decreased fertility and increased soil instability. Why would people facing bankruptcy or starvation support programs which would reduce their immediate return? The obvious answer is that they wouldn't, and therefore that any program which defers and/or diminishes yield must also provide compensatory relief to those whose expectations are sharply reduced. As Max Falque has hypothesized, the costs of such subvention may be modest in comparison to the long-term benefits to be achieved.[8]

A DESIGN FOR IMPLEMENTATION

The design for implementing ethical land policies which I offer for your consideration has four successive components. For ease of recollection, I have chosen descriptors each of which begins with a C. In sequence, commitment, control, compliance, and coercion constitute the four C's.

Commitment. Without commitment there is little likelihood that the remaining C's can constitute a successful implementation program. Many of us have seen our carefully designed programs fail because of a lack of commitment by those powerful enough to act. Because achieving commitment is critical, I shall devote most of my attention here to ways in which it is attained.

Where there are successful programs in effect, one can often find that the ecologically minded plan capitalized upon a catastrophic event to convince people of the necessity of changing the way in which they use land. The Chipko movement in Uttar Pradesh is an excellent illustration of this.

Traditionally the people living in the Himalayan villages of Uttar Pradesh had relied on the native forest for fuel and fodder. Then in the 1960s and 1970s, the state began to market the forest resource, selling clear-cutting contracts to companies from outside the region. The combination of clear cutting, a poorly designed road network to haul out the timber, steep slopes, unstable soils, and afforestation with foreign, unsuitable species set the stage for disaster. Heavy rains in successive years denuded slopes, washed out roads, and carried soil way downstream in the Ganges, blocking dams and adding to flooding. The local people saw their livelihood literally stripped away.

What were the elements here? Imminent destitution, visibly ravaged countryside, destructive interlopers, *and* a person and a movement with a vision. A local Sarvodaya religious leader, committed to nonviolence and also to the Buddhist view of man as part of nature, began talking with villagers about how they might save the remaining forest and thus their way of life. From this grew the idea of Chipko—forming a human circle around trees to prevent their cutting. Chipko succeeded in many ways: the state altered its forest policy; the women villagers became actively responsible for their destiny; the villagers planted indigenous species and are caring for them. At both the state and village level there is a greater understanding of what constitutes a harmonious balance between people, the mountains, and the forest.[9]

Without detracting from the success of the Chipko movement, we can recognize that it offered a more propitious setting than many for an ethical land policy, particularly because the commitment of the local people to the policy already existed. They needed help to realize this commitment, and it was this which Sarvodaya brought.

What if the indigenous people's view of a desirable land policy is at variance with that of long-term resource management? What if the threat is less sharply defined and less urgent? I offer Oregon's experience with its Land Conservation and Development program as an illustration. The Oregon program requires local governments to set urban growth boundaries—boundaries which may be extended as the need arises—and to retain other lands in exclusive farm and forest zones. Timber and agriculture are Oregon's leading sources of income. State leaders, spurred by the late governor, Tom McCall, became alarmed that these resources were being threatened by a gradual invasion of suburbanites attracted by the beauty and tranquillity of the countryside and, bit by bit, contributing to the loss of those characteristics which had attracted them. Oregon's law is widely heralded for its vision and its strength; the state's lawmakers are praised for their commitment to resource protection. However, what began so promisingly is currently in trouble. The commitment of local governments is proving to be to development, not resource protection.

A recent study by a group called 1,000 Friends of Oregon, the citizen organization formed to promote sound land planning, found that while the exclusive farm zones have been established by the counties as the law intended, the counties have not enforced properly the state standards for activities in these zones.[10] The state law specifies that, for a county to permit a nonfarm residence in an exclusive farm zone, the land must be "generally unsuitable for production of farm crops and livestock," and the residence must be "compatible with farm uses and not interfere seriously with accepted farming practices."[11] Subdivision of farms can occur only if the resulting tracts are large enough to support commercial farming. How have the counties responded to these dictates of the state? A survey of the 12 leading agricultural counties found that 90 percent of nonfarm residence applications had been approved, at least 70 percent of them improperly. Until 1980 the counties totally ignored the commercial agriculture standard for subdivision; in 1980, 75 percent of the applications were approved, 97 percent improperly. The conclusion? According to the study, six years after the Oregon legislature and the Land Conservation and Development Commission had adopted standards to protect Oregon farmland, nonfarm residences and "hobby farms," the bane of commercial agriculture, continued to sprout indiscriminately across land zoned for exclusive farm use. New residences were appearing on the best land as well as marginal land. Why was this happening? The principal reason comes through loud and clear from this study: counties were subverting the farmland protection program. The study called the performance of county elected officials "scandalous." If commercial farming is to be protected as the legislature and LCDC intended, the study concluded, the legislature must change the process by which farm and nonfarm dwellings and land divisions are approved.

Let us also consider the significance of ideology. How widely shared in India is the perception of man as part of nature? In Oregon do people essentially believe that each of them should be free to use his land as he wishes? Looking to other examples, to what extent have Israel's forestry and agriculture policies been shaped by Zionist beliefs? And what of the Netherlands? How is it that many of its resource policies, originally shaped to ensure survival, continue today although modern land management practices would permit alternatives? Is there a nationally accepted ideological base?

My conclusion is that a widely shared ideological base is essential. What power bloc already has a commitment to the ecological perspective, or if not an overt commitment, a compatible ideology? Not government, whose leaders respond to what is currently popular, to what will keep them in power. These leaders will respond to ecological imperatives only if this response also wins elections. My suggestion is that we seek our allies among religious leaders of all faiths. I have already mentioned the Sarvodaya movement and the Zionists. There are three recent examples in the United States of an ethical concern inspiring action by religious leaders. The first is the call for a nuclear freeze by the Catholic bishops, a call accompanied by sermons from many a pulpit. The second is the 1980 resolution of over forty Catholic bishops from the Midwest. The resolution, titled *Strangers and Guests: Toward Community in the Heartland,* includes a chapter called "Steward-ship of the Land." This chapter states principles derived from the Bible and teaching traditions of the church, which include the following: (1) the land is God's; (2) people are God's stewards on the land; (3) the land's benefits are for everyone; (4) the land should be distributed equitably; (5) the land should be conserved and restored."[12] The third example is more recent. A coalition of 64 Catholic bishops, rabbis, and heads of various Protestant denominations has urged Congress to regulate genetic engineering to "bar experiments that could change the characteristics passed on from one generation to the next ... No individual, group of individuals or institutions can legitimately claim the right or authority to make decisions on behalf of the rest of the species alive today or for future generations."[13]

Certainly there are instances of religious leaders acting contrary to the view of land management I have been urging here. For example, with the Catholic church adamantly opposed to birth control, how can it advocate limiting agricultural production on poor soils in countries with severe population pressures?

Nevertheless, I do believe the Leopold land ethic is morally sound, yet I see those of us committed to it unable to win sufficient adherents. I believe that we have a natural ally in the church, synagogue, mosque, and temple, and that this ally has a force which we lack. We need not be of any particular religious faith to recognize the compatibility of concerns and to exercise the initiative. As professionals in the land policy field, we may forget that others, even those whose ideology would lead them to share our perspective, are not nearly as aware as we of the gravity of land use choices. To achieve widespread popular commitment to a sound land ethic, we need the leadership of those who exert a moral influence. First, however, we need to seek them out and to rouse them to the issues before us.

Control, compliance, and coercion—the remaining three C's—must accompany commitment.

Control. This is the ability of some authority to ensure that land is used in accord with the adopted land use policy. The experience in the United States of over fifty years with a voluntary approach to soil conservation is one example of the failure of a policy unaccompanied by any controls. The French SAFER program, in which there is a right to preempt all sales of agricultural land, provides both control and flexibility in restructuring farm holdings to a more efficient size. Although SAFER's policy objectives do not include maintenance of long-term productivity, its control mechanism would work equally well for such an objective.

Compliance. This refers to regular, routine follow-up to ensure that policies are being observed. One of the major findings of the Coughlin study of state and local action to reduce erosion is that there is little inspection to determine whether farmers are observing the governing land management practices. A fine policy is useless if it is not enforced.

Coercion. This involves the willingness to punish when inspection reveals noncompliance. I have chosen *coercion* instead of some milder word because I wish to emphasize the importance of the possibility of retribution. Once land managers know that the authority administering a policy will enforce it by imposing penalties, compliance becomes a simpler task. What forms may coercion take? Obviously one can't force a farmer to plant certain crops in a certain manner. However, financial penalties and tenure controls can achieve the desired result. Failure to manage the land in accord with the approved policy can be a justification for termination of tenure. In extreme situations, the public may exercise the right of eminent domain to acquire property so as to achieve the public purpose of proper land management.

I wish to close with the quote from Karl Polanyi which Nat Lichfield brought to our attention in his introductory paper: "What we call land is an element of nature inextricably interwoven with man's institutions ... Land is thus tied up with the organisation of kinship, neighbourhood, craft, and creed—with tribe and temple, village, guild and church."[14]

NOTES

1. Aldo Leopold, *A Sand County Almanac* (New York: Oxford University Press, 1949).
2. Ibid.
3. Roger Sedjo and Marion Clawson, *The World's Forests* (Washington, D.C.: Resources for the Future, 1982).
4. *Basic Statistics: 1977 National Resources Inventory*, U.S.D.A., S.C.S., Iowa State University Statistical Laboratory, Statistical Bulletin #686.
5. *Woodbury County, S.C.D.* v. *Ortner*, 279 NW 2d 276 (Iowa, 1979).
6. Robert E. Coughlin, "Regulatory Approaches by State and Local Governments for Reducing Erosion of Agricultural Land," American Farmland Trust (January 1983).
7. *New York Times*, 11 June 1983.
8. Max Falque, "Protection contractuelle de l'environnement rural: Le Role du credit agricole," S.0.M.I. (June 30, 1982).
9. Shishupal Singh Kunwar, ed., *Hugging The Himalayas: The Chipko Experience* (Gopeshwar, U.P., India: Dasholi Gram Swarajya Mandal, 1982).
10. Richard P. Brenner, *Administration of Exclusive Farm Lands in Twelve Oregon Counties* (Portland: 1,000 Friends of Oregon, n.d.).
11. ORS 215.213 (3) (a), (b), (d).
12. *Strangers and Guests: Toward Community in the Heartland* (Sioux Falls, S.D.: The Heartland Project, 1980).
13. *New York Times*, 9 June 1983.
14. Karl Polanyi, *The Great Transformation: The Political and Economic Origins of Our Time* (Boston: Beacon Press, 1957).

PART IV

What Are the Policies for Managing Land—a Finite Resource—to Meet Basic Human Needs for Food and Shelter?

Chapter 14

Panel of Reporters

Charles Haar, Isaac Ofori, Harold Dunkerley, William Lim, and Earl Finbar Murphy

Matthew Cullen: Welcome to the concluding day of the Second World Congress on Land Policy. To get the morning under way, Charles Haar, the moderator for the first part of the day, has assembled an impromptu panel of reporters, all of whom have been moderators on earlier days this week, and he has added to the group Earl Finbar Murphy, professor of law at Ohio State University.

Charles Haar: I thought we would have a rather informal session this morning, that we would each take a few minutes to ruminate about the conference, where we hope it will go—general reflections on the particular day each moderator participated in. Professor Murphy and I will deal more with some of the general impressions. We won't try to summarize, because everyone's summary is different. We're all here for our common needs, but also for our individual perspectives, and it's very hard to generalize or summarize without losing all savor and individual feel.

Let me just make a few points about the conference that occurred to me, gathered from the discussions in the halls, under the tent, over the table, and so on. First, I think we have heard from a lot of different cultures and different countries at varied stages of development, so in a sense we have truly had a world congress and have had a chance to make comparative observations over a wide skein of experiences. I think for that we're all grateful to the organizers.

Second, it turns out, not to anyone's surprise, that land, as a classical economist put it, is a crucial factor of production. It turns out to be crucial from the physical and city planning point of view, not only from the sense of being the scene of all human and economic activities.

Third, what is important is not just land itself but the context within which land is found and within which land is employed— and that, of course, means the political system, the institutional and the other factors of production, especially that of capital. That is, you can have farm systems, land reform, land redistribution, but without an adequate credit system, without the provision of capital in an equitable way—whether in terms of internal savings or from external borrowing and nonrepayment—you will not be able to industrialize. There is also the problem that has been defined by the Worldwatch Institute—the whole problem of the pressures of population, of the inadequacy of our concepts, of our intellectual ability to grasp the fast-moving changes that are upon us, and so to which we bring just the tools of the past. So it is in this context that we see the common problems we all have, the problems of migration, the problems of refugees, the problems of displaced persons, and the movement to and creation of cities.

Now, within the institutions, we have to use technology and the knowledge that we have in the field of physical planning. I think that's one of the great differences between this Congress and the one that was held three years ago. There is a sense that more tools are available, whether it be through satellite pictures; whether it be through the more powerful use of the computer in getting land titles and land registration and tax assessment procedures. From the gleam in the eye of some assessor reformers to the practicalities of a dull, hard-moving bureaucracy, the role of technology in transforming what we can do with land in order to carry out our purposes of human achievement and advancement seems more prominent.

But along with that technology is the whole question of that fascinating issue of the education of planners raised on Wednesday by Professor Laconte. Students want to know what they are being trained for. When you look at the future generation and their training, you see what the problems are that face the profession of planning and that society has delegated to them — the stewardship of society's concern with the land. I think we have heard the students raise more than anything else the question of values. How do you value the present as against the future? How about the great need for housing as against the politically pressing need to preserve the environment? How do you balance the short run with the long run? What are the values for the individual profit maker as against what we call society's interest?

In addition to reconciling these different interests, how do you bring in the issue of our first day—that of equity? How do you get the dispossessed and the interest groups which have not been heard to the bargaining table? How do you get them to be able to articulate their needs, their views, and to recognize that they have this kind of bargaining power in the process of decision making about land use? Running through this is the critical issue that many have talked about—especially from the developing countries—in the panels and workshops. It is the balance between economic and, say, moral interest, the reasons that society exists. How do you hold a society together when the integuments are so weak and under so much pressure? How can you define the common interest that brings us all together, despite our differences, into this meeting? Finally there is the question of the role of the plan. How do you decide what the goals are? How do you strategize? Where do you look for your resources? What are your problems? What do you trade off? What are you going to lose? What are you going to gain? And who makes those kinds of decisions?

The question of implementation gets us into the area of politics and the technician. Is there any sense in making grand plans? Who's listening? That is one of the purposes of a conference. Different articles have been made available to us here, which we will go back and study. At a conference you have a captive audience for a few minutes; you can buttonhole a friend or a colleague from a different ministry, or even a counterpart from another country. You can share experiences and have a sympathetic ear for a little while. You can have a sense that you're not struggling alone in the Rousseauean jungle.

If we hope to see a plan implemented, we must perhaps be a little more modest in outlook, aim for something attainable, develop a strategy of success, dealing with the smaller issues within a broad interdisciplinary context. A master plan for land use without a financial underpinning in any society of scarcity will not receive much support from the political powers, or more important, from the public at large. There have been in the workshops several suggestions of how to recapture land value or how to set land prices, and how to do that in a way that will achieve consensus. In other words, the use of incentive is as important as sanction. The use of the joint venture is what we're coming to more and more in land development.

I'm always struck by how private enterprise, at least in the United States, is able to move quickly. Not that the market moves in a straight trajectory, where everything is planned and everything comes out perfectly. Rather, it's a question of adjustment, of survival, of negotiation. I suggest that our master plans too must be kept changing. In fact that's one of the great challenges and lovely attractions of city planning. It points out the need for an interdisciplinary approach to the problem of human settlements and also the need for being aware of the statistics, of the facts, of what is going on with people, in capital, in labor movements, and how to package and readjust, invent, rediscover the old, combine it with something new, hammer out some compromises, and then go ahead and cope with the situation and the rapid advance of invention and technology and population that we're all struggling with.

Finally I'd like a response to the issue of pessimism versus optimism. Do we feel—and I've heard this in the halls and corridors—a sense of doom, especially when we consider acid rain and the potential of nuclear warfare and man's inability to control the great powers that he has unleashed? Are the Panglossian optimists or the doomsayers reasonable? We all fall into these moods, depending upon whether we've succeeded in getting something through or not on a particular day.

The interesting thing to me about this conference is that even with all the problems we've heard about—the need to recycle money and to restructure the payout period of the debt level, the physical problems of cities, the problems of farmlands disappearing, the problems of the conflicting needs of the population—there seems to be a sense that we're again one world. Not only in terms of capital flow or economic resources, our common cultural heritage and future, but also in the sense that these problems that we all have together, with which we're struggling, trying to get some solutions to, give us the common sense of humanity.

Now let's hear from the moderators their reactions to their own particular day's chairing, and then we can swap some notions of what the conference has meant and what it can do, what we can take away in hopes of bettering our countries and our planning systems and ourselves.

Isaac Ofori: Monday we considered the human condition—basic needs and the land—looking at equity and growth implications of policies. In the *Boston Globe* this morning there is an editorial on housing for Boston, which is a settlement problem. The editorial drew attention to the problems facing ethnic and other minority groups in the satisfaction of the basic need for shelter in Boston. I have just been looking at the report on the seminar on the urban development policies focus on land management in Nagoya, Japan, last year. I quote the preamble to this report:

> Land is becoming an increasingly scarce resource for development, particularly in metropolitan areas in most countries ... Furthermore, skyrocketing land prices in urban areas make it imperative that urban development and land management policies are drawn up which will bring about the most efficient utilization of this scarce resource— namely land.

So, have we been doing anything useful this week, and particularly on Monday when I was moderator? My belief is that it has been a very useful week. We have shared ideas that focus attention on land. We have been looking at some of the operant dichotomies between uses of land. We have been looking, for example, at the question of whether in planning our land use policies we've put ourselves in straitjackets when it comes to the question of agriculture and urbanization. I remember Professor Taylor from London saying that once upon a time in England the policy was one of containment. Later on I chatted with him, and I said I agreed that once upon a time in Britain the idea was that agriculture was so holy that it should not be touched, and that the idea came from a book by Professor Stamps of London University, *The Land of Britain—Its Use and Misuse*. That sort of straitjacket thinking made it difficult for us to be properly oriented in apportioning land between agricultural uses and urban uses. Our discussions this week, I think, have thrown some more light on the place of agriculture and individual land use, and have also given us a bit of insight into the nature of urbanization. We have not attempted what one colleague calls benefit analysis of agricultural uses and urban uses. But the discussions somehow make me feel that we now see a large degree of complementarity between these uses.

I would not say that we have been very successful all around. In the area of housing I don't think we're very clear, apart from Dr. Shlomo Angel's paper at the education seminar on Wednesday on what their school at the Asian Institute of Technology in Bangkok has been doing about housing the poor. I don't think there has been much of a discussion of what type of housing policies we have to pursue in the satisfaction of the basic need of shelter. We know that housing is a consumer of this resource of land. It may be necessary to wait for some future deliberation on this subject.

Before I sit down I must say that I was particularly happy yesterday with the paper by Professor Strong. It brought home to me, and perhaps to others, that land policies have to be formulated with some sort of faith—faith in land as part of us and not as an object which can be played around with, without feelings towards it. I remember reading years ago reactions of some American Indians towards land. I was particularly happy that the Indians were looking religiously at land. Yesterday in a workshop I made the suggestion that in many of the African societies where we have communal tenures the whole idea of land use by the present generation is conditioned on the premise that we are but an infinitesimal proportion of those for whom the land resources are meant. I have a feeling that in many societies the living in their policies toward land are very selfish. They show little regard for what the many generations unborn may be doing after they have gone with the same resource. And—let's be honest about it—I think God closed shop years ago as far as making land.

To sum up, I would like to say that it has been a very rewarding week here, sharing ideas with colleagues and scholars in the field, getting to make new acquaintances. Let us hope that the debates about the evolution of land policies will continue to be kept alive and that before very long we shall have a chance again to sharpen our thinking on policies and policy formulation; have the chance to reexamine some of the things which we have done in the interim between this Congress and the next one. I would like to say that it has been extremely worthwhile.

Harold Dunkerley: My reactions are very immediate ones. Perhaps they tend to center a little bit more on some of the areas we didn't discuss in depth rather than on the ones we did. Let me first say that I think that there's an enormous richness of experience brought to this Congress, which is certainly one of its outstanding features. I think that the papers have been of excellent quality. But on the whole—and there are some remarkably good exceptions— we have been centering on the problems less than on the alternative policies which might be followed, the advantages and disadvantages of alternative policies.

On the day for which I was the moderator we had a very broad-brush approach. Perhaps what was emphasized more than anything else was the need to look at the land problems and the land policies at very different levels—the kinds of issues on which we had the excellent address from Lester Brown. Those kinds of issues are obviously ones which demand an international world forum. They need an awareness building up on an international scale. Many of the others are at much different levels, and show great variations between countries, down to the very local level. Perhaps there's an organizing possibility here. Perhaps in future congresses we could look at what is required at different levels.

In the program we were asked to look at such major issues as land price, land ownership, land use and productivity, and protection of desirable uses. These certainly are four aspects which go to the root of many of the things which we discussed during the week. Thinking about them in these last few minutes, it seemed to me that on the land prices, we have not gone very far toward discovering the causes of the increase in land prices, or what in fact these increases have been. It is very easy to look at specific parcels and see how the prices have moved. It is very difficult to get a broader view as to what is happening in land prices. Certainly many of the figures which are bandied about concerning prices increasing in a geometric progression would be quite impossible if that went on for more than a short while. Nobody anywhere would be able to afford any land, not even a square meter. How does the market work? The Lincoln Institute has done some excellent work in this field. Who are the actors? I think that perhaps we feel there's a need to center rather more on the mechanisms of the land markets and the differences in different places.

There is one question which came back to me many times during the course of the week. Why is it, if agricultural land is so scarce, and is becoming more scarce at a very rapid rate, that the price does not reflect this even more than it has in terms of the alternative uses, particularly in the urban field? Why is it that in fact this very vital agricultural land is being lost at the urban fringe to the extent it is, if it is so valuable? Does it have something to do with the price system between agricultural goods and urban goods? Are there biases?

On land ownership and tenure we were asked to consider at several stages if we are too much bemused by ownership. There are many different forms of constraints on the use of land. Do we need to consider this so much in terms of ownership, and get into a whole series of mystiques on this? Or should we be looking at what has occurred historically on regulating the rights of ownership so as to conform more to the public good? Bill Doebele's excellent paper on tenure, I think, relates to this question.

On land use and productivity, I think reference has already been made to the question of how we weigh the trade-offs. This enormous increase in demand for urban land reflects much higher productivity in urban areas in terms of national output in almost all the world, even in the core developing countries, even in the ones which we in the World Bank consider the poorest. More than half of national output is now produced in urban areas. There has been a drastic, dramatic change over the last few years; from 1960 to 1980 the proportion of national product from agriculture in these poorest countries dropped from 50 to 33 percent. It is still going on. How do we weigh these trade-offs? What are our techniques? What are the national policy implications from this?

From the standpoint of the work that we do in the World Bank, we are of course dealing with the Third World, and perhaps my bias is too much toward looking at the responses rather than the definition of the problem, for every project with which I deal involves urban land problems. Projects are held up by these problems. A large part of our time is taken up in discussing policies with the local authorities. During the course of the week, when I tried to think why it is that the urgency of the Third World situation is not somehow coming through, I began to wonder whether we shouldn't be thinking more in the terms in which people in the West were thinking in the last century, at the time when economics was largely about land. Do we, in fact, in our training and the kind of education we are offering to people from the Third World, neglect the area of taxation of the increase in land values? I can see no way in which the Third World cities are going to finance their urban expansion, the dwellings, the infrastructure, without managing to capture much, much more of the urban land price surpluses, the value surpluses created in part by the public expenditures and in part by the economic increase in incomes in the urban areas which this high productivity in the urban areas creates.

That takes me very briefly to the excellent session Wednesday on training. In fact, land, land policy, land taxation—all these things which used to be thought about, in England at any rate, in the last century, and here several generations ago—hardly received mention. The discussion tended to be on planning, but very little on teaching or education or higher education or the overall view of land policy, land problems. I think perhaps in future congresses, and in future consideration of what has come out of this Congress, this aspect of the response to land problems as they now appear in the Third World does deserve highlighting. We must keep to the topic of land, land policies, and separate it out a little more clearly from the more overall problems of how to get better planning in the wider sense.

William Lim: I'm going to base my comments on, first, the guidelines in the program; second, the session which I moderated yesterday morning; and third, on the very stimulating private conversations I have had with the participants here.

The first issue in the guidelines is land price. How can a government recover some of its cost through land taxation, especially in the Third World cities? In the process of development, landlords have been able to benefit a lot from the increase in land prices. Just to suggest the magnitude of the benefit landlords have been able to get—drawn from the very graphic and economically successful development experience of Singapore—in the last 20 years land prices in general have increased from 20 to 50 times. I think this is not unusual in other cities in the region, and perhaps elsewhere in the Third World. Obviously something has to be done in order to refinance public projects. Should not the benefit of the great investment and energy made by the community at large be returned eventually to the community?

In a free market economy, where we have a private sector and a public sector, as the land cost comes up in this manner, how is the government going to acquire land for a public purpose? I would submit quite strongly that in subsequent meetings we should discuss the question of land acquisition laws whereby the government acquires land from the public at a cost which is substantially below market rate, at an affordable price in the public interest, in order that the government can initiate meaningful, successful public programs. Also, how can measures that are actually implementable—a land tax in the form of a surplus or increment tax, whatever form it may take—be used, and in what way can they recapture the essential part of this benefit of profit from the landowners for the benefit of the community?

The second point is in relation to land ownership and tenure. The traditional concept of land is absolutely right, and it is really no longer the issue. I think we have a fair consensus here that most cities have various regulations governing how land can be developed: zoning, density, height control, and so on. Perhaps we should go one step further and look at landowners in the private sector in a market economy. They're only caretakers on behalf of the community, and their right has been given to them for a specific purpose, provided they utilize their facilities in response to the needs of the community. That point seems to be very well accepted. In the socialist countries, of course, the concept is a bit different. In a socialist economy, where certain people are permitted to have their own plots of land, in what way is this caretaker arrangement developed and defined? Perhaps this issue will be useful in subsequent meetings.

Regarding the third point—land use and productivity—I'd like to zero in on the question of density and intensity of development. This has been touched on a little bit by Jacques Kwak in his paper. The important thing is that, not only in the West but certainly in urban areas in the Third World, the more affluent class are demanding housing which is of too low a density, which means the land is used up and pretty soon everything else that goes with it. Of course every community is different, but I think we've got to try to find out what level of density—particularly in housing, and then subsequently in commercial and other areas—is socially, psychologically, and environmentally acceptable for the purpose of development. As we saw in the Amsterdam case and others, it is so easy, particularly in housing, to allow a lower density than a city can afford in terms of land. And acceptable density depends also on design. I would submit that very often this issue has not been discussed, although the architects tend to discuss it much more. I think in a conference like this we may have to make some definition of the ranges of intensity of development that are to be acceptable. That has a lot to do with the amount of land area that is needed for urban development.

The fourth point is the protection of desirable uses. I think the ethical approach is quite important, as mentioned in the paper by Professor Ann Strong. Public opinion changes over time, and certain things which were not quite acceptable—for example, parks and conservation areas—in many communities have now been accepted. So it is conceivable that if we say urban agriculture should be part of the land use allocation, then it can be acceptable. If not, then it will not be acceptable. However, I do have one reservation about using religious or communal groups as the sort of vehicle to get this done. From my scant knowledge of the United States, I think that perhaps most academics in the United States don't feel too happy about government action. But I think that in many other countries in the West, a community action, though desirable, may not necessarily be very effective. Perhaps in some instances a direct political action may be the more effective way. This is not to say that communal action should not play its role; but the relative importance of the roles could be reversed. So I think we have to be careful about how we define a desirable role for the public, which can be expressed by groups, or can be expressed by particular leadership, in terms of influencing public opinion toward certain ways of approaching land in other usage.

There are two other points which I will give very quickly in relation to the issue of achieving social justice and equity on the one hand, and talking about economic power on the other. Several comments have been made that seem to indicate that this is a sort of zero-sum game. This may be so, and sometimes it *is* so. But I would put it to you that it is not *always* so. We should look at the options quite carefully. Many planning actions can be taken which can achieve both social justice and economic objectives. But the time scale may be a little different. In other words, you may achieve social justice first and your economic objective later, or vice versa, but in a reasonably short period of time. Sometimes it can be simultaneous. But you can't achieve social justice without very much economic input. I'd like to suggest that in subsequent meetings you may want to look at case studies where planning action in relation to land and other planning will actually achieve both social justice and economic development simultaneously, or within a short period of time.

Last, I would like to make one observation. I feel a little uncomfortable about the optimism toward our future. The developed world feels so much the fact of war. The impact of technology, of satellites, of computers, of robots may be another way to look at how to solve problems. I'm not saying this is not going to happen. I'm saying that the optimistic environment, the intellectual environment, is not really apparent so much in the East or in the Third World. This is not the place to discuss who is right or wrong. But I'd like to express a caution on this—that technology can easily lead to a wider development gap. We talk about satellites, about computers, about robotics; this is exactly the kind of technological gap that is going to widen and make things much more difficult. I think we've got to look at the impact of this in relation to the overall context as well as what is going to happen to the cities and other areas in the Third World.

Mr. Haar: It would have been superfluous for me to introduce the moderators to you all, since you were under their benign influence on their particular days, but I should say a word or two about our next speaker. Earl Murphy is a professor at Ohio State and has long had an interest in property: the concepts of property, value, environmental law, especially as they have changed our thinking, or ought to change our thinking, if we're going to bring about a different pace of growth. He is also the president of the Ekistics Society, and so he brings quite a range of experience. I have asked him to talk about his reflections on the Congress and where we might move forward in the future, as individuals and as a group.

Earl Finbar Murphy: Many people in this room, including myself, will return home from this Congress and will be asked by an administrative superior, "What did you do; what did you learn; why did I sign the invoice that paid your way to go there?" I'm going to tell you what I'm going to tell my boss, and maybe it will help you when you talk to yours.

First of all, this Congress reinforced once again Joseph Schumpeter's great insight that sometime about 1770 there began a discourse in England and France about economic analysis, and this discourse has spread throughout the world. It didn't matter where anybody came from. It didn't matter what their discipline was. They were all part of that ongoing two-century discourse. Now, there may be somebody somewhere in the world who has an idea outside that discourse. I don't think there is, but if so, he didn't show up at this Congress. Because we focused on land, we actually covered a rather narrow range of the discourse. That's all right; you can't do everything in one congress.

What was implicit in all of the papers was the assumption that we are all operating under the definition of land that David Ricardo wrote in the 1820s: that land encompasses not just the physical substance upon which one stands but also the air and water and soil and biological life that is upon or across that land. Everything on, under, within the land. And we accept that.

We also went along with the practice that started about a decade ago of standing Ricardo on his head. Ricardo focused on the investment in land, the ability to produce money from land for consumption purposes—what we would today call the cash flow vehicle that land represents. Insofar as he was at all interested in air and water and biota, independent of their ability to produce cash, he called them free goods to be treated accordingly. And that was followed not just by the British classical economists Alfred Marshall and Stanley Jevons, but it was followed by Karl Marx. Insofar as Friedrich Engels tried to depart from it, he was never able to finish his book, and he died leaving it unfinished—his famous *Dialectic on Nature*. What has happened in the past decade is that we have begun to focus upon what to Ricardo were free goods, which we now realize are not free at all but which have a limitation, just like everything else that humanity has dealt with, and that air and water and biota are something that we need to give more concern to than we did at one time.

This has been an interesting shift, away from Ricardo and the capitalist thinkers of the nineteenth century back to Quesnay and the French physiocrats of the eighteenth century, who argued that all value came from land. Now they had a rather primitive definition of land, nothing as sophisticated as Ricardo's. And they had a rather primitive idea of what land produced. They focused upon its agricultural production. But still when we come back to this concern for air, water, biota, we are concerned with what Quesnay indirectly was concerned with. And so we found ourselves at this conference implicitly accepting the Ricardian definition but at the same time turning it inside out, or standing it upside down.

Also at this Congress we used the word *scarcity* a great deal—scarce resource, scarce land, scarce this, scarce that. But scarcity is one of those words that you have to define, and we didn't do it. Now, that's not our fault, because everyone who used the term *scarcity* had a definition. Unfortunately, the definitions are not necessarily compatible. Many people who talk about scarcity talk about a physical scarcity. But I think we have to understand, when we deal with land, that what we deal with is an economic scarcity. And that when we deal with land, we deal with hierarchies of land values that are determined in part by demographics, in part by culture, in part by the operation of the market. I think we need to do some more refined thinking on the subject of scarcity and the precise definition of it that we are employing. Once we know what we're saying, we may not agree with the way someone else uses the word. That's all right. At least we know what we're talking about.

The next point that I think is important to make concerns the discussion that grew out of the attempt to talk about tenure, ownership, usufruct of land. I think it would be very helpful to go to some of the old resource economists of half a century ago. One paper referred to them—Nathaniel Lichfield's. Those are men like S. V. Ciriacy Wantrup and Zimmerman, who focused not upon ownership, whether it be private or public or elective or individual, but upon what they call resource specificity. Why did ownership develop at all? Why did we not remain in some premarket situation? Because we needed to get a handle on nature. So we developed various concepts that enabled us to have resource specificity. It is for this reason that we are beginning to draw into the property system air and water. We're beginning to talk about establishing state registries in the trading of emission credits for air and water. Why? Because we want the resource specificity. We want to know, Where does the investment go? Where does the return come from? How do we locate the economic trade-off? We want to be able to quantify in some fungible term, such as cash, ideas which are otherwise not graspable, in which we are reduced, if you will pardon my using that verb, to the level of poetics. Poetry is beautiful, but poetry is ambiguous.

I also think we have to bear in mind that we had a couple of marvelous papers by elder scholars. I'm speaking particularly of the paper by Dr. Chang of Taiwan and the paper of Dr. Honjo. The wonderful thing about these papers is the fact that both men were talking about a world in which they had been trained to see certain problems. They had then moved into the world of action, and had applied certain solutions to these problems and had effectively cooperated with others in the solution of those problems, only to find that having solved those problems, they had created new ones. And they were turning to other people who will follow them in time, who will be the elder scholars of 2050, who will then use their knowledge and their work and their experience to solve the problems of Chang, Honjo, and others. It was a beautiful experience to watch the work of senior scholars, to see a summary of a life spent both vicariously in scholarship and actively in the field of action.

I was very much interested in the focus on soil conservation, water conservation, the actual physical tilling of the land. That's important, but at the same time we need also to focus on what all this is for. When we have a very interesting paper, as we had from Robbie Mupawose, the representative of the Ministry of Agriculture of Zimbabwe, who told us that the government pays 150 units for a certain quantity of grain which it then sells for 85 units in the urban market, that the government recognizes that a peasant has to work three to five hectares to produce in a year the cash income that a city worker receives as a minimum wage, then I think we get a great deal of insight into the extent to which soil conservation, water conservation, agronomy, or what have you, is going to be able to be engaged in on that particular land. We have to know what this land is being used for.

I was fascinated by all of the individual case studies that were presented to us. Perhaps we were overwhelmed by them, but on the other hand they were, I think, interesting, provocative. A speaker stands up and says, "Here is a plan. It's a beautiful plan. I'm going to show you some pictures. Well, ignore that structure there, it's rather bad. But the plan is very good." And you ask yourself, How do they get from this beautiful plan to that structure that we are told to ignore? Individual entrepreneurial or bureaucratic stupidity? I have come to the conclusion in my life that stupidity is structured. You have to focus upon it for institutional reasons. Mr. Lim said that many American scholars are antagonistic toward the present American government. I'm not. Because when it comes to land policy, trying to change the present American government is like trying to get a dinosaur to flick its tail from right to left or from left to right.

It's been a useful Congress. I think many of us when we return will have to explain to our superiors: I've learned a lot, but one of the things I've learned is I've got a lot of work to do. And then you can explain why they should make money available for this valuable research that you're about to engage in.

Mr. Haar: I think we've heard a very interesting group of reflections upon our experiences here. I know that your own reflections and your arguments with the speakers can be carried out under the tent and elsewhere. But the last point of Earl's reminds me there's not only the issue of what you will tell the man who can fire you or hire you or give you appropriations. There's also the question of what the Congress as a whole can do. What is its superior here? What kind of public opinion forum does it respond to?

I notice that we're beginning to ask, where has Keynes failed us? What do we do now in terms of the developing world? We have the World Bank, which lays out questions but then sort of retires quietly from the scene. The USAID works hard on these matters too, but its resources are limited. If this is a worldwide problem, and it is, is there some way that some formal research and implementation agenda can be developed? Can we work directly through a joint venture system to recognize the economic changes involving land?

Here is an example. Merrill Lynch, for its simple purposes, has been able to start a new system of taking mortgages, packaging them, and then using all its customs men to sell the securities of mortgages the way they sell stock. In this fashion they get their commissions and expand, and are in a way substituting for the savings and loan associations that in the changed economy and the changed consumer patterns of desired investment are no longer going to be able to be the sources of real estate capital, at least in the United States. Well, how do we, in this planning group, this housing group, in the public sector—how can we organize so that we recognize these new trends, these new economic forces, these new population trends? How can we do that in a way that we can get some funds? Theory is fine, but you still need some bread to keep it moving. To deal with it on a global basis, to do the kind of research on a few primary questions and then go back to the decision makers and to the public—that's what we're going to be dealing with this afternoon, and among ourselves as well.

Chapter 15

Panel of Specialists

William Doebele, Guillermo Geisse, Shlomo Angel, Isaac Ofori,
Ann Strong, Nathaniel Lichfield, Dan Darin, Sein Lin, Vincent
Renard, Charles Haar, and Peter Kimm

William Doebele: In going over the roster of this conference I counted no fewer than 44 countries represented here this week. That number and the diversity of the people who are here inevitably reminded me of a story—a story which perhaps some of you have heard, but it bears repeating, I think—of the Texan who is visiting a small village in India. In the course of his conversation with one of the villagers he asks, "Could you show me your farm?" The Indian rather proudly takes him to the outskirts and says, "My land runs to that tree, then it goes over to the large bush, to the wall, and then back to the house again." Then to be polite the Indian says, "Would you kindly tell me what is the size of your farm in Texas?" The Texan says, "I'm sure you won't even be able to comprehend this, but if I get up in the morning when the sun is rising, get into my car, drive all day long until the sun is setting, I still will not have come to the other side of my property." And the Indian smiles and says, "Oh, I can comprehend that. We have cars like that in India, too."

I think that story illustrates not only the tremendous diversity and distribution of land resources on this planet but also the enormous difficulty when talking about something as culturally defined as land of being able even to understand the problem in the same terms. The context, the baggage of tradition and conceptions that go with land has such connotations that it is very difficult to make the jump of imagination and conceive of how other people discuss it. I hope that, if nothing else has come out of this conference, mixing together such an international group has helped to increase that communication. I think we must always keep in mind that the very words *land* and *land rights* have totally different contexts, and it is very easy for conversations to cross when we use the same words but mean something very different.

With reference to the conference itself, during the last few years I've had a rather Panglossian dream, or one might say a fantasy, of someday having a conference which would be limited to only the presentation of solutions, not the descriptions of problems. No paper would be accepted without presenting an answer. No speech could be given unless it described something that worked rather than something that was having infinite problems. We all know that there are no perfect solutions. No one expects that. But there are directions of hope and possibility, and I think sometimes at these meetings we get so involved with our frustrations and problems that we overlook the things that can be done. In any case, I intend to project my Panglossian fantasy on this part of the conference, and I'm suggesting the following format.

I have asked each one of the panelists to think of not less than one, nor more than two, positive ideas, solutions, answers, or at least directions of hope and possibility, and to present them in a very few minutes to you. I would also like to propose, when we do open the discussion from the floor, that you shift gears mentally to look into your experience and your reactions to this conference, and share with us not additional problems and difficulties, not more examples of man's greed, shortsightedness, and all the other problems we deal with, but rather things that you know from your own life and work that are in fact working. Let's spend these last moments talking about successes. Even though they may be partial, imperfect, temporary, at least they're something we can all take back; and indeed it may even help, as Mr. Murphy suggests, in making a presentation to our respective superiors.

I'd like to start by giving two examples. To save time I'll speak in very simplistic terms and talk only about urban land, not about agricultural and forest land. I'd like to suggest that the problem of urban land is most fundamentally the problem of our failure almost everywhere to recover the socially created increments in value that occur with urbanization. The failure to recover these socially created values has been the thing that has made land this unique investment vehicle that we see in almost all countries and has resulted in these extraordinarily high prices of land compared to all other commodities. On the other hand, our failure to do anything about the collection of socially created value has denied to governments the resources necessary to provide adequate services, resulting, as we all know, in the absolutely degrading conditions of life which exist in the slums of every city in developing countries.

As Mr. Dunkerley suggested this morning, it may be that, unless we find ways of recovering this socially created value there will be no real possibility of cities in developing countries ever being able to provide a reasonable and decent level of services to their populations. But there are elements of hope in this. Some of you will not be surprised if I suggest that one element of hope is land readjustment, a technique which is technically complex but I think potentially very effective in dealing with this problem for a number of reasons that I won't go into here. It is in a sense a sophisticated technique of a joint venture between the private and public sectors in which the profits of development are shared. Furthermore, it is a device which is now in a state of positive evolution. Formerly it was used only to collect enough money to install services. Now in South Korea there are major experiments going on for the first time using land readjustment as a vehicle for recovering even more of this increment and using it in order to directly subsidize land and housing for the poor. A few years ago land readjustment was limited to the five countries that have traditionally been practicing it [Australia, Japan, Korea, Taiwan, West Germany]. Today it is being talked about seriously in a number of countries in Asia and Latin America, and my own feeling is that it will become quite an important tool in the next few years. Mexico City is just now carrying on a massive and effective program for real property taxation—probably the first time that has occurred in Mexican history—which has a great potential, I think, as it becomes established to deal with this problem. The Philippines is working on substantially increasing and revising their taxation structure. A few years ago South Korea passed a capital gains tax on land transactions which was moderately successful in dampening the level of increases in land prices there. And half a dozen other countries at least are considering substantial revisions in their tax programs. In 1969 and 1974 Japan completely restructured its land management system and was fairly successful in stopping what had been an almost runaway increase in land prices in that country. And at least one other major country is now also considering looking at all of its institutions that deal with land and trying to restructure them as the Japanese did. There are many other new approaches to the recovery of socially produced value of land which

I won't go into now, but I think it's something that is hopeful. There's a lot to be done, but things are going on.

The second direction of hope that I see is a growth in interest in the monitoring and evaluation of land policies. Bureaucracies, as you all know, universally oppose evaluation. If a project is evaluated, and the evaluation finds that the project has been a good one, the reaction is, "Well, that's what you're paid to do. So what?" If, on the other hand, the evaluation shows that there have been problems with the project, which is very often the case, the result can be that the bureaucracy will lose status, money, or even personnel. So it's a no-win situation, and every sensible bureaucrat instinctively and intuitively avoids ever going back to projects once the ribbon has been cut and the project is underway, because he or she has everything to lose and very little to gain by careful evaluation. And yet, if we are ever going to do anything in land policy, obviously we have to be rigorous in understanding what in fact is happening.

We're seeing some serious attempts to change this now. The World Bank in particular, which is the largest institution operating in this field, has installed an intelligently conceived and comprehensive program of monitoring an evaluation of all of its land and urban projects. Not only as to the numbers—whether so many units were built or so many hectares were serviced—but getting into the much more subtle issues of social impact and distributional effects on the populations involved. We are also seeing now what I might call a small explosion in the academic concern for the evaluation of what is being done in the urban land and housing field, a much better quality of writing, an approach which is much more pragmatic and less theoretical, and the development of a body of literature which is much more useful. Part of that, incidentally, can be found in the book [Land for Housing the Poor, Singapore: Select Books] that was edited in part by Shlomo Angel.

As a result of all this, we are beginning to learn some extremely interesting things about land in general, and in particular about the effect of land policies and land tenure on human behavior, on poverty, and on social mobility. The things that I have mentioned are not dramatic breakthroughs. They are not landing a man on the moon. But they are, I submit, significant and hopeful trends in dealing with what to me are two central issues in this field—the recovery of socially created value and the establishment of feedback mechanisms, which, in the end, are the only ways in which we can improve any solution that we propose in the area of land policies.

Now I will turn the discussion over to our panelists.

Guillermo Geisse: I'll try to follow your instruction to present just one solution. I am glad that there are eight of us here, because I really think that there is no one solution to land development problems. Besides that, solutions cannot be expected to be technical alone.

There is a variety of possible solutions, and their effectiveness depends upon the existence of concrete social forces willing to carry them out either by negotiation and in alliance with others, or by imposing them on other social agents. If we Third World planners want to improve our effectiveness, we will have to, first, have a better understanding of the overall political structures and political practices within which planning takes place, and second, reexamine current land development objectives in the light of the interest that specific social agents and institutions may have in adopting them, and not their ability to achieve them.

Latin American history has demonstrated that the main actors of change in land development processes are not the technical experts or planners but the people individually or organized in social classes or groups. Now, Third World planners have to face the situation in which land use patterns of development are to a great extent the result of the coexistence of two different social strategies centering on land. For some social agents—those within the economic demand for housing—land is a main source of wealth. For the others land is a means of survival. Land prices are the bone of contention between the two groups. Rising prices are essential for the realization of land rents but at the same time the main obstacle impeding the access of the poor to this basic resource. The poor happen to constitute the majority of the population in Latin America and Third World countries, and they are the politically weakest of all social agents. Planners in Latin America have demonstrated a sort of social commitment to the poor. Their access to land is considered essential for their integration into the modern sector of society. However, there is an implicit assumption that this is a mere technical matter which is external to the poor themselves. On the basis of this assumption, planners operate in two different though complementary manners, first, by appealing to the minority that holds most of the wealth, and very often the land, for the release of a part of it on the grounds of moral principles or out of fear of political instability; and second, by lowering land development standards in order to match demand levels of the low-income groups.

The first strategy has rarely worked. I don't know of any case in Latin America in which the upper classes gave up part of their wealth because of merely moral principles or, for instance, because they accepted that the unique characteristics of land justified the recapturing of land value increments by the state.

The second strategy has not worked so far. During the recent past the income of the poor has increased far less than the price of land and the price of the building materials. One solution, in my opinion, lies with income redistribution. And redistribution is a question of power. It is something that cannot be achieved by merely technical recommendations. This is not the power to make a socialist revolution, but to make a more democratic society which includes (1) participation of the poor in the decision-making process, which is therefore a political aspect; and (2) making the land market work also for the poor. So I am talking about democratic society in the best tradition of this country.

On an individual basis, the poor have not been able to improve their position, either politically or in the marketplace. Planners could contribute to this goal by assisting in the strengthening of local organizations centered on a land development process. I should say that planners could do much in this regard. Land and housing should be seen not as an end in itself but as a way for the poor to gain bargaining power so they can make their demands to the state as other social groups do. Also, only on the basis of local horizontal cooperation, in other words cooperation among the poor, can they obtain advantages of scale in land acquisition and land improvement that so far have also been a privilege reserved for those for whom land is a means of wealth.

Shlomo Angel: In the short time allotted to me I would like to produce the two ideas that Bill asked for. The first good piece of news is that we are beginning to gain an understanding of how the poor gain access to land in urban areas and the changes that are happening in the process of gaining such access to land by the poor and what we have to do to accommodate these changes.

Let me just elaborate on this a little bit—and this is the main thesis in the book [Land for Housing the Poor] that we just published on the subject. In the recent past, in the last 30 or 40 years, the poor have relied on informal access to urban land. This was thought of as squatting and forming slums. Now we can see that there is actually a wide variety of institutions and social agents that are acting responsibly to provide for the poor, to supply land for the poor in a variety of ways. Whether these are the quasilegal land subdivisions of Latin America, or the organized invasions or the land rental systems in a variety of Asian cities, or different forms of negotiating for land by entrepreneurs, what we find is that a set of institutions has developed during this period of rapid organization to make cheap land available to the poor, but not with the right kind of services, and not necessarily in accordance with the law. We are beginning to understand how these agents operate. And because we're beginning to understand a great variety of operations, we can start to think about the kinds of interventions that are necessary to help those agents, on the one hand, to continue to supply land for the poor, and on the other, to direct and regulate them in line with social interests at large.

Let me mention at this point that one of the difficulties is that a lot of possibilities for the appropriation of urban lands by these social agents for the poor are closing down or changing in character. This is something that we have to worry about. Many of the possibilities for squatting are no longer there. Many of the possibilities for land invasion are no longer there. Many governments have clamped down on informal acquisition or appropriation of land. At the same time there's another trend, and that is that commercial companies have gotten much better control of the land system surrounding urban areas than before. So what we are seeing is the squeezing of the land available for the poor by the informal sector, resulting also in increases in the price of informal land and the reduction of possibilities. So, there is a limit to what we can expect from tenure-granting programs on existing informal settlements, and it is likely that their supply in the future is going to be reduced.

The second point is an amplification of what Bill was saying—that previous solutions to housing problems of the poor are not working. Public housing construction is not working, and the small sites and services projects that we have still fall far short of the quantities that are necessary. The only possibility in the future is to shift housing efforts into land development efforts, incorporating housing as part of larger schemes so that if we want to build housing we don't just acquire the land that's necessary for housing the poor; maybe we acquire ten or 20 times the amount of that land and use the revenues that are generated in this process to recover the costs of housing the poor.

Finally, let me suggest that this process can also apply in the built-up areas of cities where we already have slums and squatter settlements. The example I want to mention concerns what we call land sharing. Land that is in squatter or slum occupation is divided in two. The better part is used for commercial development, and the remainder for rehousing people at higher density on that land. We have two examples, one already effectually happening in Karachi, and the other one in the process of being started in Bangkok. So this idea of using development gains actively—changing the role of government from the role of the controller of land development to the role of participant in land management and development—is the only hope that we have for creating systems for housing the poor on a cost-recoverable basis.

Isaac Ofori: What I'm going to think aloud on is not yet a solution. It's an approach. If we listen to the news coming from Africa, as far as governments and constitution making are concerned, what we shall find, perhaps strange to many of us, is that more and more governments in Africa, as they make their constitutions, have entrenched land in the constitutions. Normally they would say that the land of Ghana is to be held by the president in trust for the people of Ghana. Or they would go ahead to create setting organs, as in the case of Ghana a land commission, to hold this land in trust for the people. Now, this may sound very strange to anybody brought up on Jeffersonian principles of democracy. But I'd like to suggest why governments in Africa have found it necessary to entrench site clauses on land in their constitutions.

I think the first reason might be that there is a sense of political cohesion in all these countries. Many of them, almost all of them, had tribal proliferations during colonial times. These tribal proliferations didn't really matter, because the metropolitan power was in charge. But as soon as the metropolitan power left, these tribal divisions and proliferations began to make themselves known and seen. It has become a problem for governments to give a nation the political cohesion it needs if the land of Ghana, or the land of Liberia, is to be thought of as belonging to the nation rather than to any particular tribe.

When we talk of some of the problems of urbanization today, one of the big problems is how to prevent absolutism in the use of land. How can we prevent those who are the landlords in the urban areas from holding those of us who are landless to ransom? It is believed that when governments step in and try to at least notionally own the land for and on behalf of the people, this absolutism on the part of landowners no longer presents problems. Also, in terms of another problem of urbanization—what we call reconciling the individual's gain vis-à-vis social investment, which again is a question of unearned increment—it is believed that when governments do take a more active role in shaping land policies, these sorts of problems can be resolved.

Now, I think it is important to recognize that as far as we in

Africa are concerned, the debate should not center so much on land ownership. We think the moment you begin to look critically at land ownership—that is, the movement from communal ownership to individual ownership—there is going to be a lot of political and social upheaval. But then having said that, the question also arises whether governments are the best authority for determining in all circumstances the use of land. I'm afraid the experience of governments dictating the use of land has not been extremely satisfactory. This suggests to me that while we are trying in Africa to separate the notion of ownership from the notion of usufruct, we have yet to devise proper ways of using our land.

I have shared these thoughts with you because I believe that when we read our newspapers and hear news of Africa, it's so far away that many of us really cannot comprehend what is happening. If this little explanation, not of solutions but approaches, can go some way toward making us wiser as we read our newspapers, or more sympathetic, I think we will have achieved something.

Ann Strong: I have two widely different things to suggest. First, since people asked for pragmatic suggestions, I thought I would tell you about a report which some of you might find useful. Bob Coughlin at Penn and I worked for the Forest Service on a report which we've called "Planning As If Vegetation Really Mattered." It is a guide for small local governments which don't have access to or money for computers, satellites, or things of that sort, to take grid squares, pens and pencils, and rather rudimentary maps, and figure out what the erosion rates will be for different soils in their communities, what the yield will be from trees and crops, what people think of the land in terms of its amenity value, and what the wildlife values are. These are the four factors we tried to provide a way of quantifying, simply and by hand, so that one can then project population for the community, lay it out on the grid square, and project, in relation to the total value of the area for vegetation, what the loss of value will be in relation to where the urban population is located. We applied this technique to a small municipality between Wilmington and Philadelphia, and—given the figures which we used, which certainly one can question, but at least they provide a starting point—we were able to demonstrate that it made a very significant difference where the future population was located in terms of vegetation values.

Point two has to do with camels. I know we haven't focused on population growth here, but certainly it has been an underlying concern to most of us. I have noted that many animals have somehow learned to limit their rates of reproduction as food pressures grow. For those of you who are ornithologists, it's my understanding that raptors, particularly, will go from egg clutches of four down to one or none in periods of food scarcity. We know that elephants manage to lengthen gestation. And I recently read in a magazine on African wildlife an article which said that camels also can alter their fertility so that they produce fewer camels in times of food scarcity. I am really very serious in suggesting that animal biology may have a great deal to teach us, and I am not aware that we have made a very wide exploration of how these pressures work and exactly what the reproductive mechanism does in response to them. I'm not sure if we have anyone present who is a population biologist, but my positive suggestion is that we should look into this through some of our colleagues.

Mr. Doebele: As you see, no subject is too broad for this international Congress.

Nathaniel Lichfield: I'm departing from Bill's instruction, with his agreement, because I want to go back to the two questions in the program. Are there new ways of handling these problems? What is the most creative thinking on the future of these issues?

The most creative thinking on the future of these issues, I would suggest, is in some of the things that have come through this week —if I might put it in terms of the word used by Ann Strong in her paper, the *holistic* nature of what we're about. We've seen that when we're talking about land as a natural resource, we're talking about the whole planet. We're talking about the long term. We're talking about a subject which is a resource, a commodity, an institution. That's a big subject; and we've got to think in fundamental terms about a new concept. The other new thing that comes out, again linking to what Ann said, is the relationships. I'm going to adapt what she said, with her permission, in the following way. I think man has a relationship with himself which you can summarize in the ethic. I think it starts within each of us to have an ethical attitude toward the land; certainly to our neighbors, which is enshrined in the common law; certainly to our ancestors, to our own children, which has been so eloquently emphasized by Isaac Ofori; certainly to our local communities, which comes up in the new idea of community control in Bill Doebele's paper; certainly to the sovereign state of which we're members, as opposed to members of the neighborhood and the sovereign states within the world. So we've got that on our doorstep. And I don't see how we can tackle these issues without finding new tools and new methods.

Now I come to another method which is not new. It comes out of Ebenezer Howard. Let's forget land rent. Let's think of rent and taxes on land—rent and rates as he put it, local taxes—as one product of the soil. Let's finance the city out of that product. The question arises, then, is this the best way, the most equitable way of financing community services, because why should the product of an individual plot give you the right answer for financing community services spread all over? So it comes down to my final point. I do think if we're going to find the right methods, we've got to develop the new approaches. Here I go back to the brilliant talk this morning of Earl Murphy. We've got to go back to the classics. They said a lot of things that we're forgetting. But it's not sufficient to go to Ricardo and so on. We've got to find our own means of socioeconomic political evaluation to influence decision making. We've got to build the tools to judge the methods in relation to the perspective. That, I think, in the end, is going to give us the payoff.

I make one final concrete suggestion. I'm a keen student of what goes on in this country—the programs and policies and activities. Very often I look at what's being done in practice, and I say this doesn't match up with what one assumes to be the ethic of this most capitalist-individualistic of countries. And it doesn't. What this means, in effect, is that people finding practical solutions to problems and getting them accepted by politicians is a thing of its own. If you can get—let's call it the right solution for the moment—if you can get that into practice without too much regard for the ethics and the ideology of the society you're supposed to be living in, if we as professionals, as academics, as practitioners can find what we think is the right solution for society according to these tests in terms of the long-term perspective, I think we can transform the society. The society is transformed not so much in the political ideologies and the speeches and the programs that are never followed; society is transformed by action. Guillermo Geisse has given us one indication of action in Latin America. I'm not suggesting that for other countries. But action in the sense of getting right solutions—right, in our terms, of the long-term perspective—and getting these done, and improved, and modified, and evaluated—I think this can transform society for the long-term perspective.

Dan Darin: In 1948, during a period of cease-fire in the Israeli War for Independence, one of the underground tried to smuggle a boat loaded with armaments into Israel. That was against the rules of the cease-fire, and the provisional government was afraid that the underground was going to use the armaments to try to take power.

So Ben Gurion, who was the prime minister, gave the order to shoot down the *Altalena*, which was the name of the boat. Ever since, whenever there is a critical debate in the Knesset, whoever proposes a very debatable motion starts to explain it, and when he gets to the critical point he mentions the *Altalena*. And immediately the House is broken in half; the opposition attacks the government, the government answers back, all in regard to who is to be blamed for the *Altalena*. By that time, the issue at hand has been long forgotten, and when they come to the vote, the motion passes unnoticed.

I am afraid the issue of land ownership, whether it is public, private, communal, or tribal, serves the same purpose—the purpose of being a red herring. I'm going to speak about the irrelevancy of that issue to the problem of land planning today.

For over a hundred years the two major ideologies—capitalism and socialism—have been at each other's throats as to which of the two is the better solution for achieving equity and efficiency. For a while, followers of both thought that each could attain both. At a later stage, the market economy was associated with efficiency and the centrally planned economies with equity. At present, we know that the market mechanism is neither equitable nor efficient, and the so-called socialist regimes are neither efficient nor equitable. I dare propose that in land policy circles, at least, we should rid ourselves of that argument completely, and set aside the issue of ownership. Instead, we should seek and analyze pragmatically the issues at hand by defining the problems, setting the goals, and selecting the appropriate measures. I will give some examples.

If the problem is the concentration of plus values in the hands of landowners rather than with the society which has created them, maybe instead of expropriation of the land we can use the land tax—50, 70, 100 percent land tax—to collect this plus value. If the problem is, however, the unorganized development of the city and the lack of public finance to invest in the infrastructure, and the goal defined is to amend the situation, then maybe we can use the land readjustment advocated by Bill Doebele—and we know how successful it can be. If the issue is to secure access to the land for the urban poor, instead of expropriating the land, which usually creates conflict among the ruling classes, to which the landowners belong, maybe we could use some sort of transfer of development rights, which Professor Haar has written about. Maybe it's about time society started separating the right of ownership of land from the right to develop it.

Specifically, there are three tools that are somehow new and have all been identified recently, say in the last three or four years. I'm sure that other tools can be developed to answer specific issues. In brief, instead of going through the wall—the wall being the ownership issue—I suggest that we concentrate on finding ways of going around the wall. Maybe it's time to admit that even by imposing revolutionary policies we do not necessarily shorten the process or create a more equitable and efficient solution. Maybe by the use of evolutionary processes and mediating between all the actors involved to get them to agree, we might save time and get to a better environment, even though it probably will not be the best environment.

The last point is that, despite the oneness of the world and its problems, I would suggest that the issue be tackled on a local scale, for measures accepted in one country will be rejected in another, and an outsider with his internationally accepted description of a problem may be wrongly interpreted within the country where he is trying to solve it. Just as when the World Bank expert came to Israel and asked a cab driver to take him to the place where the Israelis go to cry, pray, and ask for redemption, twenty minutes later he found himself in front of the income tax bureau.

Sein Lin: I'm going to tell one anecdote, relate two problems, and give three solutions—all in the five minutes allotted to me. As a man was traveling in a train, he was tearing up newspapers and throwing them through the window onto the rails. When asked why he was doing that he said, "To prevent the elephants from coming onto the rails." His companion said, "But there are no elephants." The traveler said, "See! It works." The moral of the story is that we should be sure that our problems are real and not imaginary.

I will touch upon a very specific issue which runs the gamut from basic land tenure and ownership to land prices. I'm speaking in the context of Asia, so this problem and the approaches or the options may not apply to other countries. In matters of land distribution, which is a basic land tenure reform, many countries are just getting their feet wet; there are other countries which are in midstream; and there are countries which have already gotten to the other side of the river. What are their problems? Could the problems which are being faced by the people who have gotten to the other side of the stream be a lesson to those who are just getting their feet wet? As a result of urbanization we talk about spiraling increases in land values. When the land distribution programs took place, every one of the tillers was supposed to be an owner—an owner, mind you, not an owner in trusteeship. When you start a land distribution program and it ends up with a tenant becoming a steward for landownership, what would be the reaction on the part of the tenant? This is one problem.

In some countries which have had this land distribution program, urbanization has begun to encroach on prime agricultural land. Some governments have come up with a law or an executive order saying that prime agricultural land cannot be converted for development purposes. The problem then is in defining what prime agricultural land is. There are different grades and different classifications. If, for example, grade one through grade ten is deemed prime agricultural land, then the owner of eleventh-grade land gets a tremendous benefit by being allowed to convert it, to sell his land to the developers. So, arbitrarily, owners of better grades of land will suffer, because they are prevented from converting their resource.

There are several possible courses of action. One is preferential taxation. Transferable development rights, whereby a farmer who seems to have been penalized or who perceives that he was penalized has the benefit of the transferred development rights elsewhere, is another. The third is to leave the matter to the market system. Out of these choices, which one is the extreme middle, which Arlo Woolery mentioned at the beginning of this Congress? I suggest to you that these are the options. They are taking place. This does not only involve the problem of equity between the small landowners or the new tenant farmer and another tenant farmer, but also between the big landowners and the small landowners.

So these are the problems in land policy matters which are confronting countries after land reform. Those who are in the middle of the stream are beginning to feel them. For those who are just getting their feet wet, the question is whether they should anticipate these kinds of land policy problems, and how. What is the extreme middle between the free market system, or other devices like transferable development rights, and the extreme of the government edict declaring that prime agricultural land is not convertible, period? I leave it to you gentlemen to find the extreme middle.

Vincent Renard: It is a difficult task for me to talk about land problems, being a statistician and economist. First there are lies, second there are major lies, and third, statistics. And, as I heard yesterday, economists are people who know everything about prices but nothing about values. But I'll try.

This morning Nat Lichfield proposed some interesting insights in the direction of planning economies and incentives. I would like to go a little further in this direction. The idea I suggest is that a planner has to cope adequately with economics in order to have plans implemented. The only way to succeed in doing that is to reconcile prices and values when drawing up a plan. By values I mean societal values in the broadest sense, because I think if you throw economics out the window, it appears again through the back door. Two examples may help to clarify this statement.

The first is about land readjustment. That is not only a device for European countries but, as I heard in the last four days, in many developing countries as well. It looks promising where land patterns are too complicated to achieve some satisfactory developments. Any land readjustment process has to integrate the shift in land values resulting from future allocations of land. And some device has to be designed in order to redistribute land value increments resulting from the future allowed use of land. Distributing development rights through a local plan at the same time the land readjustment is implemented seems to be the most efficient tool to implement this. It is quite complicated, because you have to do it simultaneously, but this seems a precondition for good implementation. Not taking into account this economic dimension of a plan may, and often does, transform it into a purely academic exercise, supplying jobs for planners, which may be an excellent idea, but allowing no real impact on the development process.

Another illustration is the problem of funding the servicing cost and its allocation among landowners, developers, and taxpayers. Knowing that utilities' infrastructures are a major source of land value increments raises the very acute problem of linking equity and efficiency in urban planning. In this respect, equity among landowners is a prerequisite for efficient implementation of planning.

If I try to make a comparison between this Congress and the one of 1980, it looks to me as if there is growing skepticism about the efficiency of usual land planning. I suggest that a major advance would be to improve the link between prices and values, defining in this way the highest and best use of any piece of land, which is a prerequisite for satisfactory implementation of any plan. In the same direction, I would add that law should be only a tool and never a purpose by itself. I've been impressed for many years and in many different countries, especially Germany, France, and Italy, by the growth of, let's say, antieconomic legislation that has not helped planning at all but, just the opposite, has been rather a break in planning implementation. Here again, we enjoy the fact that this development supplies jobs for lawyers, but an improvement of the integration of economics in land law appears to be desperately needed.

A final remark could be added about improving consistency between land taxation and land planning. I deeply agree with what Dan Darin said to us some minutes ago, that any land tax has many different and sometimes contradictory objectives: raising revenue, minimizing unequal distribution of wealth and incomes, providing an incentive for landowners to use land according to local plans. But we have to recognize that it is not possible to reach these three objectives at the same time. Making explicit statements of the priorities in designing any land taxation system is always better than leaving shadow prices or the black market to achieve market regulations. Once again, these efforts may help to improve the convergence between prices and values. Maybe I've been too heavily educated through Cartesian thought, but I am afraid, as far as planning goes, that the way from Kafka to Descartes is still a long one.

Charles Haar: I too want to start with an anecdote which illustrates some of the problems of dealing with land prices and land values. A firm of developers was negotiating for the purchase of a large shopping center. One partner called the home office partner and said, "I have good news and bad news. The good news is that on the negotiations for the shopping center the seller has dropped his asking price from $13.5 million to $11.7 million." The home office partner said, "That's marvelous. What could be the bad news?" "He wants $100 more cash." That leads us to the statement that one person's unearned value is another person's "motherhood."

The first proposition I would put forth for terms of instrumentality deals simply with a technical device, and that is a land registration system. I think that the great need in many developing countries, including the United States, is for some effective type of registration system so that one can always know where title is and thus get the commercial market moving. We've read about the great achievements in Taiwan in this way; and the presence of the computer and the lack of a vested interest in the old-fashioned title system means that it's possible for societies to take a leap ahead. Not to have to go through the long, arduous method that we have in the United States of recording every document and doing title searches and looking for title perfecting and marketable title acts. You can leap ahead to the next phase, to the neotechnic phase of industrial development and by computerizing, at least in the more populated centers, begin to develop a system for land titles.

I recall when I was in Jakarta the general counsel to Westinghouse was complaining that he had purchased a factory in Jakarta but at the last minute two people from the village appeared with the *shamat*, who is their unofficial justice, and laid claim to the piece of land where the turbine was, saying they had the real title to it. It turned out that they actually did, but nobody had looked through some of the adverse prescription rules. He said he never again would buy land in this kind of situation. Computerization would avoid this type of thing, and would also make available credit and mortgages. It is not difficult to do, with some technical help. I think it would be useful as well for the marriage that we've been hearing about between land taxation and land titles. Once you computerize, you will also be able to parcelize for purposes of property tax assessment, and be able to keep up to date whenever there's a sale or a reevaluation of a property. So this seems to be an easy solution and one that ought to be done. Incidentally, it also has the advantage of bringing in the private sector in those societies that are looking for joint venture. You can do this through the public computer, or you can bring in perhaps a group of lawyers or real estate developers or brokers and let them form some kind of combine, so that you have the private sector involved in the transaction, and you can have a devolution to private capital in that sense.

In these days of diversification, when we read *Barron's Weekly* or the *Asian Wall Street Journal*, we know we're supposed to diversify. Andrew Carnegie had a different philosophy. He said, simply, put all your eggs in one basket and watch that basket. But I'm not so sure.

I want to make one other suggestion that relates to infrastructure. Some kind of institution, depending on the city, the government— whether it's a federalist form of government or a nationalist form with a relation to the local government—I think an urban development bank, a bank that would either finance itself in those situations through tax exemptions or borrowing from abroad, which would then lay the foundation for urban infrastructure by financing it in the form of a city program, would result in an efficient corporation outside the usual mold, and would have the great advantage of probably getting around some of the civil service and patronage issues that are dominant in many societies. The corporation, with separate financing and working through the infrastructure, would be able to deal with a problem and its solutions in a way that would meet many needs. Tied in with that, of course, is the recapture of land value, which seems to capture the imagination of academics and bearded prophets.

I'm coming back to the joint venture theory which I think we have to develop still further. When HUD was giving money—$85 million a year—to BART, which is the underground subway system in San Francisco, Congress was giving the executive branch a rough time, asking why the money was going to San Francisco, when the implicit question was, "Why not give it to my district?" We had to get planners in to prove that the land market values around those subway stations were enormous and that these values had increased as a result of the public expenditure for the subway system. I think this is something that hits the average person as being fair. People don't quite feel that inflation or other kinds of demand, or shrewd speculative ventures are subject to public recapture, I suspect. But if it's a direct result of the creation of a subway system, or creation of some other public utility which requires grand expenditures, then recapturing the value at the edges of the land which is benefited by that public improvement, is a workable project, and will tie in with this infrastructure bank.

Mr. Doebele: Just for the record, I think that it might be interesting to note to the conference that the South Korean government apparently has read Charles's writing on the urban development bank, because they have created the Korean Land Development Corporation, which carries out in a very well developed and in fact powerful form the kinds of ideas that Charles has been suggesting for many years in this area. Indeed some of you may have seen the interesting film on that corporation shown a few days ago as part of the conference.

Peter Kimm: One of the realities of speaking last is that the people who spoke before you have covered every idea that one can possibly imagine. They also have set a pattern of how one should make a five-minute speech, and I'm happy to follow the pattern. That is, we'll have an anecdote, some observations from me, and then a concrete suggestion.

The United States Agency for International Development has ongoing shelter programs in some 50 developing countries, and I'd like to say that we have made every mistake that one can possibly make. That probably isn't really true, because some of the things we're now doing may prove to be mistakes in the future. The story I will tell was told to me by someone who was present during the attempt to negotiate a settlement to the Vietnam War. At the end of a day's negotiations, the participants retreated to the home of a senior French official for dinner, and at the end of dinner the French official, in order to change the subject and to improve the intellectual tone of the conversation, said, "I'd like everybody at the table to speak to the question of the impact of the French Revolution on human history." The first person he gave the floor to was Henry Kissinger. Mr. Kissinger was not only a professor of history, he was a professor of history at Harvard, so he was able to elaborate without any difficulty upon the Mexican Revolution, the rise of the masses, and the various other impacts of the French Revolution. The second speaker was the Chinese ambassador, who, after some thought, said, "It's too soon to say."

With that frame of mind, I would like to take a look at the century in which we are living, in particular the period since the Second World War, and especially the most recent years. I think that any objective observer would conclude that what has been accomplished could only be described as a most remarkable achievement; that the world has coped with an unparalleled, unexpected urbanization with no body of experience or model to guide it, with a remarkable degree of success. And I am not in any way oblivious of the many problems which do exist and which have been discussed here. I also believe that, in the seventies in particular, an approach to the shelter problem of the poor was hammered together and articulated by the developing nations with the international agencies serving a role of bringing people together to talk about it, which in my view can and will work in any country that applies it. A formula exists, and the missing ingredient is the will to carry it out. The reason for the remarkable success that has been achieved is how close the problem we're talking about is to the survival of the individuals who are involved, and thus the heroic efforts those individuals are prepared to make to achieve the goals in question.

In this context, the suggestion I have to make—you have to remember, I work for a government and what I do for a living is work with other governments—is that the key to adjusting our strategies as we go through the ongoing crisis is the appropriate distribution of responsibility between the public sector and the private sector. So long as public sector officials are concentrating on the issue of what should be done by the government and what should be done by the private sector, and what government should do to motivate the private sector, the problems will remain manageable. It is my view that many, perhaps most, of the developing countries today are devoting an excessive amount of their time and energy to implementing projects and not enough of their time and energy to running the show.

Panel Discussion with Floor Participation

Mr. Doebele: We now move into the open part of this session. I'd like, as much as possible, to have your comments be about success stories or directions in which to move—things from your own experience which you would like to bring before the rest of us. This is, of course, the last open discussion that we will be having at this Congress. Most of you, I think, have stored up various kinds of reactions during the last four and a half days, and we are now open to receive your comments or contributions directly.

Bill Mollison (Permaculture Conservancy, Tasmania, Australia): What I feel has been very much missing from the conference is a discussion of the techniques for empowering communities instead of planning for communities. I recently attended a banking conference which explained to people in rural communities how to organize their own banking and trusteeship systems. They had a lot of excellent ideas on legal structures, banking, developmental corporations, on trust corporations, trusteeship, all of which are really applicable to the people and which people can understand. What we lack, it seems, is more such bodies in the communities where this has to happen. And what we don't have is any real involvement in communities. My own approach, and that of the bankers who are acting for these community banking systems, is that it is not only teachable but transferable to set up communities to pay back and develop their own housing. We have set up a model for a self-help housing group in Victoria which builds its own houses and obtains training in house building as it does so; and the model has been very successful. We have been to Brazil and have managed to build a small primary housing system, which should amortize itself in four years, in which the people should earn their own assets. And we have been working on a community self-financing system, a banking system not based on the general currency through which the community can provide its own money for its own housing projects. So there are three models that I know about in which people effectively pull themselves up by their boot laces. That does mean, however, that we have to be in the community and teach and model, and then send that community to the next one to get the model working.

I want to say one more thing about the difference between generative and degenerative assets. In the change from agriculture to housing, we change essentially from a land asset which generates wealth to one which degenerates. We write off. The only thing that stands between our thoughts here and some action on the ground is—the thing we need to do is to design. It is possible for us now—and we've done a few in Denmark—to build a house which is energy producing. It is no longer a degenerative asset. It is possible for us to build into the infrastructure of a community income-producing systems so that housing is not necessarily a cost. If you like, a road can be just a road, or a road can be the absorption base for a heating system which produces surplus energy for the community. A swimming pool can be a swimming pool or, with a couple of bags of salt and some insulation, it can produce enough energy for a house or two.

So I think the next thing we must do is to bring the design aspect very much to bear so that we're no longer looking at housing as a degenerative asset. We must build in—as apparently has been done in Czechoslovakia—the ability to produce food, so that enough money is saved to write off the housing for poor people, because food alone is 40 percent of their expenditure. I think we need to get just a handful of strategies. Perhaps at some conference we could have people come with their problems and have a banker, legal person, entrepreneur, sit down and work their problems right through a design strategy—a problem-solving conference.

Mr. Doebele: I might mention to you that although he is based in Tasmania, Bill does travel around the world. He is our nearest thing at this conference to Mr. Schumacher. He is involved in many things including being very active in the Nature Conservancy here in Massachusetts which has done a great deal to preserve vital agricultural land in this state.

Ted Pryor (Government Secretariat, Hong Kong): I'd like to make just one criticism, or even suggestion, and a couple of positive proposals. I think perhaps one thing which we tend to overlook, or at least have not had the time to explore, is the basic pressure on land resulting from demographic factors. Without the demographic pressures, of course, land values could hardly exist. I think we've got to think much more into the future with regard to demographic trends, particularly the question of household formation, which is turning very rapidly to small households, whereas the population rate increase is tending to level off. The impact of this, of course, is that we're getting a high rate of household formation, and that in itself is creating the pressures for land development. That is also correlated very strongly to questions of household incomes and expectations. So I'd like to make the suggestion that perhaps at the next conference we give this aspect a bit more care and thought.

I would like to briefly mention two systems operating in Hong Kong. One is a fairly old system, and the other one is a fairly new system. The old system relates to a system of land assembly which has certain parallels with the land readjustment projects in Korea and Taiwan. But in this case, what we basically do is offer a share certificate to the original landowners. They surrender their land to the government. The government provides the public uses—the roads, the school sites, the site of public housing—and a share of that land is then made available to private development. The holders of the share certificates are then entitled to bid for the private land, and in order to recover a degree of the betterment value, they are required to pay a premium which is equivalent to the difference between the original agricultural value of their holding and the value of the zone site on the date on which the transfer is made. That date of transfer might have been five or six or seven years earlier. There are certain complications to this system which have to be very, very carefully considered, but it has worked for about 25 years in Hong Kong with, I feel, a high degree of success. At various stages, we have had to discontinue it. But I think it is a system which involves the public sector as the facilitating agent and brings in the private sector, making use of their profit motivations.

The other proposal, a more recent one, which again has been

applied with a high degree of success since 1976, is what is referred to as a private sector participation scheme. This is for the provision of housing. The procedures are that the government produces the land and determines the yield of flats on a given site, the size of the flats, and the price of the flats which have to be produced. It then offers the site by open tender to private developers. Each private developer takes the price of the flat and deducts his expected profit margin, his estimate of the building costs of the flat, and the overheads, leaving a residual land value. Whoever bids the highest residual land value is then granted the site. The government then guarantees the sale of the flats, so the developer cannot lose on this. This is one way in which we've been able to bring the cost of flats down to an affordable level for the lower income group.

There are variations on this; and there are certain advantages in that this is one way by which we can draw back some of the heavy expenditures that the government has to lay out for these projects. We've got to the stage now where, in fact, we have a revolving fund to keep this project going. This is only one aspect of our housing policy which I think could be transferred to other countries.

Mr. Doebele: I would agree with Mr. Pryor about the ingenuity of the Hong Kong system of exchanging land and making land into a kind of currency for which there is then a market. In some ways it is a kind of sophisticated transfer of development rights, except that it is more than development rights. It is all the land rights. My impression is that the way it has been worked out in practice has been quite an efficient way for government to acquire land at minimum cost but in a way that is quite satisfactory to the private market. I think it's something that deserves wider attention, publication, and circulation, and we appreciate your bringing it to our attention this afternoon.

Pekka Virtanen (Helsinki University of Technology, Finland): I would like to make one comment and one proposal. The comment is that I really am happy to have participated in this Congress, which once again shows how complicated these matters are and how many facets land problems have. For example, in the very fine paper presented by Professor Strong, she mentioned that we must keep in mind children yet unborn. There is a similar thought in another paper, written by Professor Yahya from Kenya. He said that many people in power want to collect land to enhance their wealth, and for certain reasons they want to make it also unlimited so that they even register it in the names of their unborn children. So we can see the future generation in many ways.

My proposal is that a future congress should include some program of higher education on land problems. In some countries land experts exist, but in very many countries land problems are tackled by people who have not got that education, people who have acquired a good knowledge of other things but are not really expert in land. And if, let's say, amateurs try to solve land problems, you always get second-class results. You need good experts. Because many countries are lacking such expertise, I think it would be very useful to discuss these problems in a suitable congress like this one, and I propose that many good examples can be found and experience converted from one country to another.

Michael O'Brien (Kilkenny County Council, Ireland): Mr. Chairman, I'd like to say how much I appreciate the facilities which are provided here, and also the level of discussion which took place. I think I must also say that there's no truth in the rumor that, because so many Irish people are here in Boston and so many Irish people attended this conference, there isn't anybody left in Ireland. There are a few left behind. We have a fairly strong representation here at this conference, and it's only right that a developing country like Ireland should have that.

But if I could make maybe a slightly critical comment: the discussions have been academic and technical, and I'm neither an academic nor a technician. Indeed, I'm a very ordinary guy representing a county council in Ireland. Therefore, I feel that at that level, at the nonprofessional level of politics, I have on a daily basis come into contact with the conflict between the loaning of land and the purchase of land for housing and for infrastructure. I can't go into as much detail as Mr. Psomopoulos, for example. And maybe I can't express in a practical way what I feel the way the Secretary of the Department of Agriculture of Zimbabwe did in his paper. Or indeed I don't possess the provocative eloquence of Ann Strong. But speaking as a semi-politician, I think she could add another *C* to the four which she mentioned in her paper—communication—because I do believe it is necessary to communicate with politicians. I think it was Mr. Psomopoulos who mentioned that there is no point in planning if it is not understood at the political level. Essentially, it is politicians who carry out the plans that you people develop. So communication is, I believe, a very important item.

I would like to outline, if I could, in a little bit of detail one aspect of our workings in a county council as it is in Ireland at a local authority. We obviously have problems, housing problems, just the same as other countries have. We have developed a social system into our housing plans that would include the provision of serviced sites by the local authority for people with limited means. That is, people under a certain level of salary would be able to purchase a site to build a house. Of course, the lower income levels would be catered for by the local authority anyway. To do that we have, through government policy, built up land banks that cater for, or are sufficient for, housing development for nine or ten years hence. I'm sure that is comparable with the systems that operate in other countries as well. But we do not have the problem that I heard from other countries in relation to land speculation at that local authority level.

I conclude by saying that I think it is important that we should communicate, and therefore, as an extension of this conference, I'd like to see communication. Perhaps one technical representative and one ordinary representative from each country could meet the politicians responsible for land use and its development in the various countries represented here.

Haruo Nagamini (United Nations Centre for Regional Development, Japan): The one thing I wanted to add is somewhat in relation to the point raised by Professor Virtanen about developing experts in land problems, and the comments on communication just made. The brief statements made today sound rather technical and may not reflect in full the kind of sophistication or the complexities that were brought out in various discussions that took place during the past four days. What I would like to say is to recapitulate that very impressive paper presented by Professor Strong yesterday about the importance of ethical thinking. I am struck by the very scientific approach in Professor Haar's speech, which is rather contrasted by what you presented yesterday. So perhaps we should not forget all these proposals, like the right application of property taxation or land readjustment or the development rights operations; all these, I think, in many countries have been effected with good efforts, and it is exactly so in Japan, too.

There have been many political and other forces that undermined these efforts, and those cannot be implemented in a desired form. I think the final result is the people. All these good ideas should be not only discussed among the experts but also adopted in an extensive way in education, not only at the master's level but at elementary or middle-level education, so that the people's ethics can be gradually changed. I think that those who are sticking to the very expensive land in urban areas are getting old. When these rights are inherited by the younger generation, I think there is some better chance that those people might think in different ways about using this precious resource.

Takashi Inoue (Professor Emeritus, University of Tokyo, Japan): I agree with my colleague from Japan. And I want to propose my very primitive and fundamental problems through my long time in Japanese government and also Japanese academic fields. We established and planned two projects. One project perhaps you know is the Tskuba New Town of Science, which is a huge scientific facility; many overseas guests come to see this new project. For example, Prime Minister Margaret Thatcher of Great Britain wanted especially to see this project. The other one is our new international airport, Narita Airport. These two were problem projects, and underlying these problems were land problems. About 20 years ago I had direct responsibility for these projects.

The New Town of Science involved many local governments. Those governments came to our office, and we visited many times. We proposed one master plan along the lines of British new towns. Then the head of the local government asked, if some landowners refused to sell the land, then what would happen? So we answered that it would be transacted by compulsory action. Then they refused. They said they could not help us do that. They could not cooperate with us because they could not get their people's consent. So if you come to Japan you will find that many scientific establishments are scattered around a line of ten miles. We could not get the proper amount of land at the proper location for a moderate price. But if we had pushed the original plan, then what would have happened?

That is the case in the Narita conflict. At Narita we must have a 300-meter, two-direction runway suitable for an international airport. The government is now trying to get land for another runway, but local people are opposing this project. So, in this case also, how do we get the necessary land at proper locations at a moderate price? Throughout this Congress I have been thinking of this point—that is, how to get proper land, proper location, the proper price. I think it might be quite useful if you could give me some suggestions. Perhaps younger Japanese participants will come next time, and you will teach them how to do this. That is my proposal. Thank you very much.

Michael Kitay (United States Agency for International Development): I'm struck, in viewing the land situation and land problems, by the fact that in many countries, particularly developing countries, when the public sector competes with the private sector to acquire land, the rules often tend to favor the private sector. This is a paradox in many ways because, and particularly with reference to developing countries, those rules in the developing countries that help the private sector and hurt the government are often rules that are borrowed from former colonial powers, while the real cultural and social traditions in a developing country would favor the public, the tribe.

With this in mind, I have two prescriptions. One is that there needs to be a fairly serious consideration of legislative redrafting, a revision of expropriation laws, that gives the public more power to acquire land. Second, I think it is a modest proposal, but governments should be doing some strategic land acquisition one or two or three years in advance of need. This is a modest land-banking proposal. I think they could use this advance acquisition of land plus the power of the government to help finance projects and acquire land in an orderly fashion.

A. P. Parlindungen (University of North Sumatra, Indonesia): I want to tell you what land means to the villagers in Malaysia. Let me illustrate by a story. One of the villagers reported to the police that his wife had run away with another gentleman. The police said, "Why don't you run amok to that gentleman?" He said, "If you lose your land, then you run amok. I can always get another wife."

Mr. Doebele: I guess that puts land in some sort of a perspective with respect to other values.

H. T. Chang (Council for Agricultural Planning and Development, Taiwan): In my presentation in one of the workshops I tried to convey the idea that for countries with small farms on other continents, such as in Latin America, in Africa, even in the Middle East, the present smallholders are not limited so much as in Asia as to the natural resources in their respective countries. The smallness of the farms is the result of limited financial or technical resources to expand their farming operations. But Asia as a continent is characterized by small farms because they were propagated too early.

Family planning was adopted very late in our history. So I feel that Asia is one continent that is stuck with small farms. There is almost no escape. Some Asian countries are better than others, but they have small farms nonetheless, including Japan. I think Japan is the first country that tried to find ways to get away from the disadvantages of the small farm. They have had a certain success and have led the way in showing how these problems can be solved. In country after country in Asia, the problem has to be faced. Korea and Taiwan are now going through this difficult adjustment period. I won't go into this in any detail because it is discussed in my paper.

Now I would like to make a reference to Dr. Lester Brown's theme. Under such an unfavorable land/population ratio, it would be difficult for Asians in general to accept what Dr. Brown is suggesting. Although the population is so dense and the arable land area is so small, for Asia as a whole the crop yields have been kept at a low level, probably for thousands of years. Only in the last few decades, after adopting modern technology in every country, is the yield coming up. It is in a rising trend.

Therefore, it is difficult for the Asian agricultural student to agree that natural resources are declining, because to them farming has existed for thousands of years and the yield is still increasing. Now this is so because Asia is mainly rice fields, and each plot has to be flat, level. Therefore we do not have the type of soil erosion that Mr. Brown was worrying about as evidenced in the United States in some areas. The story is told by the history of thousands of years of cultivation, the yield is still coming up. Now there may come a time when what Mr. Brown is worrying about will happen, but this is contrary to what Asian agricultural students are seeing now.

Because by nature there is no erosion in rice fields, the soil erosion in Asia is caused more by a social reason than a technical reason. In many Asian countries, because of population pressures the small farmers are forced to go onto the slopes and plow up a patch of land to plant corn, sweet potatoes, bananas, and so on. But again, when a country becomes industrialized, the population of the rural areas comes into the cities for nonagricultural work. These slope-land squatters disappear. This was the case in Taiwan. I had worked on the squatter problem for many years—laws, regulations, demonstrations, education, to no avail. But when the country became industrialized, the squatters came down from the hills. No more problem.

Now this leads to my last comment. It is that this unfavorable land/population ratio will be characteristic of Asia to the last, because a country will come to a balancing point between the city, the urban population, and the land use as against the rural population and farmland; no matter what, it will come to that balancing point. For countries that have small farms to begin with because of the unfavorable land/population ratio, when that balancing point arrives, these countries will still have a smaller farm and a smaller area allowable for each family. Now, these are the problems that I feel even Japan will have to face until somehow they have been solved.

Malcolm Matthew (City of North York Planning Department, Ontario, Canada): In view of the time, I'll forego the anecdote and the comment. I have one prescription for speculation. In Canada since 1971 we've had capital gains, which taxes 50 percent of any capital increase as if it were income. In addition to that, land was being traded as a speculative commodity more and more frequently in the early 1970s. The province of Ontario introduced a speculative gains tax act which required that if a property was bought and sold without spending at least 40 percent of the sale price on improvements, 50 percent of the increase was confiscated. That, allied to the capital gains tax, meant a loss in most cases of something like 80 percent of the increment. It killed speculation very quickly. However, as soon as the problem had been solved, the act was repealed. So now we have speculation again.

A second prescription—the provision of services to land of a particular density. If anyone requires rezoning to a higher density, it is done subject to a development agreement whereby he agrees, before that zoning becomes effectively approved, to contribute to our servicing fund a levy equivalent to so many dollars per square foot. At the moment it is about $1.80 per square foot, which would be approaching $20 per square meter. That is made into a servicing fund, and that builds the services.

Mr. Doebele: That certainly was concrete and positive. I might also say that with respect to these capital gains taxes, one of the most interesting ones that has been mentioned before, but I'm not sure to the whole audience, was in Singapore, where whenever there was a change in zoning classification which resulted in an increase in the value of the land, 70 percent of that increase in value was taken back in the form of a tax. I'd also mention that the kind of very heavy front-end charges for public services which were mentioned just now as being used in Canada are also widely used in California today, and I think probably may well be spreading into other American cities as a way of capturing, even before the values go up, all of the public costs—indeed sometimes a bit more than the public costs that are going to be created by a project.

Fred Harrison (Economic and Social Science Research Association, London): I have four very quick points on the way we perceive land, because it is my view that we won't get our specific policies right and administered efficiently until we have a clearer understanding of how the land market works. I'm one of those who is skeptical about the sorts of things that are proposed at the present time.

First of all, we've heard so much about the inadequacy of food, housing, shelter—the way people have been suffering for many decades. That suggests from the planners', the politicians', the administrators' point of view the need to do something on behalf of people. If my view is correct, the problem of the inability of people to meet their own requirements arises from a distortion in the structure of the land market—more specifically, the rights to land, which have given rise to the dependence of people on help from others. The one area that I suggest would alter our perception of what needs to be done relates to the theory of wage determination. If we go back to thinking about how people's incomes are determined, we'll be able to understand that they are now pitched at an inadequate level precisely because of the dynamics of the land market. If this is true, then the land economist has a lot more to say about the theory of wages than others. This would be a fruitful area for research because it would alter completely the nature of the policies which need to be administered, the scale and the nature of the problem that confronts us.

Second, the ecological issues. We've heard about the terrible things that are going on in the world, but man does not willfully and naturally wish to destroy his habitat. He doesn't desire to create deserts or denude the forests. These are acts of desperation which are directly related to the way man has redistributed rights to natural resources to the disadvantage of many people, causing them to act in desperation and, as a result, destroy the habitat. And rather than having a million and one individual little programs designed to try and ameliorate specific problems in different parts of the world, if we understood why people are destructive, what causes them to do something that man hasn't done before in 2 million years and has only apparently decided to do in the last hundred or fewer, we will again begin to construct a program for action which is quite different from the one that we're talking about now.

I think another area of research concerns the social realities, which we're told restrict the kinds of policies that might be implemented. Are they really restrictions on the nature of research and the kinds of policies that can be prescribed? I don't believe so. We do need to look at those social realities which become constraints on action. I happen to believe that we could accomplish a great deal more. We have the example of HABITAT, where over 130 governments, in fact, were quite radical in what they were proposing, and I don't see why we as scholars or theoreticians should accept restraints at a lower level than what governments apparently feel able to do.

Last, the ecologists have been telling us that we need a new land ethic. In my view, having looked at the anthropology and the ecology literature in some depth, what we're really asking for is an old land ethic. We need a retrieval of what has happened in the past. If we look at the way man has related to his natural environment in the past, there is no mystery about what needs to be done, and we don't need a new ethic but an old ethic. Again, this is an area that needs a great deal of research, because once we've retrieved an understanding of that old ethic, it dictates the nature of the policies and the scale of the problem that confronts us.

Mr. Doebele: With that challenge, I'd like to thank you all, both for your contributions and for your patience in listening to so many and varied presentations.

Chapter 16

What Must Be Done?

José Ramon Lasuen

The topic I've been asked to talk about is, What must be done? I'm going to deal with it by rephrasing what I think you here have said should be done. Briefly, I'm trying to integrate the answers that I have been interpreting from you. In order to do so, I'm going to use a conceptual framework which consists of three elements. These are (1) the main questions that must be addressed; (2) the context in which they should be evaluated; and (3) the evaluation hypothesis that should be employed.

First, the questions that should be addressed were pinpointed on the first day by Nat Lichfield. To me, the most important question is, Should land be considered a bundle of scarce basic resources? If so, should it be managed with the criterion of sustained maximum growth—that is, long-term growth—or, on the contrary, short-term growth? Does the application of either of these criteria require a new ethic? And if so, does that new ethic require new political institutions, or can present institutions work with existing land policies? If so, do they require new instruments? Those are the questions.

Second, the context in which these questions should be evaluated should be spelled out clearly. It is extremely important to realize that we are acting in a critical period for the development of mankind. We are living through one of those major crises that take place in the world every fifty years or so, probably due to the changes in the ratios of supply and demand of raw materials and industrial products, and in their relative prices. That is to say, we are immersed in the type of crisis that has been recurring, from about 1800, every 50 or 60 years, and has been accompanied by a considerable change in the industrial structure as a result of innovations caused by variations in the availability of and requirements for raw materials and industrial products. These critical periods result in considerable changes in the world of ideas and in the structure of the sciences, of the state, and society. We have to remember that after the first world crisis of this type, after the Napoleonic Wars, the laissez-faire state appeared; around the middle of the nineteenth century, because of a crisis similar to the one we are experiencing now, the utilitarian state appeared; and around the 1930s the welfare state appeared. Right now a new state is being born. Many people are already working on the restructuring of the state, in the Western world at least. This is the critical context in which the previous questions should be evaluated—and in which your answers to these questions should be evaluated.

Third, the hypothesis. Which hypothesis should be used to understand those questions? Several speakers have been using what I would call a "land-dependent man" hypothesis. In this view man depends upon nature; nature creates man. This is the basic eighteenth-century hypothesis of Quesnay, that all the values that society creates derive from the irreproducible value of the land, from the irreproducible powers of nature. This is one perspective from which to evaluate the present problem. But there is another opposite perspective that has also been stated—though not so clearly, not so emphatically, and not so comprehensively. This is a much more modern hypothesis—namely, that man creates nature, that the effort of man transforms nature. From the first perspective derives the moral that man cannot abuse nature. Deriving from the other is the motto that neither can man be abused in the name of nature. Both views can be correct or incorrect, depending on how you use them. Taken together, both views are right. Taken separately, both views may be wrong.

That said, I will address your questions viewed in that context and evaluated from those hypotheses.

First, is land a bundle of scarce basic resources? Yes or no? Well, from a "land-dependent man" view—from the perspective of nature creating and conditioning man—the definition of land as a bundle of scarce basic resources is operational. It helps to emphasize the need to manage scarcity even in the less obvious cases. Let's see why. If nature creates man, then man can live only by not abusing nature, by taking care of nature carefully. How? Well, the notion of land as a bundle of resources, which is a modern ecological version of the eighteenth-century view, shows that all those basic scarce resources are integrated. By touching one, even the most abundant, you affect the others. Consequently, the definition shows that land use should be interpreted in a comprehensive way, as most of you have been discussing it, even in reference to the less scarce resources.

But if you take the other point of view—the point of view that man creates nature—then land should not be defined that way. Land in that perspective is not a scarce stock but a potential field of unknown resources that need to be first, discovered and second, exploited. Thus land is not a bundle of resources but a pathway leading to linked future resources.

If you take both views together, the definition of land should be: land is the reservoir of a bundle of integrated resources, as known and exploited by existing technology, that need to be conserved, but it is also an unknown collection of potential resources that need to be discovered, exploited, and related. I think that the view that most Asians have expressed in this hall refers to the need to integrate the two versions.

The second question is, Should land be managed to achieve maximum sustained growth or maximum short-term growth? Well, if man is bound by nature, certainly land has to be managed according to long-term criteria. These criteria can be pinpointed very precisely. From the perspective of efficiency, maximum sustained growth requires an equal consumption of resources per unit of output over time. From an equity viewpoint, the justice between generations requires that this percentage-constant rate of growth should be equal over time. Therefore, in a world view that sees man bound by nature, on grounds of both efficiency and equity, the maximum-sustained-growth criterion is adequate. But from the other perspective—from the point of view that man that creates nature—the application of that criterion would be catastrophic. No new resources would be discovered. There would be no incentive whatsoever for discovery, for invention, for innovation. If one links the two perspectives, the conclusion is clear: universal change is impossible, and universal conservation would be catastrophic. In fact, all societies, all civilizations which have applied the concept of conservation to everything have disappeared, just like those that have tried to change too much.

Partial conservation and partial change are necessary. From the first perspective, we need conservation. From the second perspective, we need development. By properly linking the two together, we increase the benefits inherent in the two perspectives.

Let me elaborate a bit on this point. The nonconservationists, the innovatives say, don't put any constraints on human initiative. When you run out of existing resources, that stimulates forces that will create new resources, new discoveries, new products, new everything. From the other perspective, the conservationists say, that's too dangerous. If we let people use up resources as they want, we will run out of them without any guarantee of alternative sources. By linking the two perspectives together, you integrate the criteria in a reinforcing way. Couple a conservation program for a disappearing resource with a program for developing substitutes, and the conservation program effectively acts as a further incentive for the developers. Universal conservation would be a disaster, but partial conservation, properly enforced, of resources available for existing technologies is a guarantee not only of present but of future survival, because it is a driving force for the development of the resources contained in nature but not known at present.

The third question is, Do we require a new ethic? From the first perspective the answer is no. Humanity has developed up to now only one basic ethic. I am not speaking about morals or any other sort of interpretation of the word. I'm using the word *ethic* in its most strict sense. And mankind up to now has developed only one ethic with different shades. It is the ethic of scarcity. How should man use scarce resources in society? The normative relations between equality and freedom in a limited world were first stated by Spinoza. Hence, from the first perspective, for the land-conditioned man, the ethic that is required exists, and the only thing that we need to do in order to make societies work properly is to make people aware of the existing problems. The moment that people are aware of the problem in an essential, clear way, they immediately start to apply the ethic that they know, the ethic that is ingrained in their behavior.

From the other perspective, from the perspective that man creates nature, there is no ethic at all. Humanity does not have an ethic of abundance. And we need one, because people don't know how to behave in affluence. We have gone along on the assumption that in more abundant times the only thing that we need to do is relax the ethic that we inherited, the ethic of scarcity. That is not true. You don't gain anything by relaxing an ethic; you simply confuse people.

I strongly suggest that we make people better informed so that they can act according to the ethic they know. But we must also make every effort to develop a new ethic—the ethic of abundance. And this, I think, is going to be very difficult. Meanwhile, we must use ethic substitutes. I think that we are going to develop all sorts of magics and mystiques in order to substitute for the ethic that we don't yet have—the ethic of abundance.

I jump to the next question rapidly. Does the situation therefore require new institutions? Again, from the nature-creates-man perspective, I don't think it does. We have already established a welfare state that, at least in theory, operates properly. In practice, however, it has defects. For example, the pluralist version does not totally fulfill the requirements of equality. It guarantees sufficient freedom but not enough equality. Its centralist version provides enough equality but hardly any freedom. But the theoretical model works.

The main problem arises when we analyze the situation from the other perspective. If man is seen to create nature, do the existing institutions favor or permit this change? The answer in this respect is not quite clear. But there are indications that we need a new state. In Western Europe in the last few years, a growing awareness is developing, at least in the higher-level political circles connected with academia, that a new state is needed to create the society of the future. I think this is going to be a society which is more welfare oriented than the present one. But it will certainly not be the same kind of state. The new state will be required to fulfill more functions, certainly. For instance, right now it is already accepted that the state has to help the market produce the innovations and the inventions that the market does not provide by itself, especially in Western Europe. Therefore, among the new functions the state has to provide are innovation, reindustrialization, reconversion, and so forth. But everybody agrees, too, that the state should carry on these new functions as well as the old in less interventionist ways, in a less bureaucratic and direct manner. The new state should carry on the old and new functions society requires in a more competitive and indirect way, for instance, through competitive bidding for public goods and services which permit new investments, like public enterprise zones, new development zones, compensation principles of many types. So, I would say in response to this question that from the old perspective and for the old problems, no new institutions are required. The existing state is theoretically valid; what is needed is to perfect the application of its functions. But from the other perspective, for both old and new functions a new welfare state is needed with more functions and less intervention.

Finally, which policies should we follow? Well, once again it depends on the perspectives. It is clear that from the nature-conditions-man hypothesis, the land title should be long term. Land allocation criteria over time and space should guarantee justice among generations and regions. The land distribution instruments should be the ones that have been mentioned—tax subsidies, tax rebates, tax increases, depending on the context.

From the second perspective, the solution is totally different. If man creates nature, and man has to be stimulated to conceive new relations that would permit him to cope with the existing problems and transform them by means of separating them and creating new products, services, and ways of solving problems, the title to land must be short term. The criterion for land allocation must be maximum growth in the short term rather than over the long term. And the land allocation criterion over space should be minimum cost, not equality of access among regions. The land distribution criterion should thus be competitive. This would lead to cutthroat competition, until the moment when the new technologies and institutions are developed. At this time the new developed resources should be conserved, and so the criteria should be reversed.

I think that the integration of the conclusions derived from these two perspectives must be done sequentially. In order to favor invention, the principle of change should be given priority, but once innovations have matured and new resources become old resources, new technologies become old technologies, a shift should take place from the principle of change to the principle of conservation. But not everywhere. Since the world is a unit in which some states, regions, towns, and industries are innovating while others are copying, there is one clear conclusion: the level of change and conservation cannot be the same within each state and among nations. The mixes have to be different. There is a common stock of knowledge and of problems for the whole world, but this stock of problems and knowledge is not distributed evenly over the whole world. It is distributed differentially and will always be. There will be shifts over time and over space, but it will always be differentiated. Therefore, the problem in any given place will always consist in achieving the right mixture of the principles of change and the principles of conservation. Anyone claiming universal validity for any mixture at any time must be either perverse or lunatic.

So my advice is to apply evolving mixes of development and conservation. In order to handle that task I think a new framework has to be developed which will provide answers in different contexts to the questions which Nat Lichfield raised at the beginning of this seminar. I wonder myself whether it wouldn't be a good idea to ask the Centre to take the role of providing a strategy on how this should all be studied in detail. To that effect it could create, for instance, a committee, constituted by some of the moderators and the chairmen of the workshops who already have absorbed the ideas that you have put forward. This committee could propose a design of the strategy to be followed in the future, which could be discussed in the next meeting. I think the idea has virtue, and probably the Centre is the organism that is qualified to carry it out.

In conclusion, I think that you have brought out answers to all the questions that Nat Lichfield asked of you. They can be integrated if they are perceived from the two perspectives that I have mentioned: the perspective of conservation and the perspective for development. The two need to be integrated, for separately they can be cataclysmic. And they can be integrated. I think we have the knowledge to integrate them. I think the Centre can and probably should be the institution to carry out this endeavor.

Concluding Remarks

Matthew Cullen

I'd like to ask each of you to think about this conference when you get home and to write us and make suggestions for subsequent improvements. We welcome your creative and constructive criticism, and we'd also welcome ideas for future conferences, either of a major World Congress variety such as this, or smaller regional congresses, meetings, seminars, workshops, and the like on various topics in which you express an interest. Also, please continue to keep in touch with us through Dan Darin and the *Newsletter*, especially on those topics on which you want to share your views with the other members of the Centre.

We have developed in the course of these meetings a number of initiatives for further contact, for example, through the courtesy of the chief architect of Prague, Mr. Borovicka, the possibility of a planning meeting in Prague to explore the possibility of future collaboration between Eastern and Western European specialists in the land policy area. We also have the possibility of a congress of a regional character in France. Further, we are planning to participate in a congress that will be run by the International Water Resources Association in Belgium in 1985, which will be a collaborative venture with the World Environment and Resources Council and ICLPS. And finally, we are going to respond to the initiative and challenge thrown to us by Aurelio Peccei on Monday, inviting the possibility of a group of nongovernmental representatives, private people, to meet to see if it's possible to develop a global land policy to carry out at the highest level the best use of the planet's resources. We'll meet in Geneva to begin a process of identifying those who might be involved with a view to producing a volume which might have the impact of *Limits to Growth*, a response to Mr. Psomopoulos' call for an "agenda afresh" as he termed it—a declaration of interdependence, or a statement of goals for a common future, on which we have a good introduction from the work which Ann Strong presented to us yesterday. And from that we would hope to respond to some of the initiatives suggested, and the needs suggested here, about further contact and collaboration with the political world, the world of action, and also those people whom Bill Mollison described as the walkers. He divided the world the other day for me into talkers and walkers. I have a hunch that we are among the talkers; the people who are effecting change in local communities, meter by meter and yard by yard, are the walkers, and we need collaboration with them, it seems to me. There exists the possibility of creating coalitions with those activists who are currently pressing for institutional change and reform.

Each of these congresses ends with an expression of frustration at the lack of political will. We intellectuals say we know what to do. We know some of the answers are at our disposal. We've tested them on a model basis, and some work. To those that don't work, we feel at least we have an approach. We have a reasonably good feeling about what might succeed, and all we need is either massive funding or political will, and those are sometimes interchangeable. It does seem to me that some of these institutions which have failed to adapt as rapidly as the environment surrounding them, that are calcified forms and have rigidified procedures, are now, in some parts of the world at least, responding to the pressure of political action from the lobby. As popular movements begin to alter these forms and grease them up and get them to work a little more efficiently and effectively, it may be possible to establish links that will help us implement the kinds of policy directives that we would like to formulate.

This meeting is now adjourned.

Appendixes

Program
Land: Resource for Human Survival
Food, Fiber Energy, Shelter

Harvard Law School
Cambridge, Massachusetts

Monday, June 20
The Human Condition: Growth, Equity, Basic Human Needs, and the Land

Opening Remarks: *Matthew Cullen,* Conference Chairman

Moderator for the Day: *Isaac Ofori*

Speakers: *Aurelio Peccei, Arlo Woolery, Nathaniel Lichfield*

Workshops
A. Demographic Change, Urbanization, and Ruralization
   Moderator, *John D. Montgomery,* Chairman, Department of Government, Kennedy School of Government, Harvard University
B. Land, Poverty, and Political Stability
   Moderator, *Ann Crittenden, New York Times*
C. New Approaches to Developing a Sustainable Agriculture
   Moderator, *Bill Mollison,* Permaculture Consultancy, Stanley, Tasmania, Australia
D. The Impact of Land Tenure Arrangements on Agricultural Productivity

Moderator, *Albert Berry*, Professor of Economics, Scarborough College, University of Toronto, Canada

Tuesday, June 21
Worldwide Trends and Their Impact on the Provision of Food and Shelter

Moderator for the Day: *Harold Dunkerley*

Speakers: *Lester Brown, Osvaldo Sunkel, P. Psomopoulos, Pierre Laconte*

Workshops
A. Trends in Agricultural Productivity Worldwide
   Moderator, *Peter Meredith*, Government Analyst, Department of Scientific and Industrial Research, Christchurch, New Zealand
B. Energy Development: Impacts on the Land
   Moderator, *Emilio Haddad*, Director of Planning, São Paulo Metropolitan Housing Corporation, São Paulo, Brazil
C. Forests and Deforestation
   Moderator, *Roger Sedjo*, Director, Forest Economics and Policy Program, Resources for the Future, Washington, D.C.
D. Resolving Basic Conflicts in Economic and Social Objectives in Urban and Rural Land Markets
   Moderator, *Guillermo Geisse*, President, Interamerican Planning Society; Professor, Catholic University of Chile, Santiago, Chile

Wednesday, June 22
Advanced Research Institute Workshop: Higher Education Challenges*

Moderator for the Day: *Pierre Laconte*

Special Film Session

Chairmen: *Arlo Woolery* and *Sein Lin*

Thursday, June 23
Exploding Cities and Agricultural Productivity—Conflicts at the Urban Fringe

Moderator for the Day: *William S. W. Lim*

Speakers: *Masahiko Honjo, Jacques Kwak, Blahomir Borovička, R. M. Mupawose, Eta Daróczi, Ann L. Strong*

Workshops
A. The Possibilities of Public-Private Land Pooling and Codevelopment (Land Readjustment)
   Moderator, *Takashi Inoue*, Professor, Yokohama National University, Japan
B. The Encroaching Desert: Arid Lands and Their Potential for New Communities and for Agriculture
   Moderator, *Harry Garnett*, Chief Economist, Dames and Moore, Cambridge, Massachusetts
C. Institutional Arrangements for Managing Land at the Rural-Urban Fringe
   Moderator, *Max Falque*, SOMI Consultants, Aix-en-Provence, France
D. Land Policy Categorization as a Tool in Land Policy Research
   Moderator, *Nathaniel Lichfield*, Director of Research, International Centre for Land Policy Studies, London, England

Friday, June 24
What Are the Policies for Managing Land—A Finite Resource—To Meet Basic Human Needs for Food and Shelter?

Moderator for the Day: *Matthew Cullen*

Panel of Reporters responding to what they have heard and learned from the presentations, workshops, and private conversations relating to major issues underlying the Congress such as:
   Land Price
   Land Ownership and Tenure
   Land Use and Productivity—Food and Shelter
   Protection of Desirable Uses

Chairman, *Charles Haar*, Brandeis Professor of Law, Harvard Law School

A group of substantive specialists with recent experience in other world and regional organizations will bring the best recent thinking and practical experiences to the attention of the Congress. They will address the questions:
Are there new ways of handling these problems?
What is the most creative thinking on the future of these issues?

Chairman, *William Doebele*, Professor of Advanced Environmental Studies, Graduate School of Design, Harvard University

Specialists: *Guillermo Geisse, Shlomo Angel, Isaac Ofori, Ann L. Strong, Vincent Renard, Nathaniel Lichfield, Dan Darin, Sein Lin, Charles Haar, Peter M. Kimm*

Panel Discussion Continues with Floor Participation

"What Must be Done?" *José Ramon Lasuen*

Concluding Remarks: *Matthew Cullen*, Conference Chairman

Editor's note: References to this workshop may be disregarded. This material will be available separately as part of the Lincoln Institute monograph series.

Workshop Papers

R. O. Adegboye, University of Ibadan, Nigeria

The Nigerian Land Use Act and Its Effects on Agricultural Land Needs and Productivity

Paul K. Asabere, Bentley College, Waltham, Massachusetts; and *K. Owusu-Banahene*, University of Pennsylvania, Philadelphia

Population Density Function for Ghanaian Cities: An Empirical Note

Dr. Eliezer Brutzkus, Former Deputy Director, Ministry of Interior, Jerusalem, Israel

Transportation and Urbanization Patterns

C. S. Chandrasekhara, Executive Director, School of Planning and Architecture, New Delhi, India

Urban Land Policy in India: An Assessment

H. T. Chang, Council for Agricultural Planning and Development, Republic of China

Future Rice Surplus Problem in the Asian and Pacific Region

H. T. Chang and *T. K. Peng*, Council for Agricultural Planning and Development, Republic of China

Impact of Rapid Economic Structural Change on Agricultural Development in Countries with Small Farms—the Case of Taiwan, ROC—The Unavoidable Productivity Lag

Wei-I Chang, Ministry of Interior, Republic of China

Agricultural Land Policies in Taiwan, ROC

Romesh Diwan and *Renu Kallianpur*, Rensselaer Polytechnic Institute, Troy, New York

Biological Technology and Land Productivity

Thomas J. Dreves, Harvard Law School, Cambridge, Massachusetts

Can Species Survive Sovereignty? An Inquiry into the Problem of Global Habitat Preservation

The Honorable Conrado F. Estrella, Minister of Agrarian Reform, Republic of the Philippines

The Philippine Agrarian Reform Program: A Support Mechanism to Effective Land Management

Dr. Yakub L. Fabiyi, University of Ife, Ile-Ife, Nigeria

Land Policy in the Development of Agriculture: The Responses of Farmers in Ondo and Oyo States of Nigeria to the Land Use Act

Dr. Olusegun Akanni Famoriyo, Ahmadu Bello University, Zaria, Nigeria

Impact of Land Tenure on Agriculture in Nigeria

John Forester, Cornell University, Ithaca, New York

From Equity and Efficiency to the Practical Analysis of Ambiguity in Planning Practice

Dr. Ajato Gandonu, Institute of Land Economy and Planning Studies, Lagos, Nigeria

Demand for Land in Nigeria

Urs Geiser, University of Zurich-Irchel, Switzerland

Multistage Landuse Mapping and Change Monitoring in Sri Lanka

Prof. Guillermo Geisse G., Catholic University of Chile, Santiago

Conflicting Land Development Strategies in Large Latin American Cities

Justice Milagros A. German, Intermediate Appellate Court, Manila, Philippines

Land, People, and Political Stability through Agrarian Reform: The Philippine Experience

Prof. Albert Z. Guttenberg, University of Illinois at Urbana-Champaign

The Elements of Land Policy: Toward a Comprehensive Classification

C. Lowell Harriss, Executive Director, The Academy of Political Science, New York City

Urban and Rural, Present and Future: Conflicts and Possible Devices for Their Resolution

Tokunosuke Hasegawa, Japan Sewerage Authority, Tokyo, Japan

Historical Review on the Urban Structure in Tokyo Metropolitan Region

Eric L. Hyman, U. S. Congress Office of Technology Assessment, Washington, D.C.

Providing Public Lands for Smallholder Agroforestry in the Province of Ilocos Norte, Philippines

Prof. Takashi Inoue, Former Professor, University of Tokyo, Japan

Past and Future Trends of Urban Development in Japan with Special Comments on Land Readjustment Projects

Prof. Helmut W. Jenkis, Hannover, West Germany

The Use of Land in the Urban Fringe—The Case of a Socialist Country: East Germany

Declan and Margrit Kennedy, West Berlin, Germany

Permaculture as a Survival System

Chaim Kubersky, Director General, Ministry of the Interior, Jerusalem, Israel

National Planning in the Protection of Agricultural Land: The Israeli Practice

Peter W. Kwantes, Willemstad, Curacao, Netherlands Antilles

Land Policy, Curacao

George Ledec, Office of Environmental Affairs, The World Bank, Washington, D.C.

The Political Economy of Tropical Deforestation

Prof. Hubert N. van Lier, Agricultural University, Wageningen, The Netherlands

Facts, Developments, Philosophies, and Energy in Rural Land Uses in Holland

Dr. Jacob O. Maos, University of Haifa, Israel

The Distribution of Land in Rural Settlement Schemes in Developing Countries

Dr. Peter Meredith, Department of Scientific and Industrial Research, Christchurch, New Zealand

The Factors Concerned in "Trends in Agricultural Productivity"

Bill C. Mollison, Permaculture Institute, Stanley, Tasmania, Australia

New Approaches to Developing a Sustainable Agriculture

Andres Necochea, Institute of Urban Studies, Catholic University of Chile, Santiago

Efficiency and Equity in Managing Land Resources: Educational Implications. A Latin American Perspective

Carl Ohrn, Metropolitan Council of the Twin Cities Area, St. Paul, Minnesota

A Regional Strategy for Land Use Management

Dr. Olatunji G. Olaore, Nigerian Institute of Social and Economic Research, Ibadan, Nigeria

Urban Land Use in Nigeria: The Dilemma of Harmonizing the Compulsion of Modernization with the Urban Growth Process

Aditya Prakash, Architects, Planners, Designers, Consultants, Chandigarh, India

Energy and Habitat

Prof. Hugo Priemus, Delft University of Technology, the Netherlands

Land Policy and Housing in the Netherlands

Bruce M. Rich, Natural Resources Defense Council, Washington, D.C.

International Institutional Constraints in Sustaining Tropical Forest Resources

Eduardo Rojas T., Institute of Urban Studies, Catholic University of Chile, Santiago

Agricultural Land in the Eastern Caribbean: From Resource for Survival to Resource for Development

Francisco Sabatini, Institute of Urban Studies, Catholic University of Chile, Santiago

Land Prices and National Economic Trends: The Case of Santiago, Chile, 1980-81

Dr. Yohei Satoh, University of Tsukuba, Ibaraki, Japan

Applying Land Substitution to the Orderly Use of Land

Roger A. Sedjo, Forest Economics and Policy Program, Resources for the Future, Washington, D.C.

Institutional Arrangements to Discourage Excessive Deforestation

Indra Kumar Sharma, Commission on Environment Planning, Jodhpur, India

Ecodevelopment in Arid and Semiarid Areas of Asia for Food, Fodder, Fiber, Wood, Essential Bioproducts, Shelter against Sand Storms, Parching, Solar Radiation, and Droughts

Sukardi Endang Taruna, Direktorat Agraria, Jakarta, Indonesia

The National Operation Project on Agrarian Affairs in Indonesia

Tony Taylor, College of Estate Management, Reading, England

Land Conversion on the Urban-Rural Border

Prof. Suwattana Thadaniti, Chulalongkorn University, Bangkok, Thailand

Land Use Policy of the Fringe Area of Bangkok

Dr. Alexander J. Thal, Office of Navajo Land Development, Window Rock, Arizona

Navajo Nation Natural Resources: Issues and Strategies

Prof. Pablo Trivelli, Institute of Urban Studies, Catholic University of Chile, Santiago

Access to Land by the Urban Poor: An Overview of Latin American Experience

Rachaniwan Vechaphrut, Kasetsart University, Bangkok, Thailand

The Study of Fishing Situation Around the Mangrove Forest at Changwat Phangnga

Prof. Pekka V. Virtanen, Helsinki University of Technology, Espoo, Finland

Land Reforms in Finland

Prof. Saad S. Yahya, Department of Land Development, University of Nairobi, Kenya

Revolution and Real Property: The Resilience of the Urban Land Market to Changes in African Governmental Systems

Appendix C

List of Participants

Australia
Dr. Bill C. Mollison

Austria
Robert Schmidt

Belgium
Pierre Laconte

Brazil
Emilio Haddad

Canada
Dr. Paul K. Asabere
Francois Belisle
Prof. Albert Berry
Prof. Ronald W. G. Bryant
Malcolm R. Matthew
L. C. Munn
Donald L. Newman

Chile
Prof. Guillermo Geisse
Andres Necochea V.
Francisco Sabatini
Osvaldo Sunkel

Colombia
Guillermo Anzola
Dr. Mario Calderon R.
Emilio Cera Sanchez
Dr. Roberto Rodriguez

Czechoslovakia
Prof. Blahomir Borovička

England
Martin Sulemana Abudulai
Fred Harrison
Dr. Patsy Healey
Nathaniel Lichfield
Tony Taylor

Fiji
Dr. Ron G. Crocombe

Finland
Prof. Pekka V. Virtanen

France
Oleg Demtchenko
Max Falque
Francois Garraud
Francoise Ladougne
Vincent Renard
Max Stern

West Germany
Prof. Dr. Helmut W. Jenkis

Greece
P. Psomopoulos

Guatemala
Carlos Escobar Armas

Hong Kong
E. G. Pryor

Hungary
Eta Daróczi

Indonesia
Dr. A. P. Parlindungan
Sukardi Endang Taruna

Ireland
Louis Brennan
Patrick Coffey
Joseph Connolly
John Cullen
Joseph Cummins
Patrick Dunne
Anthony Ferguson
James Flanagan
Brian Fleming

Ireland *(cont.)*
Michael Gannon
Patrick Harte
James Kelly
Patrick Kenneally
John Loughlin
Thomas Maher
Farrell McElgunn
Bernard McGlinchey
Larry McMahon
James Miley
Michael T. O'Brien
Thomas O'Reilly
Eamonn Rafter
Senator Patrick J. Reynolds
Stephen Rogers
Martin Rohan
Margaret Tynan

Israel
Dan Darin
Moshe Edry
Arthur Karney
Chaim Kubersky

Italy
Aurelio Peccei

Japan
Junko Goto
Prof. Yuzuru Hanayama
Tokunosuke Hasegawa
Masahiko Honjo
Prof. Takashi Inoue
Haruo Nagamine
Dr. Yohei Satoh

Korea
Musik Chae
Byung-Tai Choi
Yong Tai Han
Eun Jong Kim
Woo Suk Kim

Korea *(cont.)*
  Kwang Soo Pack
  Young Mog Ro
  Jei Hwa Woo

Mariana Islands
  Francisco C. Ada
  Daniel E. Aquino
  O. C. Rasa
  Ponce C. Rasa

Netherlands
  Peter van Dijk
  B. de Graaf
  Jacques M. Kwak
  Prof. Hubert N. van Lier
  Prof. Hugo Priemus
  Dick Teegelaar
  Robert E. van Unen

Netherlands Antilles
  Peter W. Kwantes

New Zealand
  Dr. Peter Meredith

Nigeria
  Prof. Rufus O. Adegboye
  Dr. Olusegun A. Famoriyo
  Dr. Ajato Gandonu

Sultanate of Oman
  Margaret Ann Chapman

Pakistan
  Parvez Qureshi

Philippines
  Rizal Ruiz Amon
  Ramon Casanova
  Hon. Conrado Estrella
  Milagros A. German
  Rosie Mercurio

Philippines *(cont.)*
  Prof. Honorato G. Paloma
  Lino Sanchez, Jr.

Portugal
  Victor R. Pessoa
  Isabel Ramalho de Almeida

Republic of China
  Hsien-Tsiu Chang
  Wei-I Chang
  Yuan-Shiuh Chang
  Kuo Chun Wang

Singapore
  William Lim

Spain
  Jose Ramon Lasuen
  Amaro Tagarro
  Jose Carlos Trullols

Sweden
  Dr. Bengt-Olof Holmberg
  Tomas Lindencrona

Thailand
  Amnuay Chumsmut
  Shlomo Angel
  Praiwan Resanond
  Suthiporn Chirapanda
  Suwattana Thadaniti
  Rachaniwan Vechaphurt
  Visith Atthakorn

Trinidad and Tobago
  Kelvin Romero

United States
  Rexford A. Ahene
  Ebenezer O. Akinosho
  Julia C. Allen
  Michael M. Bernard

United States *(cont.)*
Lester Brown
Raymond Brown
Michael Buckley
Charles C. Cook
Ann Crittenden
Matthew Cullen
Anthony A. Davis
Prof. Romesh Diwan
Prof. Bill Doebele
Thomas J. Dreves
Harold Dunkerley
Prof. Malcolm FitzPatrick
Prof. Barbara J. Flint
John Forester
Seth L. Franzman
David R. Fullmer
Annette Fulscher
Harry Garnett
Prof. Albert Z. Guttenberg
Prof. Charles Haar
C. Lowell Harriss
Ed Hayes
Robert Heroux
Alfred F. Imhoff
Huey Johnson
Renu Kallianpur
Joan Kanwisher
Jerold Kayden
Peter M. Kimm
Michael Kitay
Will Knedlik
George Ledec
Sein Lin
E. Blaine Liner
Mathew MacIver

United States *(cont.)*
Uriel Manheim
Frederic S. Marquardt
Prof. John D. Montgomery
Faith Moore
Patricia Morgan
Prof. Earl Finbar Murphy
Mary O'Brien
Carl E. Ohrn
W. Ralph Peck
Richard F. Perkins
Bruce M. Rich
E. Robert Scrofani
Roger Sedjo
Sharon Shea
Robert J. Smith
John Spears
Prof. Ann L. Strong
Michael Teitz
Dr. Alexander J. Thal
David N. Weinman
Cindy Welch
Alan White
A. M. Woodruff
Arlo Woolery
Sharon Woolery
Chang-Ho Yim
Ben Zahne
Paula Zimlicki

Zambia
Prof. Isaac M. Ofori

Zimbabwe
Robbie M. Mupawose

In Memoriam

On March 14, 1984, our very distinguished friend Aurelio Peccei died of a heart attack at the age of 75. Aside from his many other activities, he will be best remembered for founding the Club of Rome, over which he had presided since its establishment. In its memorable report of 1972, *The Limits to Growth*, the Club heightened the growing public awareness concerning the possibility of society's collapse owing to unchecked population and industrial growth.

Although *The Limits to Growth* is now regarded as a classic in its field, in the wake of its publication many criticized the report as excessively pessimistic. Yet in the years that have passed since then, the universal trends discussed in the report do not seem to be abating. Perhaps the only hope lies in the fact that awareness of the possible effects of these trends appears to be rising.

On June 20, 1983, the first day of the Second World Congress on Land Policy, Peccei made a comparison between present conditions and the circumstances described in the Club of Rome's report and concluded that there has been a decline in the quality of the human condition. The future will be the product of human beings, he reasoned, and it thus holds the same consequences for everyone, for the world and its regions have become one. For this reason, he concluded, every policy must be formulated on a global scale, including land policy.

Such an energetic and warm human being will be missed by all those who had the good fortune to meet and know him.

About the Editors
and Contributors

Matthew Cullen, an independent consultant in planning and management, assisted the Lincoln Foundation in establishing the Lincoln Institute of Land Policy. A graduate of Harvard University and the George Washington University Law School, he was program associate at The Ford Foundation and vice-chancellor of the State University of New York. He was executive director of the International Centre for Land Policy Studies from 1980 to 1983.

Sharon Woolery is the editorial assistant and conference reporter for the Lincoln Institute of Land Policy, and assistant to the executive director of the International Centre for Land Policy Studies.

Shlomo Angel is the chairman of the Division of Human Settlements at the Asian Institute of Technology in Bangkok, Thailand.

Blahomir Borovička studied at Prague Technical University. He worked for 20 years as an architect in the Project Design Organization of the City of Prague, and from 1970 served as technical director. He is chief architect of the city of Prague, and head of the Prague Urban Board. He also teaches and is chairman of the Urbanism and City Planning Department of the Prague University Faculty of Architecture.

Lester Brown is the president and a senior researcher of the Worldwatch Institute, a small, nonprofit institute concerned with the conservation of croplands, reforestation, and other world issues. He has worked at the U.S. Department of Agriculture, and has also contributed to many international meetings and conferences on population, on food, and on habitat. He has many publications to his credit, the most recent of which is *Building a Sustainable Society*. He also serves on the boards of both the Overseas Development Council and the U.S. Committee for UNICEF.

Dan Darin is an architect in private practice. As director of documentation and publications for the International Centre for Land Policy Studies, he is the editor of the *ICLPS Newsletter*, a very important part of the work of the Centre.

Eta Daróczi graduated from Karl Marx University of Economics, Budapest, with first-class honors. She has been involved in many research projects, including macroeconomic studies on urban growth in Europe, the cost of urban growth, as well as energy production and consumption in Hungary compared to other countries. At present, she is the secretary of the Hungarian National Commission for the Vienna Center of the Hungarian Academy of Sciences.

William Doebele is a professor of advanced environmental studies and curator of the Loeb Fellowship Program at the Harvard Graduate School of Design. He is also a member of the Faculty Advisory Council of the Lincoln Institute of Land Policy and of the Harvard Institute for International Development. He holds degrees from Princeton University, Harvard Law School, and the University of California at Berkeley.

Harold Dunkerley is a senior advisor for the Urban Projects Department of the World Bank in Washington, D.C. A graduate of King's College, Cambridge, he worked for the Organization of European Economic Cooperation during the period of the Marshall Plan reconstruction in Europe, and has been an advisor to governments and planning ministries, first in the Far East, then in Latin America, where he headed the Harvard Advisory Group to Colombia, and later to Africa. His most recent work is a book entitled *Urban Land Policy, Issues and Opportunities*.

Guillermo Geisse was recently elected president of the Interamerican Planning Society and is a professor at the Institute of Urban Studies of the Catholic University of Chile. He was the coordinator of the Latin American Urban Land Research Project in Santiago.

Charles Haar is Brandeis Professor of Law at the Harvard Law School. He is also the chairman of the Land Policy Roundtable and a member of the Faculty Advisory Committee of the Lincoln Institute of Land Policy. He has been assistant secretary of the Department of Housing and Urban Development for the United States federal government.

Tokunosuke Hasegawa, coauthor with Masahiko Honjo, is with the Japan Sewerage Board, and formerly worked with the Japan Housing Authority.

Masahiko Honjo, a graduate of Duke University, has worked as an architect in housing and planning agencies and as a faculty member at Tokyo University. Between 1971 and 1981 he was the director of the United Nations Center for Regional Development in Japan, a special program for training middle-level planners in the developing countries. At present he is one of the directors of the International Development Center of Japan, and is currently working on a research and coordination program in Thailand.

Peter Kimm is director of the Office of Housing and Urban Development Programs of the United States Agency for International Development.

Jacques Kwak trained as an architect at Delft University of Technology in the Netherlands. He has worked in the Amsterdam Town Planning Office and also in the Amsterdam Real Estate Department. Since 1982 he has been in charge of Land Policy Affairs as an advisor to the municipality of Amsterdam. He is also the president of the Working Party on Urban Land Policy of the International Federation of Housing and Planning.

Pierre Laconte is education and training director for the International Centre for Land Policy Studies. A doctor of law and a doctor of economics at the University of Louvain, he was also a Fulbright Scholar in the United States, and later a visiting lecturer at M.I.T. He was the chief planner-architect of the New University Town for Louvain University. He has written extensively in French and English, and has served as advisor to the Belgian delegation to the Vancouver Conference on Human Settlements.

José Ramon Lasuen is a member of the Advisory Committee of ICLPS. He is professor of economics, founding dean and honorary dean of the School of Economics at the Autonomous University of Madrid. He is also the opposition's economics spokesman in the Spanish Parliament, and a member of the Council of Europe.

Nathaniel Lichfield retired from the chair of professor on resource planning at the University of London after 15 years of professional service and now is professor emeritus. He is a past president of the Royal Town Planning Institute of Britain, a fellow of the Royal Institute of Chartered Surveyors, a chartered engineer, and a member of the Institute of Municipal Engineers. Professor Lichfield is one of the pioneers instrumental in bringing into being the International Centre for Land Policy Studies, for which he is director of research.

William S. W. Lim is a graduate of the Architectural Association in London. He did graduate study under a Fulbright grant at the Department of City and Regional Planning at Harvard University. He has been in professional private practice in Singapore since 1961 in architecture, urban planning, and development consultancy. His books are *Equity and Urban Development in Third World Countries*, published in 1975, and *Alternative Urban Strategies*, published in 1980. His present activities include a small, selective architectural and planning practice concentrating on conservation work and architecture in context. He continues to teach and write, and is presently concentrating on visual identity and architectural symbolism in urban and mass housing environments.

Sein Lin is the director of international programs of the Lincoln Institute of Land Policy, and was one of the original officers of the International Centre for Land Policy Studies.

Robbie M. Mupawose did his undergraduate study in Zimbabwe in the sciences and subsequently did postgraduate work at the University of California at Davis and the University of Maryland. He has been research officer in the Agricultural Research Stations and also general manager of the Tribal Trust Land Development Corporation in Zimbabwe. In 1980 he was permanent secretary for the Ministry of Land Resettlement and Rural Development, and since 1981 he has been permanent secretary to the Ministry of Agriculture.

Earl Finbar Murphy is C. William O'Neill Professor of Law and Judicial Administration and courtesy professor of natural resources at Ohio State University, and has long had an interest in property and environmental law. He is also the president of the Ekistics Society.

Isaac Mensa Ofori is the secretary of the Environmental Protection Council of Ghana. Educated at Manchester University and King's College, Cambridge, he was lecturer in land economy and regional planning at the University of Science and Technology at Kumasi and senior research fellow at the Institute of Statistical Social and Economic Research at the University of Ghana, Legon Acrod. He was minister of rural development and cabinet minister of the government of the Republic of Ghana. Since 1972 he has been a visiting professor at the Land Reform Training Institute of Taiwan, Republic of China, and since September 1983 he has held a position as professor of land economy in the School of Environmental Studies at the University of Zambia.

Aurelio Peccei was president of the Club of Rome in Italy. The late Dr. Peccei was a businessman-scholar of repute, having graduated from the University of Turin, summa cum laude. He spent a year in jail for resistance fighting during the last war. He had been chief executive officer of the Fiat Motor Company, based in Turin, as well as chief executive officer of the Olivetti Company. He was a member of the board of the World Wildlife Fund and the International Ocean Institute.

Panyaris Psomopoulos is one of the most renowned students of ekistics, relating human settlements to the environment. He also is an architect and town and regional planner, with exceptionally wide experience as a practitioner in many projects such as housing programs, planning studies, and large-scale development studies in scores of countries. He is editor of the journal *EKISTICS*. Formerly director of the Graduate School of Ekistics, and then director of research and international programs at the Athens Ekistics Center, he has in more recent years become its president.

Vincent Renard is a professor at the Ecole Polytechnique and University of Paris IV Sorbonne.

Ann L. Strong is professor and chairman of the Department of City and Regional Planning at the University of Pennsylvania. Her graduate education was at Yale Law School. She is a director of the Environmental Law Institute and past director of the Environmental Friends Fund. She is the author of many books, including *Private Property and Public Interest* and *Land Banking.*

Osvaldo Sunkel was trained as an economist both in Chile and at the London School of Economics, and is well-known as a specialist on Latin America. Since 1978 he has held a position as coordinator of the development unit of the United Nations Economic Mission for Latin America. His earlier career as professor of development economics and international economic relations of the National University of Chile, and his four years with the Institute of Development Studies at the University of Sussex, England, provides a fitting background. He has written many articles and books in the general area of international relations, economic development, and environmental issues in Latin America.

Arlo Woolery was for many years director of the Arizona State Department of Property Valuation, where his interests centered on real estate valuation and taxation. Since 1975 he has been the executive director and the vice president of the Lincoln Institute of Land Policy.